This book is individual

for the

G Fletcher

who as a Firefighter in the
North Yorkshire Fire Brigade
&
North Yorkshire Fire & Rescue Service
based at
Scarborough Fire Station
has greatly contributed to
Scarborough's Firefighting History

CONFLAGRATIONS

SCARBOROUGH'S FIREFIGHTING HISTORY

By
Les Shannon

Scarborough
2003

© Scarborough St John's Publishing 2003

ISBN 0-9546483-0-7

First published by Scarborough St John's Publishing 2003
Scarborough
North Yorkshire
YO12 5EU

Prepared and printed by:
York Publishing Services Ltd
64 Hallfield Road
Layerthorpe
York YO31 7ZQ
Tel: 01904 431213; Website: www.yps-publishing.co.uk

DEDICATION

I would like to dedicate this book to my wife Lynn for her patience, help and support.

Cover Credits

Design   – BP Design, York
Scarbro' Logo   – Jeff Brook Smith
Bottom Right Photo   – Scarborough Evening News (Dave Barry)

Cover Photographs

Front Top	Volvo RT and crew	– 2003
Middle Left	AFS firemen drilling	– 1939
Middle Right	The Darley' and crew	– 1901
Bottom Left	The Rem Store fire	– 1915
Bottom Right	The Opera House fire	– 1996
Back Cover	Leyland pump	– 1934

CONTENTS

APPENDIX

This page sponsored by:
LS TRAINING CONSULTANTS
Scarborough – Telephone 01723 503113

ABBREVIATIONS

ADO	Assistant Divisional Officer
AFS	Auxiliary Fire Service
ARP	Air Raid Precautions
ATV	Austin Towing Vehicle
BA	Breathing Apparatus
BT	British Telecom
CC	Chief Constable
CFO	Chief Fire Officer
CU	Control Unit
DCFO	Deputy Chief Fire Officer
DO	Divisional Officer
ET	Emergency Tender
FB	Fire Brigade
FBU	Fire Brigades Union
FE	First Engineer
Ff	Firefighter
FH	Fire Hydrant
Fm	Fireman
FP	Fire Prevention
FP	Fire Plug
Fw	Firewoman
GPO	General Post Office
H	Hydrant
HO	Home Office
HQ	Head Quarters
HX	High Explosive (bomb)
LFf	Leading Firefighter
LFm	Leading Fireman
LFw	Leading Firewoman
LRU	Line Rescue Unit
MDU	Mobil Dam Unit
NFA	National Fire Brigades Association
NFBU	National Fire Brigades Union
NFS	National Fire Service
NFSBF	National Fire Services Benevolent Fund
NRFB	North Riding County Fire Brigade

NYF&RS North Yorkshire Fire & Rescue Service
NYFB North Yorkshire Fire Brigade
OIC Officer in Charge
P Pump
PC Police Constable
PE Pump Escape
PL Pump Ladder
PPC Public Protection Committee
PSI Pounds per square inch
RFA Royal Fleet Auxiliary
RT Rescue Tender
RTA Road Traffic Accident
SCU Self Contained Unit
StnO Station Officer
SU Salvage Unit
SubO Sub Officer
SUFB Scalby Urban District Fire Brigade
TL Turntable Ladder
VFA Voice Frequency Alarm
VFR Vertical Face Rescue
WT Water Tender
WW1 World War 1

CONVERSIONS

1 inch or " = 25mm
1 foot or ' = 300mm
1 yard = 900mm
12d = 1shilling or 5p
20 shillings = £1
1 Guinea = £1.1shilling or £1.05p
1 Gallon = 5.5 litres
16 ounces = 1 pound
14 pounds = 1 stone
112 pounds = 1 hundredweight or cwt
20 hundredweights or 20 cwt = 1 ton
1 ton = 1.02 tonne

PREFACE

After my family, local Scarborough history has been a major love of my life. It followed suit that after starting a career in the fire service and finding that I enjoyed its history also, that the two should be combined.

There are only a few history books about Scarborough which is surprising when you consider what a long, interesting history the town holds. On the other hand the fire service has many books written about it, but sadly they seem to reflect London's firefighting history and ignore the rest of the country. The local newspaper often has a section on past occurrences and firefighting is a regular feature within it, therefore I am assuming that there is a lot of local interest.

Taking all this into account, a number of years ago I decided to put this right by producing a book on the subject. After many hours of research over a period of years it should have gone to print but I always felt that the story was never complete as new events were occurring and more facts were unearthed.

Surprisingly the more modern times, in particular the war years were the hardest period to get accurate accounts of. The newspapers revealed very little in case the information could be used to enemy advantage. Even the Scarborough Evening News on covering 'The March Blitz' of Scarborough referred to a *'North East Coastal Town'*, which was also the common reference for Hull. As the fire service was nationalised Scarborough Council records no longer helped, whilst national records yet again concentrate on London's war efforts. Much of the wartime research therefore has been compiled from oral records by people who were there, but this produced many conflicting reports, each person adamant their version was right. Sadly these people are dwindling in number as the years pass, making it more important that the facts are recorded in book form now.

Though using newspapers and official records for the chapters covering the North Yorkshire Fire Brigade and the North Yorkshire Fire and Rescue Service I have also drawn on my own personal experience, I started my career as the North Yorkshire Fire Brigade was born, taking part in many of the call-outs mentioned throughout the period right to 2003.

As firefighting arrangements were closely allied to the police, ambulance and waterworks in Scarborough a brief history has been included in the book, whilst the index pages cover dates and names more thoroughly.

Though I realise the story is not yet finished, and never really will be, I am now retired from the fire service and feel that now is the most appropriate time to end the book. I know there are mistakes and omissions for which I apologise in advance. I would be grateful to hear of these, as I hope in the not to distant future to release a companion book to Conflagrations, which will contain many photographs and a few firefighting tales not included in this book, along with the relevant corrections.

I must just add here a big thank you to all the sponsors who have contributed to the cost of printing this book. People are always asking for support for good causes, and it can be difficult in decided who to give to, all I can say is that I really appreciate the generosity of all the donors.

This page sponsored by:
THE AMBERLEY
West Park Terrace Scarborough

EARLY SCARBOROUGH

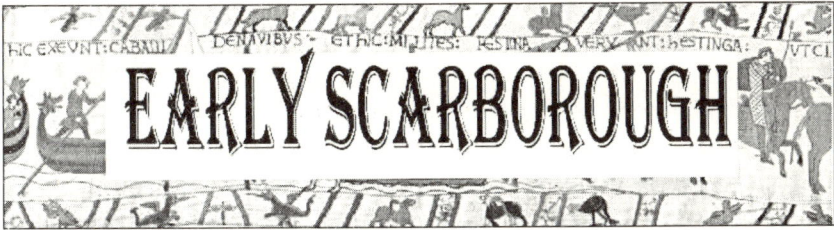

There is plenty of evidence to prove that Scarborough was suffering from the effects of fire as long ago as 1066, when it was just a small village tucked under the hillside, now known as the Castle Hill. The town was built in that situation purely for the protection that the hill offered from the elements.

At that time, in September 1066, Harold Hadrada who was in league with Earl Tostig, the Lord of Falsgrave, and their combined troops, attacked Scarborough. After bitter fighting they built a large bonfire on what is now the site of the Castle Dykes and rolled burning bales and logs down, razing the town to the ground and many of the townsfolk were slain as they tried to surrender. Jubilant at their success Harold and Tostig proceeded in their boats up the Humber to their eventual defeat at the Battle of Stamford Bridge.

After the invasion, the town quickly recovered, but not to the size it had been before. After this battle, and the Battle of Hastings, William took the throne and, due to opposition, he ordered the destruction of the troops from the north. His own troops systematically looted and plundered before destroying the area throughout 1069-1070. Evidence points to the fact that Quay Street area, which would have been almost the whole town, was again subjected to burning and destruction. This is probably the cause of the myth that Scarborough is not in the Doomsday Book, which was surveyed in 1087, due to the destruction of the town by Harold in 1066. Other theories for the omission are that the collators of the book were only collecting evidence of farm holdings, so Scarborough, being a fishing community, was overlooked. Yet another theory was that Scarborough was included in the returns for Falsgrave, which, at the time, was the major of the two manors.

The first real attempt at fire prevention since the Romans were in England was in this period, while William the Conqueror was in power (1066-1087). It was deemed that all fires and lights (as fire was the only means of lighting) be put out at 8 p.m. and a bell was tolled to signal the time. This period of lights out was known as "curfew" (from the Norman French "couvre feu" meaning "cover fire").

William had recognised the dangers from fire in wooden, closely built, buildings and, knowing they were more prone to catch fire whilst people were asleep at night ordered the "fire preventive" method. At that time England was far more densely wooded and even a small fire could quite rapidly develop into a forest fire travelling many miles through the countryside. In Scarborough it can be imagined that this system would be adopted, not with the priority being fire prevention, as was intended, but as a means of hiding the town at night, to prevent William's troops on land and unwanted visitors from the sea making surprise attacks whilst the inhabitants slept.

For many years it was assumed that in 1318 the Scots under the command of Black Douglas, a Scottish general, again reduced a large part of the town to ashes. The Scots were constantly ravaging the North after their victory over the English at Bannockburn in 1314. However whilst these facts

A section of the Bayeux tapestry depicting how fire was used as a means of warfare.

are recorded in the three main histories of Scarborough the new history by Doctor Jack Binns declares this to be a myth.

For obvious reasons, as can be seen on these occasions, Scarborough was burnt down without any attempt at firefighting. When on other occasions fire broke out, the main effort of firefighting was done by the people whose house or property was involved, aided by friends, relatives and no doubt by immediate neighbours who would have been concerned for their own property.

The only means of fire fighting available was by bucket chains from a reasonable water supply.

WATER SUPPLIES TO SCARBOROUGH

It would be useful here to include a brief look at the development of the water supplies to Scarborough in the early days, as well as the development of fire fighting, as the main medium of fighting fires was, and still is, water. Without it, the concept of organised fire fighting was unthinkable.

At the time the supposed razing of Scarborough by the Scots took place in 1316 there were two bore holes in the town, one at the rear of the house called "Paradise" and the other at the east end of St Sepulchre Street. Both these supplies gave dirty, grimy water, which, by today's standards, was completely inadequate for drinking,

The original site in Falsgrave Park of the water supplies. The building now standing on the site was probably erected in the 1700s when the area was enclosed.

and limited to the amount that could be drawn if required in a hurry, for firefighting purposes.

The Franciscan monks had come to Scarborough just before this period, and set themselves up in Friarage, on the site of the present Friarage School. They at first shared the town's boreholes but disliked the water and whilst the town was being rebuilt, they set about bringing a supply of water from a spring, (on the site of what is now Falsgrave Park, near Springhill Road).

This they did by building a covered stone trough, sloping from the spring down into the town and put outlets at the sites of the former bore holes. It is believed that the task was completed in 1319. This basic form of water supply, with some modifications, actually lasted in the town for over six centuries.

The term conduit was given to the pipe or trough, which carried the water and also the point of outlet of the water. The outlet at St Sepulchre Street was known as the lower conduit, hence the name the area acquired, and kept until recently, of Lower Conduit Street (now Princess Square).

The new supply was most welcome to the townsfolk who were now able to drink far fresher water than was possible before. Due to the amount of people drawing from the supply and the inefficiency of the stone troughs, which leaked at every joint in the stonework, the supply soon became overdrawn. The monks, in 1339, had another trough built from Springhill ending in their own property. This meant that they did not have to share with the townsfolk and that the town's supply was eased of the burden of them drawing from it.

It appears that sometime in the 1400's the stone troughs were replaced by lead piping which must have had a great effect on the efficiency of the supply it delivered. Even this, though, could not have been successful in the supplying of water in case of fire and the main source for this must have still been the Damgate stream running through the town, ponds and even the sea.

THE DEVELOPMENT OF FIREFIGHTING

The monks would have most probably assisted in the firefighting of anyone unfortunate enough to have suffered from fire. It became common, but by no means policy, in England for the parish churches, as they were classed as the administrative offices, to keep buckets, stays (ladders) and hooks (used to drag down burning roof thatching) on their premises so that there was probably an assortment of these at both St Mary's Church and Friarage.

The Great Fire of London, in 1666, apart from the poor souls who were left homeless, was in more than one way a blessing in disguise. It set about changes in both the way and the styles in which houses were constructed in ensuring they were built of better materials and further apart.

There was also legislation introduced that each parish should have available, at all times, firefighting equipment, namely buckets, ladders and hooks. The fire also helped to rid the city of the great plague, the Black Death as it was commonly known, which had swept through it in 1665. All these advantages applied to London but the rest of the country felt the effects in time.

It was soon after the great fire that an event took place that was to have more effect on the organisation of fire fighting than any other. Doctor Nicholas Barbon started an insurance company in London, known as the "Fire Office", (later to change its name to the Phoenix Fire Office). His scheme being that people would make an annual subscription to the office in return for which he would pay out a sum of money in the event of them suffering from a loss caused by fire.

A sun fire mark which was until recent years to be found at the rear of the Harbour Bar – Foreshore Road

This scheme soon had competition in that another group opened offices called the "Hand in Hand". It became evident to them that, to save money, the best means of reducing losses caused by fire was to employ people to fight the fires and salvage articles from them. Thus was borne the insurance fire brigades.

The firemen employed by the insurance companies were kitted out in elaborate uniforms; not really adequate for fighting fires, but so bright that they would stand out and advertise the company who employed them. The insurance brigade would also employ people on a casual basis to man the hand pumps at fires, often just paying them in beer.

An added incentive was that the London authorities were offering a cash bonus to the first people to arrive at a fire with a means of pumping water onto it. This resulted in the fast development of manual pumps, which if they were available had, up until that time, been no more than a box which had to be dragged to the place where it was required. London, in the early eighteenth century, became the leading manufacturer throughout the world for fire pumps.

The first improvement to this was to put skids on the bottom of the box so that it could be slid to the fire. Putting wheels onto it soon followed this. Once they were easily mobile they were enlarged and a six man a-side pump became common.

The insurance companies started to produce fire plates, or marks, which were fixed to the walls outside the insured property. These served two purposes, firstly to advertise the insurance company, and secondly, to help identify which property was insured by them. Not many people in those days were literate so it was no good having the address of a client if no one could read it.

There were by now many other "offices" springing up and, contrary to popular belief, all insurance brigades would rush to every fire in their area and work hard to put the fire out. The main reason was that if they could be seen to be the first at the scene, and the hardest working, then the client and any onlookers might be persuaded to move their policies to that company.

SCARBOROUGH'S EARLY FIRE BRIGADES

There is no evidence to suggest that there was an insurance brigade in Scarborough but it seems likely that as in most towns of its size, there were buckets and other such fire fighting equipment provided by both the parish council and insurance companies who donated them to the town. They would have been stored at either the local agents of the insurance company or at some venue such as the Parish Church of St Mary's.

The parish records of 1720 state that William Thomson, who was the castle governor and one of the two members of

A Yorkshire fire mark

parliament for Scarborough, bought and gave to the corporation a fire engine for the extinguishing of fires. Whilst it is not known what constituted this fire engine, as it was common to call anything used in fire fighting an engine, even the buckets, it may be assumed that this was a manual pump.

The Sun Insurance office had an agent in the town as early as 1726, and policies for local properties date from 1722; they presented small fire pumps to many towns to be used by the inhabitants to reduce the loss caused by fire. These pumps were available to anyone who was in need of them, regardless of whether or not they were insured by the company. It was a good advertising ploy, as if you knew their engine protected you, their name would be to the fore when considering an insurance policy. There is no direct evidence that Scarborough was at this time supplied with a pump by an insurance company but it would seem likely they would contribute to the up-keep of the existing one.

An account of a fire, which took place on the 19th November 1798, suggests that the engine was still in existence at that time; it was at the house of Mr James Clark in Merchant's Row, at seven p.m., when a little 3-year-old girl, was burnt to death in her bed. It was reported *"the fire was extinguished about 8 o'clock by the fire engines and other help."*

At a meeting of the Town Corporation on the 29th January 1799 it was voted unanimously *"That the corporation do subscribe and pay the sum of ten guineas towards the purchase of an additional fire engine for the town".*

The idea brought about some interest in the firefighting arrangements in the town as, in 1800, shortly after moving the town's affairs to a new town hall in St Nicholas St, (the site which for many years was Lloyds Bank and now awaiting redevelopment), the Chamberlains ordered that the stables in the yard at the rear of the town hall should be adapted in preparation for the arrival of the new fire engine. A total bill of £92.15s was submitted for the pump, buckets, hose, etc. whilst the engine cost £49.

Whilst there were fire marks on the walls of houses in Scarborough they were purely for advertising purposes. There are still Sun Insurance Company fire marks around the area, the most likely one to be original is above Style Plus 4, Eastborough whilst there are others in Castlegate, and Princess Street and a Newcastle mark, at Main Street, Burniston.

Two original marks were definitely in Dumple Street before its demolition (now Friargate) as recounted in Doctor Kirk's book, "A History of Fire Fighting"; one of which was issued by the Protector and the other by the Yorkshire Insurance Company.

The Protector can be dated to between 1825 and 1835, when the company was in existence, before its take-over by Phoenix. The Yorkshire mark can be dated between 1826 and 1850 as this was the only period when the design of mark was used, (the design was later changed to the more common view of the front of York Minster in 1850). The fact that the Yorkshire mark was there proves that they were purely for advertising purposes as the Yorkshire Assurance Company only ever had Fire Brigades in York and Hull.

A Newcastle fire mark to be seen at Burniston High Street

BETTER WATER SUPPLIES IN SCARBOROUGH

Scarborough was still trying to improve on its town's water supply, as ironically, the town was becoming famous for its spring waters at the Spaw. People were travelling to Scarborough for this water but when they arrived, the drinking water was of poor quality and in very short supply. In 1808 a spring at Stoney Haggs Rise was brought into use and a supply was directed into the town from there, via pot pipes.

Even before the system was put into operation it was obvious that the supply was still going to be vastly inadequate, so plans were developed to tap into a third spring at Springhill Road.

This supply was carried in cast iron pipes and deposited in a dug out reservoir in Workhouse Square, (hence the name of Waterhouse Lane leading to it. Until recently this area was known as Chapmans Yard, It has now been developed into the new shopping complex housing TK Maxx). The reservoir was covered over and was, at that time, the biggest covered receptacle in Britain, capable of holding 4,000 hogs' head or 200,000 gallons (almost 1,000,000 litres) of water.

The advantage of this system was that water could be collected and stored at night, whilst the demand for it was not so great, supplementing the amount drawn from the springs in the daytime.

THE TOWN FIRE PUMPS

On 25th September 1826, at a corporation meeting, it was noted that fire engines were falling into a state of disrepair and it was recommended that the various insurance agents be informed, especially the London & Newcastle agent.

This was followed by a report in the constitution of the corporation of Scarborough in 1827. Under the section of current annual charges, the cost of repairs to the fire engine were nil, showing that the corporation by then owned the engines but the insurance companies were still held responsible for the maintenance.

The Sun fire office transferred an engine to Scarborough from Swallow Street, London in October of that year, yet, according to their records, the corporation did not adopt this pump for at least another twenty years. This suggests that the Sun still supplied an independent pump for the town use.

Obviously the corporation's thoughts about the fire fighting equipment and capabilities changed little as in December 1839 The Hull Advertiser & Exchange Gazette ran an article:

'SCARBOROUGH – FIRE ENGINES – we are happy to observe that at last the state of Scarborough's fire engines have been taken into serious consideration, they have long been in a condition discreditable to the town, and far from the efficiency in which they ought to be. Not only so, but they have been encumbered with a debt, and detained for the money, the amount previously advanced and expended not having been returned. During the past week a meeting of respectable inhabitants was held at the Star Inn, when it was resolved to canvas the town for subscriptions, for the purpose of paying the deband establishing a company for working the engine. This resolution is now being carried into effect, and it is to be hoped will be successful. The different assurance companies, having agencies in Scarborough will be applied to, as well as inhabitants, for assistance.'

Whilst this article proved that there was a new awareness of the fire fighting role in the town, very little seems to have transpired as there is no evidence of any improvements until a number of years later.

FIRST POLICE SUPERINTENDENT

A parliamentary act changed both the face of local government and the police organisation of the town. The Municipal Reform Act of 1832 lead to the extension of government franchise to all ratepayers and eventually, in 1835, to the first town council elected by the people.

Also under the Act, policing of the town was brought into being. The nearest the town came to policing was four night watchmen, employed in 1818, who walked the town at night with an oil lamp and a rattle. Their job was to proclaim the hour and weather conditions, whilst looking after the well being of the town. The act saw, in 1835, the introduction of the parish constables, paid three guineas per year, who were employed to deter would-be felons; and by 2nd January 1836, under the recommendations of the newly appointed Watch Committee, a superintendent of the police was employed. The first police chief (the title Chief Constable did not become popular until some years later) was Mr William Robinson, paid £100 per annum, and assisted by two constables, paid three guineas per annum, who were issued with staves and handcuffs.

In June of the same year Robinson was brought before the committee for his "*reprehensible conduct*" and in July his appointment was terminated. Mr John Ramsden of Leeds filled his position; the committee was not slow at cost cutting measures as the position now carried a salary of £65.

In 1839 there were complaints heard by the board regarding the police taking bribes and, as a result, on September 9th, Mr Ramsden was also dismissed. It took until December to fill the post when Sergeant Richard Roberts of the Hull police was appointed.

SCARBOROUGH WATER COMPANY

The town supplies were yet again proving inadequate for the rapid growth that the town was undergoing and, with the advent of steam motors, the obvious solution was to pump water from Cayton Bay springs. This was a task that was going to prove costly and the council felt that they could not undertake it, so they placed the responsibility of water supplies into the hands of a private consortium of local businessmen.

By 1844 there was a reservoir built at the junction of Filey Road and Seacliff Road (roughly where Holbeck Mews is now sited) capable of holding one million gallons of water.

The system allowed for supplies to be purchased and then piped directly into individual houses or properties as well as supplying, free of charge, the two old conduit sites for those who could not afford their own piped supply. It also had fireplugs included in its length to allow a special adapter to be knocked into it, so that water could be drawn off for firefighting purposes.

It was not long before a larger, more efficient, pump was built and a larger reservoir (4.5 million gallons) constructed at Osgodby Hill Top replacing the original one. This was later to be supplemented, in 1872, by the Cayton pumping station on Osgodby Lane.

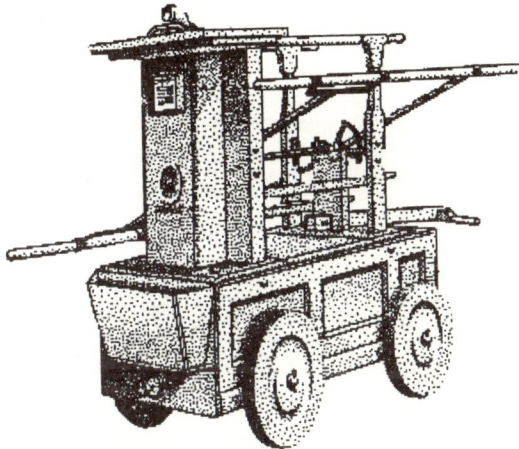

The type of hand pump that was supplied by the
Sun Insurance Company and used in Scarborough

The Town Police Clause Act of 1847 stated that:

> *"The commissioners may purchase or provide such engines for extinguishing fire, and such water buckets, pipes or other apparatus for such engines, and such fire escapes and other implements for safety or use in case of fire, and may purchase, keep or hire such horses for drawing such engines as they think fit, and may build, provide or hire places for keeping such engines with their appurtenances, and may employ proper number of persons to act as firemen and may make such rules for their regulation as they think proper and give such firemen and other persons such salaries and such rewards for their exertions in case of fire, as they think fit."*

The Waterworks Clause Act, 1847, confirmed the right of a fire authority to tap into, and draw from, private waterworks as required for fire fighting activities if deemed necessary.

So it was with these authorities in 1847 that the parish fire engines were placed under the control of a committee of the commissioners under the Scarborough Improvements Act (a body initially set up in 1805 to oversee the cleaning, paving and lighting of the streets etc.).

The commissioners appointed Mr Ed Smith, plumber and glazier, as the superintendent. He had been, since the privatisation of the water supplies, the council superintendent of the waterworks for which he received a retainer of £10 per annum. His knowledge of pipe work and water stood him in good stead for the responsibility of maintaining the fire pumps.

The local paper in May 1847 stated

> *"In the event of fire, the keys of the Engine House could be obtained upon application to him (Mr Smith) at his residence, 16 Granby-Place, Queen-Street or at his shop at Waterhouse Lane."*

It would seem that the Engine House was moved from the Town Hall, as the commissioners were an independent body and they had to find somewhere else to house the engine. A building was rented at a cost of £5 per annum for this purpose and on the town survey map (1852) the site is shown as the corner of Falsgrave Walk and Vernon Place (now the Card Store – junction of Westborough and Vernon Road).

It was not long before the first recorded use of the new fireplugs occurred (though this was not necessarily the first occurrence, because of the lack of recorded information at this time), at 5 a.m. Sunday 12th September 1847, in Mr Richards's grocer's warehouse, St Helens Square. The report stated that water from the private company plugs was used. There was £350 worth of damage caused to consumables, all of which was covered by insurance. This was the same day that 19-year-old Mary White, of Globe Street, died of burns received on the previous Friday evening. She had reached for a candle from a shelf and accidentally set fire to her nightgown.

Arrangements for the organisation of the fire brigade appeared to work well at first, but Mr Smith was a plumber, a trade that was seeing a boom as people were having water piped into their homes for the first time. Therefore, the locating of Mr Smith in times of emergency was extremely difficult as his work took him to all parts of town. He also moved house to the South Cliff area, which did not make him easily accessible; so it was unsurprising that at a commissioners meeting on 27th November 1849 a petition was presented complaining about the defective management of the fire brigade department. It was said that, since Mr Smith had been appointed, keys to the Engine House could be found all over town whilst he was never available to supervise at fires.

The commissioners set up a committee to look into the complaints and their findings were reported back on 15th January 1850. It was confirmed that keys had been in various people's possession, but had been recovered since the complaints. A set of keys kept at the police station had been sent for by Mr Smith and later returned by his apprentice leading to speculation that he had lost his set. It was also reported that since the complaints a board has been placed above the Engine House door with the names of people from whom the keys may have been obtained.

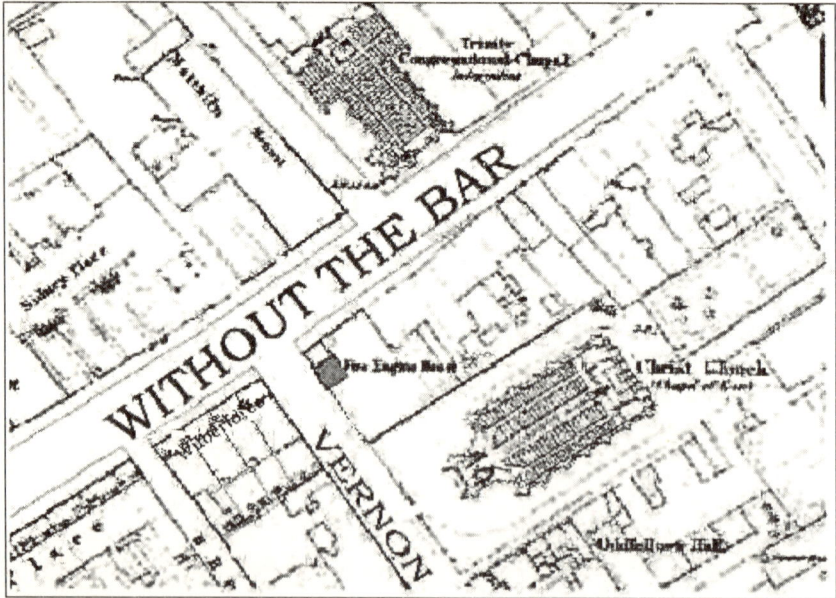

Part of the 1850 ordnance survey map depicting the fire engine house

The committee upheld the complaints and made a number of recommendations.

1) *That the employment of a salaried Superintendent be discontinued and that the charge of the engines be put in the direction of the fire engine committee (themselves).*

2) *That 6 practical men be given keys to the Engine House. The first one called to the Engine House would be required to attend the fire and connect the hose to the fire plugs, then direct operations. After the fire they would be required to put the equipment back into working order ready for further use. For their efforts they would be paid the same as the firemen.*

3) *That the fireplugs be marked clearly on the nearest wall. That the plugs should be inspected as to their workability (as the pits soon filled with mud due to the conditions at that time) and that more plugs should be made available.*

4) *That there should be a board placed not only above the Engine House door, bearing the key-holders name, but also in all 6 wards.*

5) *That all the hose should be kept properly folded on a convenient truck (handcart) in the Engine House, along with other needful apparatus.*

The recommendations were studied and implemented, but as the equipment was not getting maintained properly, they decided to appoint Mr James Thompson, local banker and agent for the Sun Assurance Company, as the new Fire Brigade Superintendent. The Commissioners obviously deemed it prudent to appoint someone such as Mr Thompson, who as an insurance agent would have a vested interest in the well being of the brigade. It was probably at this time that the corporation adopted the Sun fire engine.

POLICE UNIFORMS
In 1851, after much discussion the police were issued with uniforms, to make them more identifiable to the public. Because of this the constables wages were reduced by 1s 6d per week and the Chief's by 2 shillings.

LOWER CONDUIT STREET
There was a smell of burning hanging over the Lower Conduit Street area, (now Princess Square) on 12th September 1854, but even though it was almost midnight, little was thought of it, because it was emanating from the herring curing business of Mr James Sellers.

Inside the premises however the fire had built up over some time before it showed itself by bursting through the roof. Assistance was sent for from both the town fire brigade and the Castle Hill barracks. The latter, the 6th Regiment, were first on the scene with their camp pump, supervised by Captain Gore.

The town pump was taken from the engine house before Mr Thompson had time to get there and in the hurry the wrong hose was picked up. This was incompatible with the fittings on the pump but fitted direct to the fireplugs, which was what eventually happened.

Whilst the town brigade fought the fire at the rear of the building, Captain Gore and his men attacked it from the front. The Mayor, Mr Sharpin, assisted Captain Gore in directing the military. A joiner's shop, owned by Mr TW Crosby, located next door to the smokehouse, was also destroyed. The poor water pressure did little to help the situation, but by 2 a.m. the firefighters had started to subdue the fire.

The cause of the fire was never discovered but it was quite certain it never originated in the curing rooms.

Amongst the losses to Mr Sellers' property was his debts book containing £50 worth of debts. Neither premises were insured and therefore a memorial fund was opened in Mr Crosby's name at Theakston's Library, where donations were received for both parties.

It was stated that a high opinion can be drawn of Captain Gore, whilst Superintendent Thompson's labours were arduous and praiseworthy.

After the fire a Mr Beverley was so impressed with the efforts shown by the 6th Regiment that he made a donation of half a crown per man, plus an extra half a crown to Private J Thornhill for 'the zeal, activity and intelligence shown when in a situation of difficulty and hazard.'

There was also the cost of the 6th Regiment's clothing paid for by the Commissioners.

NEW FIRE ESCAPE LADDER

On 25th July 1855 a fire escape ladder, whose purchase was recommended by the commissioners, was delivered from London. It was said to be similar to those used by the metropolis and other large places.

This type of ladder was a fly ladder escape designed by Abraham Wivell in 1836. It consisted of a 31 foot main ladder mounted on a carriage with 4 wheels (two large ones with a 6 foot diameter and two smaller ones with diameters of 15 inches). Beneath the main ladder was a canvas chute, running to just above ground level where it was attached to an apron hammock, this was a means of lowering people to the ground. On top of the main ladder was hinged a 19 foot fly ladder which could be elevated by using hauling lines, in addition further ladders could be lashed on, giving a possible reach of 51 feet.

In London they were used not by the fire brigades but by a voluntary subscription organisation, The Royal Society for the Protection of Life from Fire. It was a fact that the insurance brigades were set up to protect property from fire and it was only a side issue that lives were saved. There was no emphasis placed upon saving life or providing means of escape so the society developed and purchased escape ladders, which having wheels made them easily transportable.

By 1843 the Society was under reform providing six escape ladders throughout London along with night watchmen who were stationed in sentry boxes. The number of escape ladders increased steadily until 1867 when 85 stations were placed into the hands of the newly formed Metropolitan Fire Brigade.

As for the new Scarborough escape, there were no premises available in which to house it so it was given temporary lodgings in the Scavengmonger's Yard (roughly the site

Manchester's wheeled escape ladder in use in 1849, this ladder was identical to the one purchased by Scarborough in 1855. Note the canvas shute under the ladder

of the present fire station). A purpose built shed was constructed for the escape at the council stables on North Marine Road.

A new regular drill system was brought into existence, with the fire brigade practising drills on a three monthly basis, supervised by Mr Thompson. Special attention was paid to the workings of the escape ladder, as the men were unfamiliar with this piece of equipment.

NORTH RIDING COUNTY POLICE FORCE

In October 1856 the North Riding County Police Force was founded, with a paid force of fifty men to cover the area. They were placed under the command of Captain Thomas Hill. Scarborough was asked if they wanted to be included in the arrangements, but rejected the offer and on the 18th May 1856 Mr Roberts was asked to resign his post as collector of taxes so that he could donate more of his time to the development of the police force. Both he and his constables were given pay rises and improved the force over the next twelve months until they had six whole time policemen, including the Chief of Police.

PORRITT & BROWN RAFT YARD

On the evening of Monday 10th November 1856 there was a strong north westerly wind blowing through Scarborough. In the raft yard owned by Porrett & Brown, located at the bottom of Blands Cliff where it joined Neptune Terrace (now Foreshore Road), there was a small fire smouldering in the furnace of the engine house belonging to the sawmill. The wind caught hold of some of the sparks from the fires embers and blew them around the sawmill floor where there was sawdust scattered. The wind helped to waft the embers that ignited the sawdust, which in turn ignited deals and timber laid about the mill. Once this was burning it was only a short time until the adjoining dwellings were alight.

The first premise to suffer was Mr J Yule's Temperance Coffee House, where Mrs Yule was sitting up waiting for her husband, who was out of town preaching, to come home. At about 11.30 she saw the fire in the engine house and alerted her neighbours before retrieving her personal belongings prior to the house being engulfed in flames.

The fire brigade was sent for and, under the supervision of Mr Thompson, the manual pump with six men aside was set into the sea, as it was high tide at that time. The leather hose was run out from the pump and the local water company's fireplug in Merchants Row. In the meantime fire was spreading from house to house.

The newspaper reported:

"It was heart rending to see the children brought out of windows in their beds, and the efforts made by poor tenants to save their furniture and effects, many of them were aged people."

Part of the 1850 ordnance survey map depicting the Blands Cliff / New Steps area

In all, there were sixteen families made homeless by the conflagration. There were a number of bathing machines parked near by, owned by Mr TW Crosby who had them unlocked and put them to the use of housing bedding and possessions of the families made homeless.

Captain Gore, the officer in charge of the 6th Regiment based at the Castle Hill barracks, turned out his men and the camp fire pump, which was also set into the sea. The soldiers and civilians worked for long periods submerged to their waists in the sea. The main fear was that the fire would spread to Blands Cliff and catch hold in the main part of town. To help alleviate this, hoses were got to work from the roof of Mr Postgate, whose property over looked the lath-house.

At half-past three in the morning the fire was still spreading and, due to his enthusiasm with the job in hand, Mr Thompson placed himself where a large piece of timber collapsed onto him. He was recovered and moved to hospital by his fellow firefighters. As Thompson was unable to take further part in the fire, Mr John Harrison, tinner and brazier, took on the supervisor's role.

By 4 o'clock the fire was at its height, the tide was going out and more and more hose was needed to keep the pumps in the sea. Eventually there was no more hose available to use, so a bucket chain system had to be set up to supply the pumps.

It was deemed advisable by several of the magistrates present (the local dignitaries and people of rank always turned out to advise others how to go about their work, sometimes their efforts were to the good but often they hindered the progress as they would be countermanding each others decisions) to send to York for assistance.

Mr T Postgate and Mr TW Crosby, acting on instructions, contacted the railway stationmaster and the telegraph attendant and within half an hour the York Fire Brigade and engines were at York Station ready to come to Scarborough. In the meantime Mr Harrison re-sited his engine and hoses to better use and slowly the fire was brought under control. By 6 o'clock they had the better of the fire.

York Fire Brigade arrived at 7.30, by special train, and even though there was not much left to do, the local men were grateful for the respite. The two York pumps 'Ebor' and 'Yorkshire' set too with the job of pumping under the supervision of the York Superintendent, Mr Taylor.

All the buildings at the bottom of Blands Cliff were reduced to a blackened heap of ruins. The raft yard was totally destroyed along with several hundred pounds worth of timber. A Mr Stanhope, who owned most of the dwellings that were destroyed luckily had them insured. It was the tenants who suffered the greatest hardship, as most of them had no insurance or insufficient to cover their losses. To make matters worse for them, looters and plunderers made good use of the confusion to help themselves, even though the Chief Constable, Mr Roberts, and his men were present.

At an Improvement Commissioners' meeting on Tuesday morning, after the fire, it was resolved that the thanks of the town be passed to Captain Gore and his men and that the chairman find some means to show his appreciation.

The Mayor visited the site on the afternoon and started a relief fund for those made homeless, suggesting that a collection be made in every church and chapel in the town. There was £10 compensation paid to the 6th Company for clothing by the Yorkshire and Northern Insurance Companies.

The site was eventually redeveloped and baths built (now Corrigan's Coney Island) and the area was added to the list of fireplugs required.

After many attempts by the North Eastern Railway company to obtain the £23 1s 7d owed to them for laying on a special train to transport the York crews, they sent a letter to Mr R Williamson in April 1858 asking him to try and obtain the money. He approached the Board with their request and they eventually decided to pay the bill in the May of 1858 (18 months after the fire).

The Bridlington six-a-side hand pump now on display at Castle Museum, York. This is a similar type of hand pump to Scarborough's

A resolution was then passed that in future, unless the Chairman of the Board or the surveyor sanctioned the request for the attendance, payment would not be made. The railway master and the local insurance agents were also informed of the resolution.

PAY RISE

In May 1857 Mr Thompson put in a written request for a salary increase to £10 per annum or he would have to resign his appointment. The committee took no action whatsoever.

Mr Thompson obviously never carried out his threat as in the August of the same year he found and reported faults in the large (number two) pump's valve chamber and suction hose. He was told to get an estimate of the cost for repairs.

By September the estimate was submitted and the board told the surveyor to go ahead with the repairs. To help finance the venture the possibility of selling the small (number one) pump was to be looked into.

WEST SANDGATE

West Sandgate, in 1858 ran from the present junction of Foreshore Rd – Eastborough through to the Leeds Hotel, whilst Merchants Row started at the bend of Eastborough and ran up to include what is now Merchants Row. On the 3rd March that year at 1 o'clock in the afternoon a fire was reported at the 'Old Factory', a four storey building, West Sandgate. It was occupied by Thomas Shaw and used for making and repairing sails.

Superintendent Thompson was sent for and the fireplugs in the Bolts were brought into use. Also in attendance was the Commissioners surveyor, Mr A Taylor, who also tried to organise the fire fighting efforts. Some of the other firefighters were Firemen Chatwin, Harrison, Reed, Temple, and Police Constables Whitehead and Wood.

The building was soon alight throughout and much concern was given to the fact that it might spread into the adjoining properties of Mrs Cammish and H Pearson and Mrs Rowntrees boarding house. It was even considered it could spread to the Dolphin Inn and a sweet shop opposite, but, with the efforts of the fire brigade and the help of the officers and men of the 9th Regiment, it was confined to the one building.

At the height of the fire at about 2 o'clock the York Fire Brigade was requested to attend by the Mayor. It was 3.30 when they arrived by train, too late to render any help, as by this time, all that was left was the blackened walls.

The cellar of the building had been leased by J & T Race, fishermen, and by Mr Readman, fish curer. Mr Shaw lost his entire stock in trade – sails from 19 boats, eight of which were double sets, the majority of which belonged to Filey fishermen and were worth up to £300 per set – valued at approximately £3000 and also his accounts books.

After the fire Superintendent Thompson reported to the Commissioners that 100 yards of hose was required to replace hose damaged at the job. He was told to claim from Yorkshire Insurance Office, which was a debt that seemed to take some time to recover.

The Commissioners also recorded a vote of thanks for the 9th Regiment and offered compensation for soldiers clothing; this seemed to be another debt that was outstanding for a long period of time.

Yorkshire Assurance asked the Commissioners to pay the North East Railway for transporting the York Fire Brigade but it was decided not to pay. The reason being was that it was the Mayor and not the board who had requested them, and they had, since that time, passed a resolution that only the Chairman or Surveyor could request York's assistance.

NEW STEPS FIRE

In the same year, 1858, New Steps (the steps which now run from Foreshore Road, to Merchants Row, at the side of the St Thomas's building) was a well used main thoroughfare, with houses and warehouses running up the side where the St Thomas's buildings now stands. On the other side, at the corner of the sands, was a stable; beyond that, running up the steps were cottages and houses with The Bolts running off at right angles to New Steps, in a long line, at the rear of Neptune Terrace (now Foreshore Road buildings).

The large building extending up the steps on the site of the present day St Thomas's building was owned by Thomas Weddell, who let out the building to various people. "Prospect House", a boarding and lodging house, was accessible from about half way up New Steps, projecting forward to the sands. It occupied the upper three floors of the building and was leased by Mr Charles Campion.

The floor below the lodgings was used as a furniture warehouse and mattress makers and was leased by Mr Sutcliffe. The floor below this was also leased by Mr Sutcliffe and sub-let. It was used at the rear as a wood turner's shop by Mr James Skelton and to the front as a wareroom by Mr W Wear, where a quantity of ships sails and other products of the same type of material were stored.

Below this was a cellar, which was actually at the sea-front ground floor level, occupied by Messrs T & J Ward as a coal depot, where there was approximately 50 to 60 tons of coal stored.

On the evening of Saturday 18th December, two policemen, Police Constables Murgatroyed and Jowsey, were on duty in Carr Street (now the part of Eastborough running from Blands Cliff to Leading Post Street) when they detected a strong smell of burning and an investigation of the area lead them to the top of New Steps, where flames were seen issuing from a window in Mr Sutcliffe's warehouse.

Police Constable Jowsey ran to the Town Hall/Police Offices on St Nicholas Street and informed Chief Constable Roberts, who in turn sent constables in various directions to locate Mr Thompson and his firemen.

Meanwhile Police Constable Murgatroyed aroused the Campion family in Prospect House, which consisted of Mrs Campion, her daughter and son-in-law, Mr and Mrs Shaw, with their eighteen-month old baby, two nieces, a young daughter and three sons.

It seems that in the confusion Mr and Mrs Shaw each thought the other had taken the baby, and it was only when Mr Shaw tried to return to find his watch (a valuable object in those days) that, in the dense smoke and darkness, he put his hand on the baby's head and recognised it for what it was.

The sons slept on the upper floor and such was the extent and rate of spread of the fire that, as the last son was leaving, his foot went through the bottom tread of the stairs as it burnt away from below, but luckily he managed to drag himself out.

In the short time that it took Mr Thompson and his firemen to arrive at the scene of the fire with the engine, the whole of that part of town had been awakened and gathered round to watch the incident.

Even the prompt and good supply of water from the fire plugs did little to stop the rapid spread of the fire, which was fanned by a strong south westerly breeze and fed by the contents of the various store rooms. The building was almost certainly lost, but Thompson and his men worked hard to contain the blaze which, with the height and extent the flames were going to, was an extremely hard job especially with the surrounding property being close. On the opposite corner of New Steps and the Foreshore, below the cottages on The Bolts, was a stable containing two horses which were rescued and removed to safety.

By 2 a.m. the streets of Leading Post Street, Merchants Row, The Bolts and their adjoining avenues were so thick with smoke that the only means of access to the fire ground was via Blands Cliff.

At about 2.30 in the morning, the fire was at its fiercest which was the time the roof eventually collapsed, falling through the floors of the whole building and sending sparks and flames hundreds of feet into the night sky. The efforts of the firemen were then wholly given over to protecting the buildings on the other side of New Steps and The Bolts. The flames on many occasions completely engulfed these buildings and the watching crowd gave these buildings up as lost more than once. The residents of these buildings had been evacuated and attempts to regain admission to try and save belongings were futile, as the heat from the fire proved too strong for them.

The severity of the heat can be ascertained by the fact that furniture was burnt inside houses on Merchants Row. Flying burning particles of straw and other pieces of debris set fire to chimneys as far away as Globe Street. The roof of the Royal Oak Inn, St Sepulchre Street, which was constructed of tar, gravel and paper, was only just prevented from catching fire by its owner Mr Cottam, when large amounts of burning rubbish lodged on it.

Chief Constable Roberts at one point noticed, from his position on the sand, that due to burning rubbish on the roof, it appeared that the fire had spread to a house at the head of New Steps and was devouring the whole of that house also. Luckily this was not the case and a few well-placed squirts of water alleviated the situation.

It was said that, looking in the direction of the fire from the Princess Street – St Mary's Street vicinity, the fire seemed to be in Palace Hill or Merchants Row, such was the height of the flames.

As was usual in those days, thieves and vagabonds were busy in the confusion looting and ransacking the dwellings along the other side of New Steps and The Bolts, which had been hurriedly evacuated in fear of the fire spreading and the effects of the thick dense smoke. The absence of the military, not only for firefighting but also policing of the properties was very much noticed. By 3.30 the likelihood of further spread began to diminish and the firefighters got the upper hand of the fire.

PUBLIC INQUIRY

Mr Campion's belongings were insured with the County Office but to nowhere near the value of the belongings lost. His daughter's belongings, which included many beds etc. as she and her husband,

Mr Shaw, were about to set up business as lodging keepers themselves, were totally destroyed and they had no insurance whatsoever. Mr Skelton lost everything in his warehouse and was uninsured.

On Monday 20th December at the police court, before Mr Byron, Mr Fowler and Mr Brown, there appeared William Sugden, a man dressed as a sailor, from Cardiff. He was charged with stealing a pair of wellington boots and baby linen whilst pretending to assist with firefighting. He pleaded guilty and was sent to serve two calendar months hard labour at the Borough Gaol.

The Mayor opened a subscription for Mr Shaw and payments were accepted at Theakston's Gazette offices, St Nicholas Street, at Mr Rowntree's Drapery in Newborough Street, and at Mr Walker's boat builders, Sandside.

There were rumours spreading throughout the town, even as the fire was burning, that Mr Sutcliffe had more to gain from the fire than the others and in the lack of solid evidence as to the cause of the fire these grew stronger.

The insurance companies heard of these rumours and approached the Borough Coroner as to holding an inquiry into the affair. Subsequently, on the 23rd December, an inquiry was opened into the origin of the fire in New Steps. The Borough Coroner, Mr Easton, opened it by saying whilst it was unusual to hold an inquest when there was no death involved, he thought it fit and proper in this instance to do so.

Mr Collinson, solicitor, representing Mr Sutcliffe, said that the Coroner did not have the powers to call this inquiry. To this the Coroner replied that he was within his rights, quoting clause 52 of Henry 111 Chap; 24. He also said this type of inquiry (without deaths) was common in the Metropolis and saw no reason why one could not be conducted in Scarborough.

On reflection, it seems the Coroner was misinformed, though it was true that Mr Serjeant Payne, for London and Southwall, had held inquests where no fatalities had occurred in London. He had reintroduced the practise on 21st August 1845, after an absence of such practices for hundreds of years. He was forced to cease the practice in 1853 by the council who did not consider that they had sufficient authority to hold them.

In fact there was a case taken to court in Manchester in 1860, after the fire on New Steps, where the high courts deemed it unlawful. By 1888 the Act was rewritten and Mr Payne's son, now the Coroner of London and Southwall, resumed this type of inquiry. Therefore the Scarborough Coroner was incorrect in saying that it was a regular practice in London, as it had been halted five years earlier.

Mr WR Woodall, solicitor, represented the interests of the insurance companies. The inquiry lasted four days with a break over the weekend and Christmas period. The main theme was trying to ascertain the whereabouts of Mr Sutcliffe on the night and morning of the fire. On the 30th December the jury returned a verdict that the fire was started by an incendiary device in the warehouse of Mr Sutcliffe, by persons unknown.

At a meeting of the Watch Committee on 18th January 1859 a sum of £1 was awarded to Chief Constable Roberts for his efficient services rendered at the fire with a further 10 shillings each for Police Constables Murgatroyed and Jowsey.

The lists of donations for Mr and Mrs Shaw, quoted in the newspaper, by this date was extremely long. The paper also stated that the Shaw family had been enlarged by one since the fire.

PAY RISE AND PROMOTIONS
The firemen asked for an increase in salary to £1 and for suitable clothing to fight fires. They also requested hose and a key (to connect the leather hose) plus a town plan showing the whereabouts of the fireplugs (there were now 41 plugs throughout the town), be kept at the police station.

There were some doubts raised by the Commissioners as to the number of firemen present at the New Steps fire and it was necessary to ask the Borough Surveyor to devise some means of recording the attendance of firemen at fires.

After some months deliberation a set of rules and regulations were drawn up to help monitor the attendance. In the meantime an ultimatum in writing from Mr Thompson for a salary increase to ten pounds or else he would resign his appointment was again delivered to the Commissioners. At first it appeared that they might react favourably but a fortnight later, at their next meeting, a vote was taken rejecting the pay rise. The Commissioners asked for a retraction of the letter or else they would deem the appointment vacant. However, though there is no record of such a retraction, Thompson continued in his position as Superintendent.

In December 1859 he requested that fireman J Harrison be appointed foreman of the number one engine whilst fireman S Rawlings be branch pipeman and that fireman E Reed be appointed foreman of the number two engine with fireman W Bland as its branch pipeman.

TINDALL'S IRONMONGERS

A fire, which occurred at 80 Newborough Street, had a far more reaching outcome, than was at first realised. It was 25th April 1861 when a fire was discovered at Tindall's Ironmongers (now the site of PriceLess Shoes shop), fireman W Jackson who lived at the rear of the premises, was informed of this so he alerted Superintendent Thompson and the fire brigade.

The Scarborough Gazette reported the incident by stating Mr Thompson was very energetic and showed much exuberance, and mentioned that Chief Constable Roberts assisted. The Scarborough Mercury's report was totally different, making no mention of Thompson, it said that the Chief Constable was extremely hard working and was the first person that dare enter the fire.

At the end of that year the Improvement Commissioner's powers ceased and were transferred to the local board. How they organised the fire brigade seems to have been influenced by the reports from this fire.

SEWER COMMITTEE

The local board placed the fire brigade in the sewer section of the sub-committee, this might seem unusual but it was in fact the Street, Sewer, Building and Fire Committee. The thinking being that builders knew the limitations of structures and building materials and therefore, how they would react in fire.

They also terminated the engagement of Superintendent Thompson on 1st January 1862, giving him a month's notice and a pension of £5 per annum. His responsibilities were passed to Mr Roberts who became Superintendent of the Police and the Fire Brigade. He was given an increase in salary of £5 to cover his extra work duties. The month saw letters to the committee from both Thompson and Roberts signing themselves as superintendent of the fire brigade.

THE ALBION
An incident took place on the vessel 'Albion' (captained by Mr Simpson) in the harbour on the morning of 7th January 1862 and whilst Thompson was fighting the fire he was informed that the cabin lad was still aboard. A thorough search was made and the lad was found, in his bunk, unconscious and in a poor state; he was rushed to hospital where he later made a full recovery. The vessel was burning inside from stern to hold, and in time the flames broke through hatch and deck. By the time the fire was out the boat was destroyed but thanks to Thompson's efforts there had been no risk to the surrounding vessels.

An official report stated that the fire was started by the misuse of a stove, but there was strong speculation in the town that an incendiary device had started it. The latter theory was strengthened by the fact that whilst the fire fighting was going on, one of the lengths of hose was deliberately cut.

Thompson reported the matter in full to the committee who then had an advert printed stating:

> "REWARD of £5 to person or persons who may give such information as shall lead to the conviction of the person who cut and damaged the hose belonging to the Board on the 7th instant during the fire attended in the harbour involving the vessel Albion.   10.1.1862"

Meanwhile Mr Roberts reported to the committee that he had made a thorough examination of the fire engines and found that they were all in a poor condition. He then had them overhauled and painted except for one, which at the time of repairs was in use at the fire on the Albion, but this was repaired and painted soon afterwards. He reported that the fire escape ladder was also in a poor state, mainly due to the location in which it was kept, as the shed was damp, and mould was growing on the ladder attacking the canvas under it, which in turn was rotting.

At a meeting on the 6th February 1862 the local board directed the police to make periodical inspections of the fire plugs as it was found that, with the poor street conditions, they were filling up with dirt and mud, making them useless when they were needed in an emergency. It was also decided on the recommendation of Mr Roberts to move the hand cart and hose to the Town Hall / Police Station, the reason being that it would be more readily available in the event of fire, making use again of the old fire engine house at the rear of the Town Hall.

Other decisions made were the appointments of police constable Bennett as Deputy Superintendent, and Mr EO Tindall to maintain the engines hose and escape.

TALLOW WORKS FIRE

Tuesday 15th July 1862 saw a fire at Mr Foster's Tallow Chandlers, located between Cross Street and Dumple Street, backing onto the Market Hall (now Market Place). The alarm was raised just after midnight by passers by. Firemen were assisted by Sergeant London with his men, plus the 10th Hussars, which were stationed at the Castle Barracks, who brought the camp pump.

Luckily there was no wind which allowed the fire to be contained, but there were fears that the Market Hall was in danger of being engulfed, especially as the glass in it was cracking from the intense heat. After this fire Chief Constable Roberts tendered his resignation but the Watch Committee refused to accept it.

An onlooker watching the fire was Captain Woodall. He observed the firefighting methods, wondering whether they could be improved especially as firefighting was now under police control. The local gentlemen and dignitaries were no longer able to organise and dictate the running of firefighting as the firemen and police would only take orders from within their own ranks.

Captain Woodall devised a scheme to help the gentlemen overcome any feeling of inadequacy by suggesting a volunteer brigade. He first approached the council who put it to a fire brigade sub-committee who instructed him to canvas support for his idea.

Firefighting had become a fashionable hobby of the upper classes, later boosted by the friendship of the Prince of Wales with Sir Eyre Massey Shaw, London Fire Brigade Chief. A special silver helmet was produced so the Prince could attend large fires in London to help organise the firefighting.

PUBLIC MEETING

A public meeting was held at the Town Hall on 6th December 1862 chaired by the Mayor. The first volunteer was a bricklayer, Mr Moore, followed by another 35 men. A uniform of fire helmets and red jumpers was suggested and Mr Jancourski and Mr Bright offered a guinea each, as a subscription to the scheme.

There was another meeting held the following month at which another nine volunteers were enlisted and a provisional committee was set up consisting of Captains Woodall and Symonds, plus nine others. The committee was empowered to draw up rules and regulations to put before the council committee for acceptance on the running of the Volunteer Brigade. It was suggested that it might be easier if the volunteers were sworn in as special constables to give them powers necessary to perform their duties ready to commence in the April.

As if to strengthen the necessity of a volunteer brigade, a fire occurred at 8 p.m. 21st February, in a house on Regent Street, which took all the Fire Brigade plus police officers to handle. Just as the fire was brought under control another alarm was raised to the Drugs Warehouse, near the Old Gasworks, off Sandside. Due to the Regent Street fire Sergeant London was despatched with only a small number of men to handle the next blaze, luckily it was no more than a bad chimney fire. After these incidents Mr Roberts commented on the importance of a volunteer brigade in circumstances such as these.

Captain Woodall's enthusiasm with the brigade never waned and after election to the council in 1863 he was appointed on to the Fire Brigade sub-committee in 1867, going on to become Mayor on four occasions, retiring from the council in 1889.

He was born in 1831 into a well known local family and served his country in the Crimea until his return to his St Nicholas Street home in 1857. His interest in the fishing industry encouraged him to have the Olympia building constructed at the foot of his gardens (now St Nicholas Cliff Gardens) as a fisheries exhibition. The house and gardens were purchased from his family at the turn of the century and changed into public gardens and the present Town Hall. Captain Woodall retired to London where he died in 1905.

NEW CHIEF
Mr Roberts offered his resignation again in 1865 on ill health grounds and retired on a pension of £70 per annum. The Watch Committee looked for a man who was forward thinking, and to this aim brought in Mr William Pattison (33) who had started his career in Newcastle and later Beverley. He carried out the job of police and fire chief for twelve months before the committee decided that it was still in the public interest to unite the jobs, and paid him the year's back pay.

UNIFORMS FOR THE FIREMEN
Chief Constable Pattison made sweeping recommendations for the brigade including the firemen should be supplemented by all the police force, which had under the same recommendations increased from 10 police constables to twenty plus the twelve part-time firemen.

Uniforms were ordered for the firemen including: – 12 red serge tunics, leather helmets, belts, 13 axes and hose keys, 6 hose clips plus a Superintendent's helmet, tunic and belt. The total cost was £33.2s.6d.

SCARBOROUGH POLICE STATION AND GAOLS
All the improvements meant that the police offices outgrew the Town Hall and it was decided to construct a purpose built police station. This new station was on the site of the gaol, on Local Place, (corner of Castle Road, Tanners Lane (now St Thomas St)), which was to move to new premises on Cemetery Rd (Dean Road). This gaol had been located here since the demolishing in 1841 of the original gaol sited in the old town bar.

Whilst the new police station was under construction it was decided to extend the building programme to include a new Town

Hall on the same site. This move gave rise to some local scandal at the time, as it was maintained that the Borough Surveyor had vastly under estimated the cost involved. He pleaded that it was having the Town Hall added to the original costs which made the difference; whilst the Watch Committee maintained the extra costs were incurred by the footings being far deeper than had been allowed for. The footings, which followed the line of the original Borough boundary wall, were, in fact, twice as deep as originally planned. Whilst still protesting his innocence, the Surveyor resigned.

On 1st January 1868 the Town Hall was transferred to the new premises.

MR BIRDSALL'S

All was quiet in the town centre in the early hours of Sunday 25th September 1869 when, in the warehouse premises of Mr Birdsall, fish dealer, of Market Street a fire was smouldering. It went unnoticed until just before 1 a.m. when a niece of Mr Birdsall, who was sleeping in a room overlooking the warehouse, was woken by the smell of smoke. On further investigation she saw, through the window, flames and thick smoke circulating around the warehouse area. She immediately aroused the neighbourhood with her screams of 'FIRE'.

Chief Constable Pattison, his constabulary and firemen were soon on the scene, only to find the streets packed with onlookers. At about this time the fire broke through the roof aided by the highly combustible materials stored in the warehouse, such as fish boxes, wood, straw and sawdust, which were all used in the packing of fish.

Surrounding properties were also filled with flammable materials, so efforts were made to empty them, especially the gunpowder from Mr Glaves' gunsmith shop, and petrol-based products in Messrs Coulson and Wells, chemist warehouse.

By the time hose was run from Blands Cliff the roof had collapsed, so the main efforts were placed in protecting the surrounding property. To achieve this much of the work was done by directing jets from rooftops. The newspaper report made a special mention of Fireman Bland's efforts on the roofs. Throughout the operation the hose kept on bursting partly due to the good water pressure from the plugs, but also due to the age of the hose. The onlookers proved useful as they assisted in repairing the hose.

At 6.30 a.m, the fire had sufficiently died down to stop applying water, but at 10 a.m. it flared up again, a further two hours of firefighting was needed to completely extinguish the fire.

The fire brigade sub-committee met shortly after the fire to investigate the cause of the frequently bursting hose. It was ascertained that in the past 24 years only four lengths of hose had been purchased; so there was little wonder that they burst when subjected to strong water pressure. Chief Constable Pattison was given permission to obtain more hose.

As was the practice in those days the Chief Constable made a claim for expenses incurred by the brigade at the fire from the insurance companies (The Sun, Phoenix, County, London Liverpool & Globe, Yorkshire and Atlas). He included the cost of the new hose but the insurance companies thought it was excessive, as it was the responsibility of the Board to supply the hose. They therefore presented a united reply to the committee objecting to the claim. At the next meeting the committee stood by the Chief Constable. The committee resolved to send a letter to the insurance companies stating that a new hose and reel were to be bought and not only should they foot the bill, but they should also pay towards the future upkeep of the appliances.

Yet again the committee backed the Chief Constable, in August 1870, when after a fire at the Royal Hotel, Fireman Hutchinson passed a remark that the Chief was the worse for drink. Mr Pattison then brought charges against the fireman for blackening his character, which resulted in the committee dismissing Mr Hutchinson and demanding he give up his uniform.

SOUTH CLIFF FIRE STATION

Throughout this period the town was growing rapidly with an influx of people, a large number of the elite were buying property in the South Cliff area. At a residents' committee meeting for that area, held in 1872, it was decided to approach the Fire Brigade Sub-Committee and one representative was given permission to sit in on the sewer committee meeting. The representative put forward the argument that the South Cliff area was not covered by fire equipment and, in the event of a serious fire, it would take the brigade some time to get there.

It was agreed there should be more fireplugs fitted in the area and that a fire station, under the authority of the police, be opened on the South Cliff providing:

1 hose reel, 500 feet of canvas hose, 12 canvas buckets,
1 branch pipe,
1 standpipe, 4 wrenches, 1 crow bar, 1 pickaxe and
1 felling axe,

at a cost to the Borough of £69.5s. The possibility of providing a fire escape ladder for that area was also to be considered.

By January 1874 the South Cliff area had its own sub-station at 7 Alga Terrace, which the corporation rented at £16 per annum. Police constable McKenzie was the officer in charge of the police and fire arrangements, and he was charged a rent of 2s. 6d a week to live there. In addition Mr Lund who owned the adjoining coach house and shed offered them for use as storage for the appliances and hose.

To help pay for these improvements the committee decided to sell off, by public auction, two old fire engines and other appliances that were stored at the scavengermonger's yard. (This was possibly the old number one small manual pump and the manual pump supplied by the insurance company.)

As part of the improvements to the brigade the committee decided to seek a new location for housing of the escape ladder in a more central position. In addition the hose and reel were moved from what was by now called the engine house, on North Marine Road, to the entranceway of the new Town Hall on Castle Road where they were more accessible.

TALLOW CHANDLERS TWO

Yet again the tallow works in Fosters Yard (next to the Market Hall) was the scene of a fire. The building had been completely rebuilt since the fire of 1862, and was now owned by Messrs Hood and Newman.

At 9 p.m. on the 6th March 1874, boiling fat from an upstairs boiler leaked out and set fire to surrounding articles and due to the highly combustible nature of the contents of the building, the fire soon spread. Mr Newman was the first to notice the blaze, his reaction was to make a dash into the building and retrieve his books in which many outstanding debts due to him were recorded.

This page sponsored by:
North Yorkshire Fire Service Sports & Social Club

In the meantime someone else who had also seen the fire reported it to the police station.

There was concern for Mrs Parkinson in the adjoining property, as she was crippled and unable to get about on her own. With the aid of onlookers the firemen effected a rescue; the building was then surrounded with hose, requiring Chief Constable Pattison to take up a position on the Market Hall roof. Luckily it was a calm night with no wind otherwise the fire could have spread throughout the closely confined buildings. Once again the tallow works had to be demolished and rebuilt.

SPA GRAND HALL

St Mary's Church was running a four-day bazaar in the Saloon and Concert Room of the Spa, commencing Wednesday 6th December 1876. The object was to raise funds to cover debts, amounting to £1,035, incurred in renovating St Mary's and Christ Church.

By the evening of the third day, the debts had almost been covered and it was with great anticipation that the organisers were looking forward to Saturday, the final day, and hopefully a large excess on the money required.

At around 10 p.m. on the Friday evening as the vicar, Archdeacon Blunt, was making an announcement about the day's takings to the small crowd that was gathered around a lady noticed that there were drops of molten lead falling onto the floor in the centre of the Saloon. She reported it to the duty policeman who told her "*it's alright*", he thought that the lit gas jet had got too close to the lantern (Gasolier) cover and the joints had melted. Someone else drew his attention to the occurrence again and still he could foresee no danger.

Such was the rapidity of the fire spread that it was only minutes later that the Archdeacon had to order everyone to evacuate the hall and asked them to take an article of value to safety. It seems that as the evening was drawing to a close the lights had been extinguished except for the central one in the Saloon. This caused the gas pressure to build up giving a far stronger flame, which melted the joints on the lantern and set light to the heavy drapery of the hall.

The panic stricken crowd had not managed to leave the building before particles of burning material were raining down on them, setting fire to the stalls which were ready for the last day of the

From a print of George Farrington Harnibrook's painting of the Spaw fire

event. This meant that there was no time to rescue many of the articles the Archdeacon had wished to save.

One of the valuables which was rescued was Sir Noel Paton's painting 'Man of Sorrows' valued then at £6000, which was on loan to Mr Hare of St Nicholas Street to exhibit in his gallery. He had lent the painting to the organisers of the bazaar as an added attraction. It seems that Mr Jones, the agent in charge of the painting, was already on his way home from the bazaar when his attention was drawn to the large pall of smoke hanging over the Spa building. He immediately ran over the Cliff Bridge and back to the Spa and, ignoring all attempts to stop him, he entered the Saloon. In amongst the smoke, debris and general mayhem he managed to locate the painting and then, assisted by three other men, rescued it and carried it back, undamaged, to Mr Hare's gallery.

Within thirty minutes of the evacuation the entire Saloon was ablaze, the flames fanned by a strong south-westerly wind.

Bringing two hose carts, the fire brigade were quickly on the scene; they consisted of the Chief Constable, Firemen Bland and

Cockerhill, plus Police Constables Mackenzie and Stubbs. There was a line of hose running from the Prince of Wales Hotel from which the south end of the building was drenched whilst another hose was working on the west side.

News of the outbreak spread around the town with such rapidity that the local paper, the Scarborough Gazette, made comments about the speed of arrival and number of people watching the inferno from paths, walks, cliff tops, sands and even a flotilla of boats in the bay. They likened the scene to the firework displays held at the Spa, which at that time were famous throughout the country, commenting that the fire was much more spectacular.

Further hose was requested from the Railway Company, which arrived, directed by Mr Bearup the Stationmaster. Captain Krane and his Coastguard also worked extremely hard, assisting wherever possible. The Mayor, Mr Hart, also felt it his duty to be present to organise the work force.

A photograph of the morning after, taken by Henry Osguthorpe

Within an hour of the discovery of the fire the roof collapsed, this allowed the firefighters to turn their efforts wholly to protecting the other parts of the complex. This was a major task and did not give the firemen a respite from their labours. To these ends the officers and men of the gunboat 'Pheasant,' which was at anchor in the bay whilst on fishing patrol duties, also attended the fire lead by Lieutenant Hope. They removed the wooden floor of the promenade under the balcony stopping the fire from spreading to the gothic saloon next door. By midnight the fire was subdued, leaving the building completely gutted with just a hollow brick shell left standing. The onlookers went home leaving the firemen in their cold, wet clothes, to keep their long night vigil over the remains and occasionally playing water on the outbreaks in the debris that flared up.

In the cold light of day the bazaar organisers were quick to cast blame on the Cliff Bridge Company, owners of the Spa, for the incapacity, carelessness and negligence of their employees, and made a claim for £700 for goods destroyed. The company ignored the claim and assessed the overall damage at £5,897 16s 8d. After a long argument with the insurers they received £3,837 15s.

NEW HOSE REEL

A new hose reel and hose was ordered and delivered from Merryweathers of London late on Saturday 22nd October 1876. A fire broke out early the following morning at Mr Jayes, Shoemaker's workshop, on St Sepulchre Street; as the new equipment hadn't been unpacked the old hose and reel were taken. The in-experience of the police constables and poor condition of the equipment showed when too much pressure was applied and the hose burst causing water damage and more fire damage occurred than need have done.

A hose reel cart. Note the hose wrapped around the axle

None the less, despite the efforts shown by the firemen at the Spa and the inexperience of the police at the Jayes fire, on 20th December, six of the part-time firemen were dismissed and replaced by policemen who were to perform fire fighting tasks in their off duty time.

LOCAL REFERENDUM

It was becoming more and more evident that the water supplies to the town were inadequate. There was major expensive renovation required to upgrade the system and the council, having seen how lucrative supplying water could be, set about discrediting the private consortium. They maintained the work was beyond the financial means of any private company.

There was a local referendum held to give the council the right to supply the local water. To ensure their victory the council said that, when the votes were counted, all the no-votes (blank returns) were counted as a vote in support of the council.

Unsurprisingly, they won the referendum and in 1878 they again became responsible for supplying the water to the town. They had a new borehole sunk at Irton and two new reservoirs built at Olivers Mount, all this became the basis of the present day water supplies.

FIREMEN ARE NOT ALL SAINTS

At 1.30 on Saturday 27th December 1879 Robert Milner discovered a fire in the schoolrooms of All Saints Church as he delivered orders for his father's butchers shop. He ran to get Mr Wells, the key holder, and they opened the boiler house door to find the fire bursting out at them. Alerting others, they ran off to get help. Mr Milner went to get the vicar, Reverend Brown-Borthwick. The vicar sent one man to get the coastguard, another to the railway station to fetch their brigade and hose, organised by the Station Master, Mr Bearup, and someone else to the police station on Castle Road, to fetch the Chief Constable and the fire brigade with their hose cart. The Volunteer Brigade also arrived to give assistance.

There was more than enough hose at the fire, but a poor water supply did little to assist the situation. Plus with all the small groups of organisations, no one was taking overall responsibility for the running of the firefighting operations, with each group doing what it saw best, and not co-operating with each other.

The Railway Station team appeared to be doing very well until the water was cut off and redirected to another team's efforts; it took ten minutes of arguing to get it reinstated. By 3 o'clock the schoolrooms were almost devoured and the fire was nearing the main church area. The Reverend had had enough of the local firefighters and took it upon himself to telegraph the York Fire Brigade to come by train, with their steam engine, to assist in the firefighting.

By this time the Chief Constable's men had given up trying to save the schoolrooms and were concentrating on saving the church itself. They found that the Reverend and his helpers had been removing the valuables from this area and had told the Verger, Mr Stephenson, not to allow anyone to enter in case of looting. Therefore when Fireman Bartliff was ordered to assess the church by the Chief Constable he was not admitted. He stood and waited till the Reverend and his helpers arrived and entered the church and tried to gain admittance with them but the verger was too quick and again stopped him from entering.

Fireman Bartliff once again tried to rush in, but was stopped as the Reverend threw a bucket of water over him. That was the end of the fireman's patience and he took a swing at the Reverend, felling him. The crowd of onlookers, seeing what had happened, rushed forward to assist the fireman. There followed a stand up battle between the Reverend and his helpers and the fireman and his supporters, which lasted some minutes before two volunteer firemen (Captains Kitching and Nesfield) stepped in and soothed the situation.

The Reverend and Verger retired to Mr Wells' shop and the firemen were allowed to enter the church and fight the fire. Because of the lack of water they were forced to remove much of the roof to get close to the fire. At around 5.30 the York Fire Brigade, consisting of Chief Constable Haley and 10 policemen came galloping from the Railway Station to Falsgrave with the steamer belching smoke and sparks, ready to tackle the blaze. However they found that, without the interference of the Reverend and his party, the local brigade had managed to put out the fire and save the church.

The schoolrooms were only insured for £350 and the Reverend had to set up a building fund to raise £3,500. The new building was opened on 17th December 1880.

NEW EQUIPMENT

There were many purchases made throughout 1880, a Merryweather hand pump in September, followed by new hose – the hose which had been lent out to the council for swilling down the sewers had been totally ruined. There were also hand lamps and a Tynedale's respirator acquired on a trial basis. By December the Committee had made their decisions and 500 feet of hose, four hand lamps and two respirators were purchased.

The Tynedale respirators were quite an advanced idea at the time and were supposed to be the forerunners to breathing apparatus. Professor Tyndale and Sir Erye Massey Shaw developed them in 1875. It was thought that by filtering the air, it would be possible to work in smoke, the misconception arose as it was not fully understood at the time that a fire needs oxygen to burn, and it was the lack of oxygen to breathe that kills people in fires.

The respirators proved useful however as they allowed a fireman to make a quick entry and retreat in fires without causing as much discomfort as had previously been experienced. Whilst their popularity never continued they became the basis of the respirators issued by the Home Office in the Second World War as a gas mask.

CONCERN OVER APPLIANCES

It seems that the location of the fire escape ladder in September 1883 was causing some concern because an article in the local newspaper read as follows:

> 'How many people know where the town's fire escape ladder is kept? Of all the things that are wanted promptly, if they are wanted at all, the fire escape is the one respecting which a delay might be most serious....
>
> The fire escape at Scarborough is, we believe, kept in a shed somewhere near the disused jail in Cemetery Rd. A more out of the way and unsatisfactory position it would be difficult to find. When a fire breaks out it is usual at once to send information to the police office and a number of policemen and firemen go to the scene of the conflagration. They take the hose with them but not the fire escape, and if the escape is needed the fact would only be discovered when they get there, and back they will have to go for it....
>
> We would suggest that our fire escape should every evening be brought out into some prominent and central position, say in or near the railway station yard.'

Whilst the fire brigade did not take the idea on board straight away it was definitely noted.

It was however, recommended that the fire plugs be fitted with plaques on the walls near by to help the firemen locate them, especially in bad weather when they could be covered in snow. One hundred and twenty plaques costing £1 per dozen were ordered, some can still be seen in certain locations in the Borough, displaying F P, (over the years many have been replaced by plates showing F H, and more latterly with the H plates which are now standard throughout the country).

TOZER PUMPS

A Tozer hand pump was ordered in 1884, this was a hand pump mounted in a bucket. Alfred Tozer, Chief Fire Officer of the Manchester Fire Brigade, took out the patent for these in 1864. This type of pump became very popular and were placed in areas were today it would be expected to find fire extinguishers. Mr Tozer, in proclaiming its virtues maintained that one pump alone in 21 years of use in the Manchester Brigade had saved over £100,000 worth of property.

Mr Tozer came from a family of distinguished firefighters. His father Robert was an Insurance fireman in London for 30 years, Alfred Robert was Chief Fire Officer of Birmingham, for 29 years, followed also by Alfred Robert for 20 years, William was Chief Fire Officer for West Bromwich and Charles William was 2nd Engineer for Birmingham.

The efficiency of the pumps could be seen in their use at a fire at the Old Bowling Green House, (now the site of St Mary's Lodge, Queen Street) where the Convent was under construction. It was 10.30

A Tozer hand pump

a.m. 5th February 1885, when the fire brigade was sent for, to attend a fire that was thought to have originated in a wooden beam built into a chimney breast. The firefighters found the fire to be raging in a bedroom and the chapel; two of the hand pumps were put to work, one upstairs and one down. They were trained on the fire for two hours, by which time the fire was extinguished.

A human chain saved many valuable religious paintings and sculptures by shuttling them outside to safety.

FALSGRAVE STATION

At the same meeting at which the pump was ordered a new sub-station was recommended to be opened at Falsgrave; the Chief Constable recommended the renting of Avenue House, on Avenue Road, at a cost of £15 per annum to the council. The house was to be occupied by a constable at a rent of £6.10s per annum. The constable would run the police office and fire station. The full council referred it back to the sub-committee and it seems that the police and fire station was opened at 56 Falsgrave Road, the premises of Mr Judson, from whom they rented at a cost of £18 per year. (Now the site of the Yorkshire Quality Paperbacks book shop. This was the location of the Scarborough Police branch, not to be confused with North Riding Police offices opened in Sitwell Street in the same era.)

A new escape ladder was delivered which was initially intended to go to the South Cliff area, but the council had a change of heart and drew up a contract with the North Eastern Railway Company giving the fire brigade permission to store the escape ladder in their yard.

Discussions took place on how to improve the turn out times for fires and there were a few schemes brandished, one being that the firemen would be paid a £2 annual bonus to live

A set of three hand grenades

within a quarter of a mile of the Town Hall. Another idea was that the council should approach the insurance companies, asking them to pay the costs of keeping a fireman on night duty at the police station so that he would be available there between 10 in the evening and 4 in the morning. Fireman Ed Reed was paid an extra £6 per annum to maintain the hose and look after the equipment.

1887 saw the introduction of hand grenades into the brigade. These were a sealed glass bottle or vessel of approximately one pint capacity, filled with water and sodium bicarbonate, or salt water. Their design and shape was such that they smashed easily when thrown on to a fire; they were patented in the USA in 1871 and were eventually available in this country from 1877 onwards.

Surprisingly, despite their commercial success which lasted over forty years, they were not particularly effective, as the additives to the water did little, if anything, to the firefighting properties of the water, thus an ordinary bucket of water would have been just as effective.

The Scarborough Brigade ordered a dozen of the bottles for each station from Water & Woodhouse. At the same time a new hose reel and standpipe were ordered from Merryweathers.

FIREMEN'S HOUSES
In October 1887 an agreement was reached with Mr Bradford, property owner, from Weaverthorpe, that the Brigade would lease six houses (numbers 9 – 19) in Sandringham Street. The Council in turn would sub-let them to firemen. There was also an estimate obtained for the fitting of call-out bells in the houses, connected directly to the police station.

With the new houses being provided for the firemen in January 1888 came a new set salary of fifteen shillings plus extra for attendance at drill practices. New uniforms were costed and a dozen leather helmets were ordered. Estell Rawlings, North Marine Road, was commissioned to produce a dozen jackets.

FIRE PREVENTION
The forerunners of Fire Prevention visits were introduced in 1887 when the Chief Constable was required to visit theatres in the town to advise on their fire safety. An example of what was expected can be seen in the recommendations for the Spa theatre:

1) Four outward opening windows to be placed in the rear wall of the gallery.
2) Hose and hydrants require regular checks.
3) That all gas jets should have guards fitted.
4) That the locks in a door should be removed when there was a performance.
5) That fire fighting appliances should always be easily at hand.

The fact that the Chief Constable had been requested to check the fire precautions probably came about as a result of a fire at Exeter's Theatre Royal that year when nearly two hundred people were killed. Local authorities already held the power under the Theatres Act of 1843 to inspect places of public entertainment, but very few authorities carried out the inspections. After Exeter's fire it would seem that Scarborough was sufficiently shocked into taking up their responsibility, surprisingly they were in the minority.

In 1888 the location of the escape ladder at the railway station was starting to cause concern as it was found that instead of it being in a prominent position as had originally been intended, it was, in fact, locked up in a remote corner of the station yard where hardly anyone was aware of it. An approach had to be made to the railway company to have it moved into a more prominent accessible position.

At last South Cliff was reconsidered for an escape ladder and on 21st August 1888 an estimate for £78 10s was accepted from Merryweathers for a single telescopic 50 foot fire escape.

There was a shed built to house the new escape on land at the rear of the Crown Hotel Stables, on Crown Terrace Back Road (now the premises of T&S Motors), at the cost of £44 17s 6d. At the same time the old escape underwent a major overhaul after which it was replaced in its shed in the corporation yard.

THOMPSON'S PAWNBROKERS

A fire occurred in the premises of Mr Benjamin Thompson's pawnbroker's shop, Eastborough, (in what is now the Jolly Roger Public House) in the early hours 2.30 a.m. on 15th September 1889.

Police Constable Barker, the beat constable, who noticed smoke issuing from the shop front, raised the alarm. He immediately alerted the neighbours, but of Mr and Mrs Thompson and eight children there was no sign.

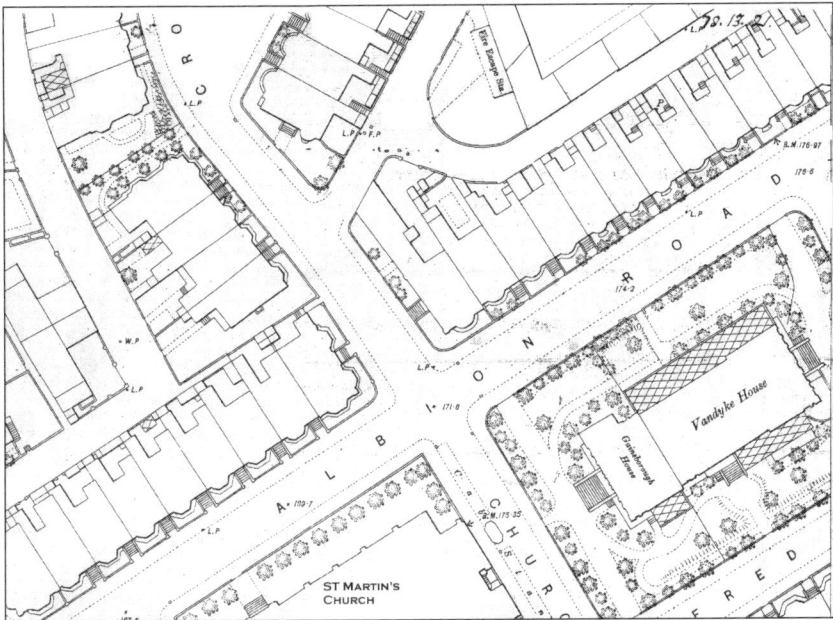

Part of the 1890 ordnance survey map depicting the location of the escape house.

At the front of the shop, on the ground floor level, were the storerooms of pawned articles whilst to the rear were rooms, which the family occupied.

Mr Ellis, one of the neighbours, had joined police constable Baker in trying to alert the household of Mr Thompson when a child was seen at one of the upper windows. The men tried to climb the drainpipes to rescue the child but were unable to scale the wall. Police constable Bowes also arrived on the scene and, on seeing the situation, dashed off to get the Fire Brigade.

Someone eventually brought a ladder and this was pitched to the window where the child was last seen. Mr Ellis then, via the ladder, entered the room that by now was full of dense smoke. He discovered three children in a bed, so he tied them up one at a time in the bed sheets and passed them through the window to police constable Barker who carried them down to safety.

By this time the rest of the family had become aware of the danger which they were in and were trying to escape the flames. Mrs Thompson and two children descended the stairs to the room where

Mr Ellis was and escaped through the window. Once all the family were safe Mr Ellis and Mr Thompson escaped through the window onto the ladder, just in the nick of time, for the fire broke through the floor on which they had been standing as they clambered to safety.

Chief Constable Pattison, arrived with the fire brigade only some ten minutes from the alarm being raised. Even with the brigade in attendance it was obvious that all firefighting attempts were futile. The roof collapsed at about five o'clock and every effort was put into protecting the surrounding property, which by this time had been evacuated. It was three hours later before the fire was finally subdued, by which time the entire contents of the shop and house were completely destroyed.

Fortunately the property was insured and Mrs Thompson realising that life was more important than property, stated that without the aid of Police Constable Barker and Mr Ellis there was no way she and the two children with her could have survived. The Royal Society of Protection of Life from Fire later gave an award to Mr Ellis for his actions at the fire.

Chief Constable Pattison recommended to the sub-committee that there should be ladders placed around the town which were easily accessible in the case of emergency. It was also recommended that the master of the Workhouse (now part of St Mary's Hospital site) should have a duplicate key for the escape ladder shed on Trafalgar Street West, where it was then kept, to save time waiting for the police-firemen to reach the location.

In the following January there was an order placed for three 28 foot and seven 22 foot ladders. These were positioned around the town.

HACKNESS HALL
On Monday, 10th February 1890, just before 4 a.m. a servant girl who had been sleeping in the south wing of Hackness Hall heard crackling and, upon opening the door, she was engulfed in smoke which filled her room. She roused the other female servants who were asleep in that area and they raised the rest of the household.

The butler and other male servants attempted to bring the fire under control, but it had a strong hold on the laundry area. They managed to get a small manual pump to work and also set about removing woodwork between that wing and the rest of the building. By 4.30 they realised the fire was out of control and as

Lord Derwent was away at the time they awoke the guests that were staying in the house. Help was sent for from Scarborough and from the villagers who lived around the hall.

Scarborough's brigade was informed of the fire at just after 5 o'clock and within a few minutes they had an engine, pulled by a team of five horses, prepared and on its way. Chief Constable Pattison filled a cab with as much hose as he could get hold of and also set off, arriving at the fire just a few minutes in front of the engine. His first action was to dam the stream running through the village so that the engine could receive enough water to get to work.

In the following four hours the villagers and servants helped to remove the part of the roof that united the two parts of the building, whilst the Chief Constable and his men continued to pour water onto the fire. After four hours they had finally managed to bring the fire under control, but it was at the cost of the whole south wing which was devastated and needed to be rebuilt. The cause of the fire was put down to a stove, which had overheated in the laundry room.

PAY RISE
Firemen's salaries were substantially increased in 1893 by £2, on the understanding that they would refrain from collecting Christmas boxes, this was an expected donation from members of the council and public, much the same as the voluntary Christmas tip given to people today. The corporation introduced a scale of payment for fires, which was expected to be reclaimed from the insurance companies.

There were four more ladders ordered to replace those in accessible places around the town. These being longer than the original ones, two at 30 foot and two at 35 foot. Two were to be placed on the South Cliff, one at Falsgrave Police Station and one at Harcourt Place.

In 1895 Chief Constable Pattison requested better uniforms and he arranged for sample helmets of leather and brass to be made available for the committee to examine. They chose the leather helmets, which proved to be a very wise choice, as in the years to come the brigades using brass helmets had to convert to leather. Due to the advent of electricity, firemen were receiving electric shocks through their helmets and it was found therefore that the leather was far safer to wear. It is not known whether the committee

This page sponsored by:
North Yorkshire Fire Service Sports & Social Club

made the decision with foresight or whether it was made on financial considerations. An order was placed to provide a dozen new leather helmets, a dozen fireman's tunics and a dozen pairs of trousers, from Messrs Reynolds of London.

WILLERSLEY HOUSE

A fire occurred in a hayloft of a coach house at the rear of Willersley House, Filey Road, property of Mr Johnson on the 15th February 1896. Sergeant Anderson was informed at the South Cliff sub-station of the fire and contacted the Central Police Station via telephone to turn out the hose and reel. Mr Anderson then proceeded to the fire with a hand pump, which despite its size and lack of water helped to restrain the flames until the Chief Constable and Inspector Kettlewell arrived with the hose.

Hose was connected to a hydrant and ran out, it was then discovered there was not sufficient hose to reach the fire and more hose had to be sent for; by the time this arrived the roof had burnt through. Mr Johnson blamed the fire brigade for the loss of his roof and about a ton and a half of hay and straw, so he made a claim to recover the costs. The Council's reply was that it was his own fault that there was not a sufficient water supply to the premises. This was the start of the era when the gentry and local press began to use the fire brigade as a political instrument.

Superintendent Pattison with the Scarborough police force c1890

THE FIRE KING

On the Saturday morning of 7th November 1896, at the Hull Drug Store (now the site of the County House jewellers, Westborough) the message boy, Master Goodill was sent on an errand into the cellar. As there was no other means of lighting, he took with him a lighted taper. It seems that at some point he dropped it amongst the straw and debris on the floor.

When he realised he had started a fire he attempted to put it out himself. He continued unaided for some time before he ran up the stairs and informed the manager, Mr Sherwood, who notified the duty policeman at the top of Huntriss Row and a message was relayed to the police station. Police Constable Paul at the police station in turn conveyed the information to Chief Constable Pattison, before he was allowed to operate the call out bell. Unfortunately some time was spent in locating the Chief Constable who was in the Town Hall at the time.

It was just after 11 o'clock when the alarm had been raised but it was a half an hour later before the fire brigade eventually arrived with the hose reel cart. The fire was burning ferociously despite the earlier efforts of men with buckets of water.

Hose started to arrive at half-hour intervals as more firemen found out about the fire and attended it. Anxiety was shown as explosions started, when the fire and water got to the chemicals, it was feared that the building would be lost and that the fire would spread to the surrounding buildings. It was extremely fortunate that the London and Yorkshire Bank next door (corner of Huntriss Row) had been built to a high standard to withstand fires. There was some smoke and water damage to the bank but none to the structure. On the other side of the Drug Company was the Bar Chambers which suffered some damage and Mr Kirkness's shop, which was adjacent, actually caught fire.

Just after mid-day the Marshall and Snelgrove private fire brigade arrived to give what assistance it could, and despite the fact that their hose did not fit the town hydrants and had to be held in position, this seems to have been the turning point of the firefighting efforts.

The private fire brigade took up a position in the bank chambers and poured water onto the rear of the stores whilst the Scarborough Brigade, under the Chief Constable, attacked the fire from Westborough. Despite the intense smoke a local solicitor, Mr Cross, played a garden hose from his office window, next door to the Drug Company, onto the fire.

By 1 o'clock, even though there were still renewed outbursts of flames following explosions, it was felt that the fire was well in hand, but it continued to smoulder for sometime after.

It is evident from the various newspaper reports that there was a growing public awareness of the lack of adequate firefighting facilities in the town. One report stated:

> *'It is perhaps just as well, to judge from the experience of Saturday last, that conflagrations of a serious kind are of rare occurrence in Scarborough, because the fire which broke out in the premises of the Hull Drug Company clearly demonstrate that we have practically no up-to-date means of extinguishing a really serious fire, while our methods are of the most primitive kind.'*

It went on after reporting the fire to conclude:

> *'While all will admit the energy and zeal with which they worked, we could not help thinking not only that the brigade could have been earlier on the scene, but that they were but ill provided with mechanical means for getting the fire under when they did arrive. We are sure that after this lesson the Fire Brigade Committee will introduce the necessary reforms. Two or three engines of the best type is what no corporation should grudge, even if their services are seldom required. Fire is not the kind of danger one can afford to consider after the event.'*

Just over two weeks after the Hull Drug Store fire the brigade were again having a difficult time on their hands at Taylor & Sons, 37/38 Newborough, a printers and publishers (now the location of Tricolo's restaurant). The workers had smelt burning for some time, but thought it was friction burns in the machinery. It was not until a small girl who lived at the rear of the premises came to tell the manager that she could see flames that they realised the building was on fire. The building was evacuated immediately, and on leaving, the workers turned back to see the sky alight with luminous smoke.

The fire brigade was soon in attendance but they had great difficulty in getting to the seat of the fire. They dare not enter the building through the ground floor because they were frightened of the upper floors giving way due to the flames and weight of the printing presses; strategic fire fighting positions were made in back yards and alleyways and from the Star Hotel in King Street. From the hotel the firemen were able to rescue Mrs Taylor, who was an invalid, from the burning premises.

So intense was the fire that the coastguards and Marshall & Snelgrove private fire brigade aided in the firefighting efforts.

CO-OP

Mr Benson was returning home from teaching his Sunday-school class on 25th January 1897 when he noticed smoke billowing from the chimney of the Co-operative store where he was manager. (The corner of Victoria Road and Belle Vue Street, now Squires.) He knew that no fires should have been burning and went to investigate; when he looked through the windows he could see the shop was well alight. He ran to raise the alarm at the Police Station on Castle Road and the Chief Constable immediately put in the call-out bell and sent volunteers, George Hall and Herbert Garton, with the hose and reel to attend the fire.

Meanwhile, as there was no sign of the firemen attending the scene of the fire a runner was sent to Falsgrave Sub-station requesting their presence. Police Constable Head proceeded with the Falsgrave hose reel, arriving at the same time as the Chief Constable and as no firemen had yet arrived, they, along with several volunteers set up the hose and had almost extinguished the flames when the first fireman could be seen strolling up Victoria Road, with his hands in his pockets, smoking a pipe.

The first fireman was followed eventually by a full complement of men, but this was at 5 o'clock, three-quarters of an hour after the fire was originally reported. A member of the growing crowd who felt so frustrated by the little attempts that were being made to fight the fire threw a large wooden box through the window, wrongly thinking he was helping the fire escape from the premises. He had in fact fuelled the fire by allowing oxygen in to feed it.

So bad was the damage that the premises had to be demolished and completely rebuilt, at a cost of £2000. There was much pomp and ceremony at the re-opening of the Co-op on 17th December that year. The building must have been fated, as yet again it was badly damaged in December 1914 due to the Scarborough bombardment of the First World War.

ATTEMPTS AT IMPROVEMENTS

The whole matter of the fire brigade was discussed and whilst it was agreed that the situation needed improving, the wheels of bureaucracy rolled slowly. One of the points raised was that the ladders which were placed around the town were in the habit of appearing at places other than where they belonged; so permanent mounts were put at the following locations enabling the ladders to be fixed and always found there:

> 2 ladders in North Ward at the old Corporation Yard, North Marine Road
> 2 ladders in Central Ward at the old Town Hall passage, St Nicholas Street
> 2 ladders in North West Ward in a passage adjoining 20 Gladstone Street
> 2 ladders in East Ward on the Almshouse wall, St Mary's Street
> 2 ladders in West Ward on Mr Drake's wall, St Johns Road
> 2 ladders in Mr Bentley's passage on Ramsdale Road

For the use of Gladstone Street, St Johns Road and Ramsdale Road walls an annual payment of £1 was paid.

The engine house was to be assessed by the Borough Surveyor with a view to enlarging it and enclosing the existing pinfold to accommodate the hose, engine, appliances plus an attached cottage. This is the site of the present fire station on North Marine Road.

INSTANTANEOUS CONNECTIONS

Sixty six aluminium instantaneous couplings, costing £47 16s were ordered from J Morris of Manchester. These were a push fitting that allowed the hose to be connected together without having to screw them together or connected with a key.

In March 1897 the committee watched the men drill using the new couplings and were so impressed by the speed with which the men could get to work that a large order was placed with Morris for the converting of all the hose, hydrants and standpipes to instantaneous connectors. In the Second World War these hose connections became standard throughout the country. The Home Office British Standards of 1950 recommended that for hydrant outlets the standard throughout the country be screw thread connectors.

To this day Scarborough is almost unique in that a large amount of the hydrants are still of the instantaneous connector type. Appliances standing-by at Scarborough are supplied with special standpipe otherwise they would be unable to obtain water in the event of fires in this area.

The order to Morris was for more than £150 worth of connectors, this was forty gun metal connectors at 10 shilling each, ten scissor connectors at 14 shillings each, four hundred and fifty hydrant connectors at a total of £100 and four standpipes to be adapted to fit the connectors at 7s 6d each.

The ownership of the land on which the escape shed, on South Cliff, was sited changed hands in August 1897 and the new owners wanted the corporation to vacate it. After much negotiation it was decided to rent the land, to permit the escape ladder to remain there, at a cost of £20 per year. Consideration was given at this time to the siting of an escape station on Falsgrave, but nothing came of this.

The Sub-committee again looked at building of a fire station at the old Corporation Yard on North Marine Road. The Borough Surveyor was requested to draw up building plans for the site.

MASONIC CLUB

On the afternoon of 9th August 1897 a number of members of the Masonic Club, St Nicholas Cliff, were relaxing in the reading rooms, amongst their numbers was Councillor Fletcher. Some members smelt burning and on opening the doors to investigate, the reading room was immediately filled with smoke causing the members much anxiety in trying to reach the fresh air.

Club Steward, Mr Hinchcliffe, battled his way through the smoke down the stairs to the basement, and on reaching it found a builder, who had been working there, fighting the fire.

A maid who had been washing in the basement had stacked the copper (a boiler used for heating washing water) full of wood, she had then left it whilst she went for lunch. A piece of burning timber had fallen from the fire onto some old newspapers stored next to it and had, in turn, set fire to more papers and empty cigar boxes in a cupboard, from where the fire spread rapidly around the basement area.

Mr Hinchcliffe assisted the builder until they were both overcome by smoke and it was only by breaking a window at the rear that they could make an escape. By this time the Fire Brigade was on the scene, followed soon after by the Marshall & Snelgrove private brigade.

It took both brigades nearly two hours to bring the fire under control, by which time the basement, including the kitchen, spirit store, wash house and various other stores were totally gutted. A gas pipe near the meter had melted sending a large jet of fire throughout the area, which caused many problems in quelling the flames. At ground floor level the fire had broken through into the committee rooms and had damaged a number of partition walls but the main damage at this level was caused by water from the hoses. However, the reading rooms, billiard room and Masonic Temple were saved from damage.

The club had only just undergone refurbishment and the decorations had been very expensive.

HUNTRISS ROW

It was only a week later that the brigade was again busy just across the road at Mr Butlers, Opticians, Huntriss Row (now the site of Yorkshire Bank). Chief Constable Pattison was supervising the fire when the Marshall & Snelgrove private brigade arrived. Mr Pattison refused them admission saying *'He didn't want their help; and when he did he would send for them.'*

Mr Wilson who was in charge of the Marshall & Snelgrove brigade saw smoke coming from the offices of Messrs Bradly and Davis, over the opticians. He organised his men to lay out their hose up the stairs, causing much damage with the water, only to find there was no sign of fire as it was just the smoke percolating through from the shop below.

Mr Pattison on quelling the fire below went to see what was happening outside the shop, when he saw the damage being caused by the hose laid up the stairs he became very disturbed. He took his anger out on the Police – Firemen for letting the Marshall & Snelgrove brigade enter the property.

At the same time Councillor Sinfield, the Chairman of the Fire Brigade Sub-committee, was arguing with a crowd of people outside the shop about who was in attendance at the fire first and what right the private brigade had to be in attendance at the fire.

The Scarborough Gazette newspaper reported the incident saying that:

'...Marshall and Snelgrove a brigade which, (was) called into existence by the foresight and thoughtfulness of the firm for the protection of their own property, has nevertheless been placed at the disposal, freely and ungrudgingly of all who might need its services. It is well equipped with modern appliances, and its members are courageous, energetic, and well trained...'

It went on to say:

'There is no V.C. to be obtained for being drenched by water or scorched in a fire, though there is the risk of rheumatism and broken bones. One thing, however, is certain, that the town heartily appreciate the action of Marshall's Brigade on various occasions, and we take this opportunity of conveying their thanks to them.'

There was much condemnation of Mr Pattison and continual reference to having the 'Chiefs' wings clipped', was made. The report continued with:

'We would also like the town to address itself to the question of the efficiency of the present appliances and provisions existing for the extinction of fires. The fire at Mr Johnston's stables in Filey Road, one Saturday night some months ago, disclosed a disastrous state of things, and there has seldom been a fire anywhere which has not, owing to lack of water or unsuitable, or insufficient hose or appliances, or scarcity of men, disclosed the fact that the existing system is sadly deficient.'

The Gazette's onslaught on the brigade continued as a report later in the year, on 25th November stated:

'What about Scarborough; we are miserably behind the times here and we tremble to think what would happen if ever there was a big fire.'

It went on stating the various scenarios of fires, which might take place in the town.

TROUBLE AT T'DRILL

After local elections Councillor Fletcher was elected as Chairman of the Fire Brigade Sub-committee and he promised to make radical changes to the fire brigade's organisation.

His first change was to increase the men's drills from quarterly to monthly. He instilled a competitive spirit by timing the men in their drills and hydrant checks, which seemed to work well.

A view looking down Castle Road towards the castle. The Town Hall and Police Station are on the right. The curved building on the left is the site of what is now the Kam Sang Restaurant

Drills had been carried out on a Saturday afternoon but on Saturday 8th February 1898 Councillor Fletcher ordered Chief Constable Pattison to put the alarm bells in at 10.30 in the evening. On inspection by the Chief Constable one fireman was found to be totally drunk whilst two others were the worse for drink.

The committee dismissed the drunken fireman and the other two were cautioned and ordered to appear before Councillor Fletcher for a severe reprimand.

A report in the Scarborough Gazette on 17th February 1898, less than three months after their attack on the inadequacies of the brigade stated:

> 'The Fire Brigade: a new institution and one that is certain to answer admirably…'

After detailing the drill practices, it expounded:

'Alderman Cross and Councillor Fletcher who witnessed the practice expressed themselves highly pleased with the efficiency of the brigade.'

An enlargement of the previous photo detailing the fire engine house

BROOKS FIRE

At around 12.30 a.m. 8th June 1898 a beat policeman doing his rounds went up Queen Street, trying the doors as he went. He found nothing out of place and proceeded on his way along Market Street and into St Sepulchre Street.

Within twenty minutes of the policeman passing a commercial traveller was making his way back to his hotel, The George, Newborough, when he noticed that the whole of the shop area of Mr J Brooks, barber and tobacconist, Queen Street, (between Market Street and Newborough, the site of the Department of Social Security) was ablaze. The traveller ran across the road to the George Hotel and stirred the boot boy, Mr Howe, to raise the alarm.

It seems that as Mr Howe arrived on Queen Street, Mr Jackson from the saddler shop opposite also came into the street. Mr Howe ran to the police station and informed the duty personnel; at around the same time the local lamplighter arrived on the scene and blew his whistle to try to raise help.

A constable on duty in Durham Street heard the lamplighter's call and raced back to the police station in time to collect the hose cart, which the sergeant was preparing after being informed by Mr Howe of the incident. He then rushed with it to Queen Street, arriving at the fire within ten minutes of the initial discovery of the blaze.

In the meantime Mr Jackson had been banging on the door of the shop and the neighbouring premises to wake up any occupants inside. The adjoining properties were evacuated but no sign of life was seen from inside the Brooks' premises.

As the hose cart arrived on the scene, someone was spotted on the roof of the Queen's Head Hotel next door. As he slid down the roof he was recognisable as Mr Brooks and the firefighters shouted to him asking about the safety of his wife and children but his replies were inaudible.

Brooks eventually dropped off the roof at the rear of the Queen's Head, sustaining minor cuts and bruises, and was brought out through the inside of the building.

In the meantime Brooks' place on the roof seemed to have been taken by Mr Howe in an attempt to gain access to the second floor of the burning shop, to try and attempt a search of the premises but he was unable to reach the burning building.

Shortly after Chief Constable Pattison arrived with the firemen, the crowd informed them that the occupiers of the buildings had all been removed to safety.

Heroic acts were performed by the firemen in quelling of the fire, which was made more dangerous by the constant explosions caused by fireworks, which Brooks had stored in the shop for sale.

There was some criticism later about the firemen's work but the general public did not realise the severity and danger of the conflagration. The building was well alight by the time the firemen reached it, the stock in the shop consisted of fireworks and smokers' materials, and the furniture was mainly made from bamboo. All the doors were open throughout the premises and the upper windows were also open, allowing a free passage for the smoke and fire, also feeding the flames with a constant supply of oxygen. The back way to the shop was only accessible via the roofs of other properties which increased the time it took to get water onto the fire from that side. The firemen had a difficult task and had to work extremely hard to extinguish the flames.

After an hour the fire was only smouldering in the shop area, but was still burning strongly at roof level and a ladder was put up to the bay windows to gain a position from which to throw a jet of water.

By 3 a.m. day was breaking and the fire was well under control. One of the firemen stepped off a ladder through a second floor window only to reappear very quickly and in the night air his whisper, as low as it was, sent a shiver through the spines of everyone present. His voice carried so that everyone in the crowd below heard him say to the Chief Constable

'Gov,nor, there's a woman and child here.'

Mrs Brooks was on the floor of the second room that the fireman had entered, laid dead in the position of trying to cover the baby to protect her. On further inspection in the back room of the same floor, one by one, more bodies of dead children were discovered, five in all. Some of them had been burnt badly, others were untouched by the flames but they had succumbed to the dense smoke. Two of them were laid on the floor with their arms outstretched as if begging for help. Two boys were found in one bed and a girl was found on another bed. The doctor at the incident did his best to reassure the small crowd that all would have died from suffocation and not as a direct result of burning.

The police ambulance men went back to the police station to fetch the wheeled and hand stretchers and the bodies were removed one by one, the baby being laid on the breast of Mrs Brooks even though the Doctor had had to disentangle them on his first examination.

The victims of the fire were:

Mrs Jane Brooks	aged 42
Mary Ellen Brooks	aged 13
Mildred Brooks	aged 11
Darrell Brooks	aged 8
Douglas Brooks	aged 5
Elsie Brooks	aged 3
Ida Brooks	aged 15 months

THE AFTERMATH

At midday on the morning after the fire Chief Constable Pattison left town to start his annual holiday in Derbyshire with his invalid wife.

An inquiry was opened into the fire the following day (Thursday), conducted by the Borough Coroner, Mr Taylor, with a twelve man jury sworn in to listen to evidence.

Mr Taylor outlined the case as he saw it, that is:

That on the evening of Tuesday, Mr Brooks had been out for a drink returning home about midnight and retired to bed only to be woken by his wife who said she had heard burglars. He got up and went downstairs to investigate and found the shop ablaze. He was unable to get out of the shop by the street door because of the flames so he returned to his wife and climbed out of the bedroom window to try and get help.

Because of the fact that Brooks was storing explosives (fireworks) on the premises without a licence, the coroner had to inform the Home Office who recommended that an inspector of explosives be present to investigate the case thoroughly.

The whole court was then moved to the Borough Mortuary for the formal identification of the bodies by Mr Brooks and for the jury to view the bodies. On returning to the courtroom, Mr Brooks took the witness stand and confirmed the coroner's outline of events. It was also revealed that on entering the shop when returning from the public house, he had left a half smoked cigar on the counter in the shop. He spent many hours in the witness box and never gave a satisfactory answer as to why he did not help his wife and children out of the inferno. The inquiry was adjourned to the following Wednesday.

Mr Brooks was taken from the courtroom and had to be protected from an angry mob that had gathered outside. He was whisked away in a closed cab and taken out of town to await the rest of the inquiry.

A strong feeling started to build up in the town about the state of the fire brigade and the lack of the fire escape at the scene of the fire until later on, even though there were two in the town.

A special meeting of the Watch Committee was held on the Thursday evening and it was proposed to send to Derbyshire and order Mr Pattison to return to Scarborough to explain his reasons for leaving the town so soon after such a serious incident. On his return, yet another special meeting followed and Mr Pattison apologised for any inconvenience he had caused, saying that, as the opening day of an inquiry was purely a formality, he felt his presence was not required until the second day.

After he left the meeting it was proposed, and seconded, that he should be asked to resign his post as Chief Constable and Superintendent of the fire brigade due to his gross neglect of duty. The motion was passed unanimously.

THE FUNERAL

On Saturday 11th June the funeral took place of the mother and her six children. The seven bodies were placed in five coffins and were taken from Mrs Vasey's, Mrs Brooks' sister's house in Elders Street. At 3 o'clock, when the cortege was due to leave from Elders Street, the police were required to clear the crowds to make room for the three hearses and the long line of mourners' coaches. The streets were lined with thousands of grieving town folk all the way to the cemetery in Dean Road.

Mr Brooks was not in town at the time as the feeling of the people had grown to such hatred that the police had advised him to stay away, as they could not guarantee his safety. There were many scuffles

COPYRIGHT BY J. WATERS, EQUESTRIAN HOTEL, ST. THOMAS STREET, SCARBOROUGH.

The view from the Equestrian Hotel, looking down Elders Street, at the funeral cortage

at the funeral as the crowds rushed the coaches trying to discover the whereabouts of the widower.

The bodies were placed in two graves, which had to remain unmarked, as they were paupers' graves and still remained unmarked to this day.

Mr PATTISON

At a meeting of the full council on the following Monday the decision of the Watch Committee to ask for Mr Pattison's resignation was confirmed. It was stated that at the fire he was continually smoking a pipe and whilst he was removing the bodies he was smoking a cigar.

Mr Pattison sat through the meeting and when interviewed afterwards he denied that he ever had a pipe with him at the fire. He said he asked someone to give him a cigar, as he was feeling sick after the events that had just gone before him. He also said that, at the time, he had no intention of resigning.

Mr Pattison tendered his resignation on the Wednesday evening.

THE INQUEST

The inquiry resumed on the Thursday evening with the court and surrounding streets thronged with people. The next stage of the proceedings was for the jury and officials to inspect the scene of the fire.

On return, Mr Brooks again took the stand to give evidence. Various drinking partners who confirmed that he was not too much the worse for drink on the evening in question followed him on the stand. The meeting was adjourned at 11 o'clock until the following Wednesday.

There was a crowd of over 2000 people outside and the police thought it prudent to keep Mr Brooks in the police station overnight for his own protection, allowing him to leave town again in the morning.

There were more meetings in which various events were revealed, such as the fact that the commercial traveller, who had first discovered the fire, was arrested by the police for being drunk and disorderly. His explanation was that after the police/firemen, arrived they were dithering about trying to connect the hydrants, which to his mind, they seemed to have no idea how to do, and he simply pushed them aside in his excitement to help. He made a statement that he had been out at sea until 9 o'clock, after which he went to the Exhibition (probably the Olympia) at which he said no drink was available, and from there he went to the Balmoral where he had two pints. He refused to say were he had gone from there, much to the amusement of the onlookers.

Mrs Brooks' sister revealed that the relationship in the Brooks household had at times been strained, and that her brother-in-law had been known to hit Mrs Brooks. The police detective who examined the bed Mrs Brooks slept in stated that he thought Mr Brooks had never been in the bed that evening. The Home Officer Inspector of Explosives said that, whilst the local licence for storing explosives had expired, the Home Office themselves were satisfied that Mr Brooks was registered for the sale of such goods.

At day three of the meeting, part way through the enquiry, Inspector Walker entered the meeting to inform Chief Constable Pattison and the other firemen that a fire had broken out in St Thomas's Walk. The speed at which they left the court to attend the fire impressed all who saw it. It was not long before information was returned to the court stating that the fire was only small and would soon be dealt with; the children at the house involved had left a candle burning which had set fire to a box.

There were a total of six meetings to discuss the evidence, at the end of which the coroner summarised the events to the jury and said that in making their verdict they had to remember that *'cowardice was not a criminal offence'*. The summing up lasted from 6 o'clock until 10.40. The jury then went out, leaving crowds both inside and outside the courtroom waiting for the verdict. The jury returned at five past midnight and gave their verdict, saying that, whilst there was no evidence to suggest any deliberate lighting of the fire, they felt Mr Brooks action in not making the slightest attempt to save his family made him guilty of culpable negligence.

The coroner said he agreed with their findings but it was not classed as a criminal offence. He made a statement that he could only attribute the actions to gross cowardice and sottish drunkenness. He said:

'Brooks had left his house for the purpose of self-indulgence. He went to public houses and took beer, and at another played billiards, and then retired to another house and indulged again in drink, and after that went to another house and indulged in fish. During that time he had left his wife at home, and this indicates the self indulgence".

He hoped it would be a warning to Brooks and that he should lead a far different life in future.

Brooks sat with his head bowed throughout the coroner's remarks and was then ushered through to the police station so as not to let the crowds outside catch a glimpse of him. He left the town and moved to Rochdale.

POST CARDS
There was another appearance in the court in connection with the Brooks fire on the 10th January 1899, but this time it involved Mr J Waters, the publican of the Equestrian public house, St Thomas Street. He had seen a business opportunity in selling post cards of the funeral cortege from photographs taken from the Equestrian looking down Elders Street where the procession started. He had come to an agreement with Mr E Stead, photographer, of Aberdeen Walk, regarding the production of the post cards and both parties had their own views as to how much was due to them. Mr Stead's case was found proved and he received ten pounds compensation from Mr Waters.

IMPROVEMENTS
After these events Councillor Fletcher was able to shake the council into dramatic improvements of the brigade. Within weeks a definite site was set aside for a new fire station (the old Corporation yard in North Marine Road, leased to Mr Percy, behind the Merchant Seaman's Hospital – the site the station occupies today). However, the official acceptance was not made until December 1899.

The two escape ladders were to be made more readily available by keeping them in a prominent position at night. The South Cliff ladder was to be kept at the rear of St Martins Church, whilst the other was to be placed on land opposite the police station (now the location of the Fire Safety and Advice Offices). At all incidents the brigade attended the escape was to be one of the first appliances in attendance.

TYLER'S BOOT STORE
Whilst the flurry of recommendations were going back and forth, on the morning of Sunday 15th July, at just after 3 o'clock, Police Constable Philpot was walking up Westborough when he came across a fire at 122 Tylers Boot Store, (now The Card Warehouse). He sent Police Constable Warriner to report the fire at the police

station, whilst he alerted the neighbourhood, which included more than fifty people in the adjoining Balmoral Hotel.

In the meantime Police Constable Warriner had reached the police station where Inspector Lee put in the call-out bell to rouse the firemen. The two then set off back to the incident taking with them the hose and reel, which was connected to the hydrant at the end of North Street, opposite the Windsor Hotel (became the Old Bar hotel, then the Huntsman and is now the Next clothes shop), directing the water onto the front of the building. When the rest of the firemen, under the direction of Inspector Walker, arrived they connected into the hydrant in Huntriss Row and took the hose through the premises of the Scarborough Brewery Company next door, and placed themselves in a window on an upper floor from where they could reach the fire. Another hose was run out and through the Windsor Hotel. By the time this was in place on the top floor the Marshall & Snelgrove private brigade arrived and took charge of it.

It took the joint efforts of the brigades until 5.30 a.m. to control the flames, by which time the rear western end of the Balmoral Hotel roof plus many of the top floor bedrooms were burnt away. Damage was caused to many of the other rooms by water and in the cellar most of the wine was made undrinkable by the heat.

At Tyler's, which had been a four storey building, there was nothing left of the roof, floors or internal walls, with just the front and back walls left standing. The building had been heavily stocked in anticipation of the summer trade, plus the week's takings had been left behind in the shop. The brigade and Mr Beaumont, Tyler's manager, made a search in the remaining embers as soon as the fire had subsided sufficiently. But due to the dangerous condition of the building it was called off, and as they walked away a large section of brickwork fell right where they had been searching.

Questions were asked at the next committee meeting as to why the escape ladder was not one of the first appliances at the scene as recommended. Councillor Fletcher said that he had attended the scene whilst the firefighting effort was going on and he was satisfied that if the escape had been required it would have been in attendance in good time.

GOODBYES

Mr Pattison worked his time out until September when he had to retire. Inspector Walker took over as temporary Superintendent of the fire brigade until the new Chief Constable arrived. There were many glowing reports and commendations made about Mr Pattison and he received many retirement gifts from the various committees he had dealt with over the years. One such gift was a gold watch presented to him in the police courts, inscribed:

> *'Presented to Mr W Pattison by members of the Scarborough Police and Officials of the Corporation on his retirement as Chief Constable, after 33 years service. September 9th 1898'*

Mr Pattison died in February 1906.

NEW CAPTAIN

Chief Constable Henry Riches filled Mr Pattison's place. He took over a police force of 47 men, including one police constable who was privately funded; a much-improved force from the one Mr Pattison had inherited thirty three years previously.

He was also given charge of the Fire Brigade, but his title was to be Captain and not Superintendent like his predecessors.

Fletcher and Riches worked well as a team and there was a flurry of proposals for improvements going before the council over the following twelve months. Included in these were:

That a new hose cart should be ordered from Merryweathers costing £109 5s. to replace the hose reel.

Mr Stuart, the patent holder of fire alarms, was invited to Scarborough to discuss the possibility of the installation of street fire alarms. He was a partner in Messrs Stuart & Moore, who had supplied street fire alarms to London.

Permission was sought for Councillor Fletcher and Chief Constable Riches to tour the country looking at fire stations and obtaining ideas to the best design for one.

Tenders for the new station were invited.

Firemen were to be insured against accident with the Yorkshire Fire Brigades Friendly Society, at a cost to the council of £3 10s. per annum.

A full-time foreman should be employed and the position to be advertised nationally.

RESULTS

From these proposals came new equipment, the firemen were insured and by 22nd September 1899 there were six street fire alarms put into use in Scarborough after being fitted by Shaw and Co Electrical Engineers, Stockport. These were said to be accessible in any part of Scarborough, within five minutes of discovery of a fire. They were sited at:

1/ Westborough – York Place junction
2/ Westbourne Grove top – close to the Ramshill Hotel
3/ Seamer Rd and Falsgrave Rd junction – near Chapman's shoe makers
4/ Prospect Rd and Raleigh St junction – near Chapman's butchers
5/ Dean St and Trafalgar St East junction – close to the Workhouse
6/ Sandside at the bottom of Eastborough

They were all connected to the police station in Castle Road.

Falsgrave – Seamer Road Corner, a street fire alarm can be seen on the extreme right in front of what is now the Tap and Spile

A NEW STATION

There was a report in 'Fire & Water', a fire brigade journal, showing the proposed designs for a new Scarborough fire station stating that:

'Scarborough was a progressive town to be building a station to the standard of stations as yet only found in City brigades.'

There were council deputations to other new stations at Manchester, Salford, Rochdale, Leicester and Kilburn to study modern fire brigade needs.

The plans showed that the station would consist of a watch room with a callboard for street alarms and communication with firemen's dwellings, which were within the vicinity of the fire station. Above the appliance room would be the Superintendent's and a resident fireman's rooms, and a store for spare fittings etc.

The Superintendent's rooms would consist of a sitting room, three good bedrooms, bathroom, kitchen and usual offices. It was intended that the other rooms would be occupied by a married on-duty fireman with a single fireman lodger.

The hose tower was to be 63 foot high with racks and a pulley system for hoisting hose, which could then be heated by steam coils from a boiler in the tower base.

The tower top could be used as a lookout post and would have an alarm bell under a domed roof.

There would be a repair shop at the rear with a washhouses etc. and also a trough for hose washing purposes.

There would also be room left to build stables if the council decided to keep horses on the station in the future. It was estimated that the cost would be £3000 to build Scarborough Central Fire Station, exclusive of the purchase of the site. In addition there was to be a sub-station to be built on the South Cliff with rooms for a fireman.

Tenders were invited for the building of the new station and in anticipation of the station been built a meeting was held on 27th October 1899. It was also proposed that a rent of five shillings a week be charged for the Chief Constable's house in the new station when it was complete. This was rejected on the grounds that a Chief Constable should be a respectable person and not have to stoop to living in accommodation of only five shillings so a higher levy was set with his wages being adjusted accordingly to meet the extra.

By 12th January 1900 all the tenders were in and the following were accepted, that is:

Messrs J Bastiman & Sons	Bricklayers work at £1429
Mr J Hargreaves	Tile & Slaters work at £ 99
Mr T B Jowsey	Carpentry & Joinery work at £ 690
Messrs E Percy & Co	Plumbing & Glazing work at £ 150
Mr Henry Pickup	Smith & Founder's work at £ 288 14s
Mr F Thompson	Painters work at £ 41 11s 8d

On 15th February 1900 both Bastiman & Son and Jowsey withdrew their tenders on the grounds the prices were rising too quickly. Bastiman said the present cost was now ten per cent higher than the one he submitted by tender.

The next highest tenders were looked at and it was found that Bastiman's re-estimate was still lower than the nearest tender so they retained the contract and the joinery work went to Mr John Barry. Mr A J Lowe was awarded the heating contract and Messrs Walker & Hutton the electrical work.

James Wood's tender of £180 10s 4d for alterations to 6 Alga Terrace to make a new fire station for the South Cliff area was also accepted.

The Town Council approved the purchase of a steam fire engine and authorised the borrowing of £450 to enable them to obtain a Shand Mason 'Patent double cylinder' vertical steam fire engine, capable of issuing 350 gallons per minute of water to the height of 160 foot with a one and one eighth inch jet.

The invention of steam fire engines had taken place many years earlier. However there had been a reluctance to obtain them because Sir Eyre Massey Shaw, the ex-London Fire Chief, believed that they made firemen lazy, as pumping by hand was no longer required. He also maintained firemen would tend to stand at some distance from the fire and let the pressure of the pump throw the water at the fire instead of crawling up close and applying the water to the fire. These ideas were not discouraged by the firemen of the day either as it was feared that with no one required to pump the handles on the manuals it would lead to the loss of jobs, or at least the loss of their free beer allowance. However, over the years of the 1890's, new ideas were slowly becoming accepted and, taking the lead from the London brigade, the smaller brigades were following suit.

On 12th May 1901 Chief Constable Riches was instructed to advertise for an expert foreman to instruct and train firemen and to take charge of fires in the absence of the Chief Constable. He was to be offered 38 shillings per week raising bi-annually to 42 shillings. Coal and gas were provided free of charge and he was to reside in the Central Fire Station, paying 4 shillings a week for accommodation. (The accommodation was that originally planned for the Chief Constable, who had managed to persuade the committee not to make him live on the station.)

By 4th July there were three men short-listed for the job:

Herbert Benson   of the Fire Station, Idle
William Birkbeck   of Pollard Street Fire Station, Manchester.
George Law   of Branch Fire Station, North Evington, Leicester.

It was Mr Birkbeck who was appointed on 15th July 1901.

All the plans did not go through unopposed though. At a public meeting regarding the purchase of the steam pump a Mr Yeoman opposed the financial outlay stating that there was not sufficient need for one. He went on to say that it would not be used for anything else, plus it would fall in to a state of disrepair and would not be useable when required.

At a Council meeting in June 1901 it was stated by one of the councillors that the Fire Brigade and new station (under construction) was nothing but a white elephant. He went on to say that at Fletcher's Firehouse a wall was removed in front of the station to reveal that the engine station floor was four foot lower than that of Mr Percy's, a coaching house adjoining. He continued to say that the gap in the pavement to allow entry to the station was far too wide, as it was the same width as Huntriss Row, which was a main thoroughfare.

Councillor Fletcher remained unperturbed by all the comments and earned himself the title of 'The Scarborough Fire King', a name which was to stay with him for many years.

Horses to pull the new pump and escape ladders were to be supplied by Jewison, cab proprietors, of Lower Mill Street. They were contracted to keep two horses ready for the use of the fire brigade at £28 a year, plus extra if needed out of the area and four horses were required.

Mr Jewison's house at 27 North Marine Road was rigged up, like the firemen's houses, to an electric bell system, so he could be called in the event of a fire. (Surprisingly most fire brigades throughout the country, including the larger city brigades never purchased their own horses but leased them from 'Job Masters' (cab firms)).

The contract was not an easy one for him to keep up, as he was to discover; a fire occurred in Westborough in February 1902 for which he had no horses available and so had to pay Foxtons for the hire of two shire horses. For his efforts he received a sharp rebuke from the committee and was warned his contract would be withdrawn in the event of similar circumstances occurring.

A photograph of the Scarborough fire brigade
Left to right standing are: Firemen Bland, Smithson, Reed, Chief Constable Riches, Fire Engineer Birkbeck, Firemen Jefferson, Robert, Craven, Wardell and Wood
Left to right seated are: Firemen Reed Junior, Thacker, Councillor Fletcher, Firemen Lilley and Dixon

The front elevation of the station taken from H W Smith's, Borough Engineer, plans

CENTRAL FIRE STATION

The 30th August 1901 was the date set for the grand opening of the new station.

The orders of events were that at midday the Mayor, Councillor Darley, was to meet the rest of the Corporation and dignitaries at the Town Hall (which was still operating from Castle Road.) Amongst the guests were:

Earl of Londesborough   Lord Hawks
Sir Everand Cayley   Miss Helen Bower
Miss Iris Darley   Mr W Pattison
Aldermen:
                Cross, Tonks, Smith and Gawnie
Councillors:
                Fletcher, Broadwood, Sanderson, Parie, Bland,
                Sinfield, Hudson, Gibson, Maynard and Taylor
Deputy Town Clark   – Mr S Jones
Borough Engineer   – Mr H W Smith
Borough Accountant   – Mr T M Fawcett
Water Engineer   – Mr Millhouse
Borough Treasurer   – Mr Sayer
Borough Coroner   – Mr G Taylor
Chief Collector of Rates   – Mr R Cole
From Shand Mason & Co   – Mr J C Hudson
Shand Mason & Co   – Mr A Elliott
Contractors:
                Mr Barry, Mr Percy, Mr Lowe and Mr Hargraves
Surveyor   – Mr H Chapman
Clerks of Works   – Mr J Oats
                            Mr J E T Graham
                            Mr F G Smith
Chief Constable of Norwich   – Mr E F Winch
Supt of Dewsbury Fire Brigade   – Mr Warwick
Scarborough Chief Constable   – Mr H Riches
Scarborough Fire Brigade Engineer – Mr W Birkbeck

Scarborough fire station on it's opening day

At ten past twelve they proceeded to the new station on North Marine Road where a large crowd was waiting to greet them.

Councillor Fletcher, on behalf of the Fire Brigade Committee then officially welcomed everyone. He thanked the Mayoress, Mrs Darley, for consenting to perform the opening ceremony. She then, by pulling on a rope, opened the fire station doors which revealed the new Shand Mason steamer inside. Her next task was to christen the steamer 'The Darley'. (It was a recognised practice in those days to give names to fire engines.)

On the same day, the South Cliff Fire Station was also put into use. It had a direct connection to the central fire station by a telephone line, which Mrs Darley used to contact that station also.

An exhibition of fire fighting techniques was then performed in the yard. Jets of water were sprayed up the tower using water pumped through the manual pump (which, according to the programme, was the one bought in 1802); the escape ladder was used to perform a life saving drill, plus other ladder drills.

The dignitaries returned to the Town Hall where they removed their fancy regalia, and then followed the steamer to St Nicholas Cliff where more displays were performed. The Earl of Londesborough started the first test, which was to create 100-psi pressure of steam from cold water within seven minutes. This was followed by various displays of water reaching different points on the buildings round about. Due to the poor weather, which was continual drizzle, the crowd was not too bothered by the spray from the jets.

A luncheon was then held at St Nicholas House (the location of the present Town Hall; this building was being made ready to become the new Town Hall) where there were fifty guests. In the speech made by Mayor Darley he said that he hoped the fire brigade and new equipment would be the means of saving life and preserving property. He went on to the amusement of the guests to say:

'He hoped the youngest Darley would have a useful career.'

In his reply, Councillor Fletcher said that his job was almost complete; he had had to stand by the ship in all storms and tempests. This was a reference to opposition on the council and the many adverse references made in one of the local newspapers.

VASEY'S FARM

Before the official opening of the station, its new amenities had already been put to use on the 28th August. At 1.30 a.m. Mrs Vasey of the Gables, Valley Road called the police station to say a haystack was burning fiercely at Vasey's Farm, Stepney Road.

The Chief Constable telephoned Mr Birkbeck at the fire station and put in the call-out bells at the firemen's dwellings and whilst they were preparing themselves, he arranged for horses to tow the manual pump and two hose carts to the scene.

Birkbeck organised a water supply, which had to be pumped from various iron tanks around the area.

South Cliff fire station as it looks now

Once the fire was brought under control the majority of the firemen were sent back to the station leaving Birkbeck and two others to keep watch over it whilst it burnt itself out. They remained at the site overnight returning to the station the following day.

BELLE VUE SAWMILLS

Whilst all the upgrading of the brigade was taking place, there were still fires to be tackled, the most notable occurring just before 9 a.m. 29th July 1901 at the sawmills of Messrs Wade & Son, which were located between Belle Vue Street and Sherwood Street.

When the fire was first noticed a message was sent to the police station who dispatched the reels and hose carts straight away, to arrive on the scene at around 9.30 a.m, at the same time as the Railway fire brigade arrived under the command of Station Master G Brown.

By this time, the fire had spread rapidly to the whole of the interior of the sawmill, due to the large amounts of dry timber stored inside, sending up great volumes of smoke high into the air. The brigade's hose seemed futile

The 'Darley' and crew, hose cart and crew, escape ladder and crew

against the large tongues of flames spreading out from the building. Cracking of the timber as it burnt was likened to that of artillery fire. By 10 a.m. the brigade did not seem to have had any success in controlling the fire. Flames grew so much that they spread along the roof and gradually replaced the smoke so that the whole of the building was a raging wall of flame. Heat thrown off was overpowering, but the firefighters never let this bother them and, with great personal discomfort, they battled on to get the upper hand

As well as losing the sawmill they were to lose the two adjoining buildings. The whole block was owned by Wades and, as well as the sawmill, was occupied by various other firms who had leased the premises.

Mr Flinton leased one building as a joiner's shop. Stored in it were large amounts of finished door and window frames for the new workhouse. Another building was leased to Mr S Manson, a building contractor. Amongst stock he held was about £650 worth of fittings for the Remnant Store (Boyes). Both these workshops were well stocked with timber and burnt readily with the convected heat from the sawmill.

The sawmill was comparatively new and, as well as the timber, it held a large amount of heavy woodwork machinery which had been purchased brand new when the building was built and was extremely valuable.

Private fire brigades of Messrs Rowntrees and Marshall & Snelgroves arrived at just after 10 a.m. bringing their hose carts with them and whatever help they could offer. This meant that the firefighting operations were capable of having ten jets of water sprayed on the building from different quarters.

The scene was a great attraction for the local people who came from miles around, especially as it was in the school holiday period. Most of the crowd dare not venture closer than Gladstone Road or Victoria Road due to the extreme heat. Many people watched the occurrence from other parts of town, where the rising smoke and flames were seen to give off quite a spectacular display.

It was reported that at one point Councillor Fletcher (Scarborough Fire King) appeared amongst the crowd and as he made his way to the front was greeted with a half humorous cheer.

There was a frightening occurrence when the heating boiler inside was heard to explode with a terrifying noise, after which the roof began to collapse bit by bit as the supporting walls gave way. The collapsing building sent sparks showering up into the air to be carried around the town.

Great volumes of water was played around the outside to protect the surrounding buildings and it seems this held the fire within the confines of the yard, helped by the fact that it was a calm, windless, day.

By noon the fire was eventually brought under control but it was noted that, if the steam fire engine had attended, the job would have been made much easier, but no more successful.

It was believed the fire had started in the boiler house of the building, a location where there had been problems before as on 17th August 1897 a pipe or valve, it was never decided which, exploded, severely scalding Mr T Brown and slightly injuring Mr W Emmerson.

A NEW CHIEF

In July 1902 the ambitious Chief Constable Riches surprised the council by tendering his resignation to enable him to take up the post of Chief Constable of Middlesbrough, (he held this post for 28 years until his retirement and he died in 1953 in Bournemouth.) The Council advertised for a new Chief Constable and received 53 applications. After some consideration it was Mr William Basham, (34) previously Chief Inspector of the Lincoln Police Force, who was appointed to the position.

Before Mr Basham took up the appointment the firemen submitted a letter signed by them all, asking that Mr Birkbeck be appointed as the Captain. The committee took no action however and Chief Constable Basham was offered the position when he started.

After being at Scarborough for a year Mr Birkbeck received a new uniform to differentiate him as the Engineer.

Chief Constable Basham had been in office less than a month when he was paid to travel to London and Salford for the purpose of inspecting various engineering

The 'Darley' and a crew, of firemen at the rear of Scarborough fire station

works, for the construction of a new horse drawn combined hose and fire escape ladder. The order was placed with Messrs J Morris & Sons, at a cost of £222 10s.

COSTLY ERROR

At 2 a.m. 23ʳᵈ October 1902 police constable G Rumford, on duty in Newborough, noticed the coffee room of the George Hotel was on fire. He tried to rouse the occupants and was joined in his efforts by Mr Jackson, a saddler, who lived near by. It took nearly fifteen minutes before they managed to alert them and start to evacuate the hotel.

In the meantime Police Constable Bailey arrived at the scene. He decided, whilst the other two were rousing the residents, to run to the fire station to alert Mr Birkbeck and the fire brigade.

Mr Birkbeck prepared horses in case the steamer was going to be required whilst Firemen Reed (junior) and Reed (senior) were preparing themselves. When all three were ready they proceeded to the fire, taking the hose reel and handcart with them.

On arrival they discovered Police Constable Rumford had managed to rouse the landlady's son, Mr Besford, and the hotel porter who opened the door to the policeman, just as the fire brigade arrived on the scene.

They entered the premises and knocked down a door leading to the coffee room. On entering they found that the area was well stocked with furs and eiderdowns (there was a trade convention being held in the hotel that week, and these were their products). The stocks were burning ferociously but with the hard work of the three firemen, assisted by the policemen, the fire was soon under control and extinguished completely shortly after.

It was at this point, whilst Mr Birkbeck was congratulating the firemen on a job well done, that he was informed of a problem in the back yard.

After the firemen had entered the building Mr Besford had returned upstairs to warn the rest of the family and staff of the fire. By the time they were awakened there were great volumes of smoke travelling up stairs. He assumed that the whole stairway was on fire, so he led the party to the fire escape on the top floor.

The type of fire escape was a canvas tubular chute, which was stored, rolled up, in a room. (It was intended that when it was dropped from a window people at ground floor level would pull it out at an angle to the building, allowing people to slide down it. If there was no one to hold it the first two people who descended did so by climbing down a rope running through the tube and then they could hold it taut to allow others to escape.)

As there was no one at ground level Mr Besford nominated two servant girls to climb down the rope and gave them orders to pull the chute taut, at an angle to the building. When they were out Mr Besford asked if everything was all right and when he received an affirmative answer he assisted his mother, Mary Ann (69), to climb into the chute.

Unfortunately, the girls were not holding the chute, as they had seen a group of hotel staff on a roof and went to their assistance by fetching a ladder. Mrs Besford fell down the 50-foot drop with no one pulling the chute taut, landing with full force in the back yard.

Totally unaware of what had happened to his mother, Mr Besford then assisted his aunt, Mrs Walker (60), off the ledge. She also plummeted to the ground and landed on top of Mrs Besford. Mr Besford's sister followed, then the laundress and finally Mr Besford, all landing on top of one another. All received serious injuries from the fall and Mrs Besford was to succumb to these and die a short while after.

Use of the fire escape chute had been totally unnecessary, as, if they had stayed in their rooms for just a few minutes more, the smoke would have cleared. The great amount Mr Besford had seen coming up the stairs was just the initial effects of the firefighting operations.

NEW ESCAPE LADDER

The new escape ladder was due for delivery in April 1903 and a request was made that an engineer should be sent with it from the manufacturers to instruct the firemen in its use.

A contract to supply the horses was also renewable at this time and Foxtons won the order, although £40 per annum more expensive (plus extra if more horses were required). Their premises were off

The horse drawn escape ladder passing the railway station followed by the 'Darley'

Vincent Street and backed adjacently onto the fire station, so a doorway was knocked through and a ramp constructed, in the station yard, to allow the horses to be brought to the station more rapidly.

There was some concern over the discipline of the firemen, and after some deliberation, the committee deemed it necessary to delegate their powers, under the Town Police Clauses Act of 1847, over to the Watch Committee.

The Darley – Scarborough's steam fire pump

THE WATCH COMMITTEE

The Fire Brigade coming under the jurisdiction of the Watch Committee, as they already ran the Police, made Mr Basham's job as Chief Constable and Captain of the Fire Brigade much easier. This allowed decisions to be made for both sections without the need for consultation between committees.

Recommendations that came from the first reports of the combined committee proved that it was the police who were going to have the stronger influence. The Chief Constable recommended that four of the part-time firemen (auxiliary firemen as he referred to them) be dismissed, using the funding to enlist extra police as part-time firemen. Within the month ten policemen were retrained as Police/Firemen, also retrained for firefighting duties were the constables in charge of South Cliff and Falsgrave sub-stations.

To consolidate the police influence Mr Birkbeck was enlisted to the Scarborough Police Force at the rank of sergeant whilst still carrying out his usual duties.

There was a strong letter of complaint received from the Head Postmaster in 1905. It seems that the beat policemen had taken to using the street fire alarm system as contact points to the police station; this in fact was a flouting of the law, as they were not licensed to be used in this way. The practice had to stop whilst a licence was applied for.

A recommendation put to the committee in 1905 was that, as there were problems with Foxtons supplying horses for mobilising appliances to fires due to the fact that they were in constant use taxiing, a motorised, self-propelled, fire engine be considered. The committee said they would give some thought to this. What actually occurred was that two horses were kept on permanent hire and allowed to graze on the land, belonging to Jowseys, adjoining the station (now Rymer Schorah).

This scheme with the horses proved to be successful and over the following years two horses were permanently stationed next door but under the ownership of various contractors as Messrs J Robinson & Sons and Jowseys all held the contract at different times. In 1907 it cost the brigade £40 to hire the horses plus extra if more horses were required to pull the appliances out of town.

There is a story told about one of the horses, that after the contract was given to another operator, the horse in question was used on a milk round. One day the steamer came charging past on the way to a fire, and the horse forgot it was no longer involved. It set off and gave chase to the steamer, milk bottles flying everywhere, and was hotly pursued by the milkman it had abandoned. (It must be said that this story is common to most towns where horses were used by the fire brigade.)

QUEEN HOTEL

One of the most spectacular fires seen in Scarborough occurred on 9th April 1906 at one of the longest established hotels in the town, the Queen Hotel on North Marine Road, which filled the gap between the hotels that the Cricketers Pub now occupies. At that time it was one of the largest hotels in the town having 100 plus bedrooms and was owned by the Hudson Hotel Ltd, which also owned the Crown and Royal hotels.

At a little before 5 a.m. the live-in barman was woken by crackling noises and on investigation, he found the staircase totally ablaze. He managed to rouse a maid who he helped escape through a window and sent her to the fire station to raise the alarm. He then tried to get to other parts of the building to alert the manageress and cook, but found it impossible to get anywhere near them, so he made his exit through the same window the maid did. Luckily, due to the time of year, there were no other people in the building.

At 5.28 a.m. the fire brigade was alerted and straight away Mr Birkbeck and his assistant took the hose cart to the scene, leaving a message that as soon as there were enough men available they had to proceed to the fire pushing the normally horse drawn escape.

Five men were soon at the station and hurried to the scene with the escape to arrive only minutes after Birkbeck. As they arrived, the manageress and cook managed to make their own way out of the burning building.

Four water jets were put to work and by this time the fire had spread up the stairs to the extent that it had broken through the roof. It was decided that there was sufficient pressure from the hydrants and there was no need for the steam engine. Despite the hard work by the firemen the fire had managed to spread right across the roof by 6.30 a.m. There were few people walking to work at that early hour, but those who were, were treated to a magnificent pyrotechnic display in all parts of the town.

Unable to contain it, the fire spread into the roof of the adjoining building to the south end of the hotel (now the Balloon Box), and a large portion of the roof had to be removed to counteract the spread.

By 7.30 a.m. the roof started to collapse, causing a crash that could be heard some considerable distance around the town, sparks rose high into the air amidst an almighty roar, which erupted as the roof caved in. Luckily, at this time there were no firemen on the roof, as only minutes before they had been shinning along it, taking many risks to gain better positions from which to fight the fire.

Once the roof had collapsed the fire was much easier to contain and it was not long before the firemen had the fire under control, although the jets were played onto the building until mid-day. There were firemen left at the scene well into the next day watching for further outbreaks.

A fireplace hearthstone, in the manageress's sitting room, was blamed for causing the blaze. A fire had been left burning overnight, and because of bad workmanship – the hearth being built on timber, this eventually set alight. This was a common cause of fires in that period.

Queen Hotel seemed somewhat ill fated in that it suffered another fire some years later; it was also damaged by bombs in the Second World War leading to its eventual demolition in 1964.

POMPIER LADDERS

Whether or not as a direct result of the Queen Hotel fire, Chief Constable Basham was given permission to purchase a 'Pompier' ladder set; this is what is known as a hook ladder and was used by fire brigades up until the early 1970s.

These ladders had originally been made in France, but were introduced into this country from America at the turn of the century. They had been developed by American firemen for the famous 'Hook & Ladder Companies'. The ladder was a single length, sometimes hinged in the middle, with a long metal bill on the top end. The idea was to hook the bill over the upper floor windowsill and ascend to that level, where the ladder was raised to a window on the next floor, and so on.

NATIONAL FIRE BRIGADES UNION

Scarborough Fire Brigade was accepted as a forward thinking brigade for that period and as such, it was a member of the National Fire Brigades Union (NFBU). This was not related to the Fire Brigades Union which is the main union for serving firemen today, but was a federation made up of fire brigade superintendents, Chief Constables, Watch Committee members and other people with interests in the running and organisation of fire brigades.

One of its main aims was to standardise the way firefighting techniques were developed and the types of training firemen underwent. As a means of achieving this competitions were run annually, with member brigades encouraged to enter. Various types of competitive drills were held including hose cart drills, steamer drills, dividing breaching drills, hydrant drills and ambulance drills.

In July 1907, the Yorkshire branch of the society held its annual meeting in Scarborough. The council gave the facilities of the Castle Yard over to them. There were two arenas

CHEEKY BOY. A 'OUSE AFIRE? 'OUSE AFIRE?

CONSTABLE. NOW NON OF YOUR KIDDING WHERE.

CHEEKY BOY. GARN IN T' CASTLE YARD BARMY

A cartoon from the Scarborough paper

roped off for the competitions and a four storey wooden house was built for a ladder and rescue drill.

At 1 p.m. Saturday 20th July, members from thirteen various brigades met at the railway station and formed a parade, marching in order of their length of service in the union. The whole parade was led by Chief Constable Basham, followed closely by mounted police, the horse drawn wheeled escape ladder and steamer and the Scarborough band. They marched down Westborough, Newborough, up Queen Street, along Castle Road and into the Castle Yard. As they entered the Castle the president of the union, the Earl of Londesborough, inspected them.

Various drills were performed and the Scarborough team was unlucky not to win the steamer drill; they would have done so but for the fact that someone had forgotten to shut a lid and the team was penalised by three seconds. A temporary wooden house was then set on fire and when the flames had a good hold the Scarborough Fire Brigade put on an entertaining demonstration of rescue and extinguishing techniques using an escape ladder.

Prize giving was performed by Lady Ida Sitwell, who after giving out the prizes, made a special presentation of a gold medal to the Scarborough Fire Brigade for their burning house display.

That evening there was a dinner laid on at the Grand Hotel for the officers and officials. In proposing the toast the Mayor of Scarborough said that he felt it would have been more appropriate for Councillor Fletcher to make it, after the good work he had done for the development of the brigade in Scarborough. Both he and Councillor Fletcher, Scarborough's Fire King, who was also present, received loud applause. One of the after dinner speakers stated that Scarborough had been a magnificent venue for the union and suggested that it was the ideal place to hold a national meeting of the union at which members from the whole country could attend. The Mayor replied to this, saying it would be a good idea to see this happen.

NFBU CAMP

After the success of the visit of the Yorkshire Branch of the NFBU to Scarborough in 1907, it was decided by both the Corporation and the union to hold the national gathering at Scarborough. Once again the Castle Hill was used as a base, but this time there were 3,000 representatives attending, spread across a ten day period and using the Castle as a campsite. National camps had been held annually over the previous nine years, but this was the first time they had taken place in the north, usually occurring in or around London.

Representation was present from almost 30 fire brigades and included amongst the attractions was a motorised fire engine, which did several tours of the town, and firework displays from the Castle Hill. On the Sunday a church

The Rotherham Cup winners – note the cup and other silverware on the footplate

parade was formed by the firemen, marching through the town from the Castle to the Valley where an open air service was held on the slopes near the Valley Bridge.

Scarborough Fire Brigade was successful in winning the Rotherham Cup for the four man steamer competition and there were numerous other competitions run throughout the following days. Another 'house' had been built for the rescue drills. The house was put to use in a simulated incident involving a cask of petroleum, a box of explosives and two trapped men, with the officer in charge having to decide the best way to effect a rescue of the men. There were points awarded for use of equipment, speed of rescue and ingenuity used to decide on the winner.

Points were also awarded to the various brigades for their camping capabilities and inspection of the tents was made on a daily basis. General Baden-Powell (later to become Lord, and famous as the chief of the Boy Scouts) visited the camp on one occasion and inspected the men and the various fire appliances that were there.

After the rally was over the Borough Corporation realised that the event had been something of a financial disaster. The Corporation had agreed to pay for the illuminations and fireworks (which had cost £175), but they were to charge the union for the manual labour costs of the camp. The actual costs of this were £150 but the Borough Engineer was instructed to only charge £30 and the Corporation covered the difference.

In 1907 the Rural District Council sent a letter to the Watch Committee saying they were not prepared to contribute to the upkeep of the Scarborough Fire Brigade and would not pay the expenses of the brigade for attending fires in their area. The committee decided to withdraw their co-operation with the rural area. They would only attend fires when a guarantee of payment was received before they left the fire station i.e. there was an insurance policy covering the property involved allowing the brigade to reclaim their expenses from the insurers.

ST OSWALD'S CHURCH
Between the two visits of the NFBU to the town the Scarborough Fire Brigade was busy, not always living up to the prestigious name they started to make for themselves.

Assistance of the Scarborough brigade was requested out of town in January 1908 when a fire in St Oswald's Church, Filey, seemed too much for the Filey brigade to handle on their own. On Sunday 19th Mr T R Cammish was taking some flowers to a grave in the churchyard at about 8.30 a.m. when he saw that there was smoke coming from the church roof. On closer inspection through a window he could see that the organ was burning ferociously.

He immediately ran across the Ravine Bridge and summoned help from the vicar, Reverend A N Cooper, who managed to alert and enlist the help of about 40 fishermen to set up a bucket chain at the incident. Whilst this was going on, Mr F Gray, the captain of the Filey brigade, was informed and he turned out his men along with the manual fire engine. When they arrived they set into water at Church Farm, nearby. The fire in the building by now had a good hold and it was feared that the whole church would be lost.

Solid oak timbers in the roof were dry, as was much of the wall panelling. Combustion of this caused fears that once the roof was burning well, it would send streams of molten lead onto the workers, so as a precaution, a telephone message was sent to Scarborough for them to provide assistance of manpower and the steam fire engine.

Scarborough Fire Brigade received the call at 9.40 a.m. and, as was the procedure at that time, the brigade could not leave the Borough without the permission of the Mayor. This caused a delay whilst the Mayor was located to give his consent.

Once permission was gained, Chief Constable Basham and Fire Engineer Birkbeck readied the steamer and hitched it up to a team of horses. One of the horses was less than happy with its task of pulling the engine and started to play up, nearly going into the window of a shop opposite the station and again at the Nottingham Pub (now the Indigo Alley). When it reached the police station at the top of St Thomas Street it fell over, pulling the neighbouring horse on top of it. This necessitated the return to the station where the horse had to be unhitched and replaced with another one; a group of bystanders heckled the firemen all the time whilst this was going on.

When the engine and its team of men and horses eventually got under way it took a further forty minutes for them to reach Filey. There was little wonder that by the time they reached the fire at 10.45 their services were no longer required, although they did remain to help clean up before

Filey Fire Brigade

returning to Scarborough in mid-afternoon.

Filey brigade with its group of helpers had done a marvellous job of containing the fire. Whilst the organ had been totally destroyed and also a large portion of the roof above it, they had managed, with some considerable effort, to keep the fire at that end of the church and not let it travel to the other parts.

A central heating pipe was attributed to the cause of the fire. The system had only been fitted the previous month. A pipe entered the church through the floor next to the wood boarding which surrounded the organ pipe it started to scorch and eventually burst into flames. At 6 p.m. the previous evening the caretaker, Mr G Killingbeck, fired up the boiler and stoked it up at 10 p.m. and again at 6 a.m. on the Sunday to ensure the church would be warm for the morning service.

There was around £1,000 worth of damage caused but luckily, the vicar and churchwardens had increased the insurance premiums only shortly before, after seeing the cost of the repairs to the fire damaged Selby Abbey.

ST HELEN'S SQUARE

Not long after the Filey fire, the Scarborough brigade was again able to prove its abilities, though the location and type of fire brought back memories of the Brook fire only ten years previously. This time however there was not the fatal outcome of the Brook fire, which had occurred around the corner in the same block of buildings.

At 4 a.m. 15th May 1908 the duty Police Constable at St Helens Square junction with Newborough saw that the shop at the corner was well alight. Information was relayed to the police station about the fire, who forwarded the message to the fire station. The hose cart and horse escape were dispatched immediately under the charge of Chief Constable Basham and Fire Engineer Birkbeck.

When they arrived at the scene of the occurrence they found that three shops were involved in the fire, all lock-ups, therefore there was no one sleeping inside them. The property consisted of a large sweet shop, commonly known in the town as 'Under the Dial' because of the clock that protruded out into the street above the shop, owned by Messrs J&E Sage. Next door, in St Helens Square, there was a hairdresser's shop, owned by Mr J Croft. On the other side of the sweet shop in Newborough was a fruit shop belonging to Mr C Simpson.

Three water jets were immediately set to work from the hydrants and firemen started the battle to control the fire. So extreme was the heat above the hairdressers that the walls started to crack, causing fears that the fire would not be contained, but would spread into the adjoining property in St Helens Square, of Mr E Hodgson.

Police Constable Allan was working up a ladder outside the hairdressers when the person footing his ladder was called away. Shortly afterwards Police Constable Allan caused the ladder to bounce sending the foot of it sliding across the footpath leaving the police constable hanging from the windowsill screaming for help. With some effort the ladder was re-pitched to the window and Police Constable Allen came down with nothing hurt but his pride.

The fire was believed to have started at the rear of the sweet shop where there was a thin wooden partition between that shop and the hairdressers. There was a stove next to the partition, which having been left lit but unattended, had burnt through the partition causing the highly flammable contents of the hairdressers to make the fire situation worse. The upper floors were used as storerooms and in the stores of the hairdressers were fireworks, which also aided the rapid spread of the flames.

'Under the Dial'

Even though it was the early hours of the morning, word soon spread and there was a large crowd watching the operations by the time the fire was quelled at about 7 a.m.

Two firemen stayed at the scene for the rest of the day, controlling any outbreaks of flames as they occurred. The sweet and hairdressers shops were completely devastated by the fire whilst the fruiterer was only damaged at lower levels by the fire but the rest of the property sustained much water damage caused both by the firefighting operations and burst water mains.

'Under the Dial' and the fruit shops were covered by insurance but Mr Croft's hairdressers shop unfortunately was not. All three shops were later demolished and made way for the building that now stands there containing the public toilets.

HACKNESS HALL

Yet again Hackness Hall was the scene of a serious fire when, on the Sunday afternoon 16th January 1910, a passer-by noticed smoke coming from the Hall. He immediately informed Captain F Johnstone who was one of the few people left at the Hall, as the rest of the occupants and guests were at Sunday service. Word was sent to the church where the service was called to a halt so that the guests and locals could lend a hand extinguishing the fire.

Lord Derwent, who was 81 at the time, had to be escorted from the church to the house of his agent, Mr J Little, to recover from the shock.

The burnt out shell of Hackness Hall

By the time help arrived, the whole of the top storey of the building was aflame. A messenger was dispatched on horse back to the Scarborough Fire Station with a request for the steamer to attend. In the meantime the locals and other helpers set about removing what valuables (paintings, statues, books and even a full size billiard table) they could reach to a place of safety, namely the lawn.

Chief Constable Basham alerted Fire Engineer Birkbeck and six firemen, before helping to prepare a team of four horses and the steamer for the journey. Once ready, the steamer and its crew departed, whilst Chief Constable Basham went ahead taking a cab. In Scalby Mr Cooper overtook him in a motor car. Mr Cooper insisted that, for the sake of expediency, the Chief Constable should accompany him for the rest of the journey in the car.

At Roscoe Street, one of the team of four horses stumbled and hurt itself, recovered and carried on only to stumble again in Scalby Road where the firemen decided to unhitch it and proceed with only three horses.

On arrival at the Hall Chief Constable Basham quickly assessed the situation. By now the entire Hall was ablaze, and it was evident that a plentiful water supply was going to be needed. Chief Constable Basham therefore enlisted local help to dam a stream that ran through the village, so that water could be provided for the steamer.

It was 5 o'clock by the time the steamer arrived. The horses were exhausted with the extra workload put on them and were unable to pull the steamer into position. Mr Leadley, Chairman of the Scarborough Board of Guardians, helped commandeer some cart horses and used them to place the steamer near the, by now, plentiful supply of dammed water.

By 5.15 three jets of water with a good pressure were being directed at the fire. A request was sent to Scarborough for the Assistant Engineer and two more firemen to attend the fire, which they did with great haste.

The main building was blazing from end to end but a concerted effort was put into saving an extension wing, which was newly built after the last serious fire at the Hall, almost twenty years previously.

Development of the fire by 10 p.m. was such that the main part of the roof began to collapse in sections causing loud crashes and sending sparks flying through the air. The stables seemed to be safe at that time as the wind was blowing the fire in the opposite direction to them, but water jets were played on them as a precautionary measure.

Fire spread in the Hall continued to gain momentum, with the firefighting efforts making little, if any impact, as it was starting to spread through the roof void of the extension into the servants' quarters. Finally the firemen started to win the battle and by 1 a.m. the incident had been brought under control.

Water was played on the fire until 6 a.m. when the steamer was turned off. However at 7.30, there was a further outbreak of flames as the fire rekindled itself in the servants' quarters, so the steamer was re-fired and the flames were once again brought under control, finally being completely extinguished by 10 a.m. By 11a.m. the brigade were leaving the scene, arriving back at Scarborough at mid-day.

As the Hall was one of the first buildings in the area to have been lit by electricity, rumours soon spread around the district that it was the wiring that had caused the devastation. In actual fact, the fire was put down to a chimney fire starting at the first floor level caused by wooden floor joists running into the flue wall catching alight. This theory seemed to have been borne out by the reports of a smell of a burning chimney an hour before the actual outbreak was discovered.

Later Fire Engineer Birkbeck commented on the good running of the steamer as it had worked without a hitch in a situation it had never before encountered. Chief Constable Basham said:

> *'I would like to pay a tribute to the manly and self sacrificing way in which the members of the Fire Brigade worked, even against hope. Their efforts were heroic.'*

Hastily saved belongings from Hackness Hall scattered across the lawn

A letter of appreciation was received by the Watch Committee from Mr Little, thanking the brigade for their hard work.

Luckily Lord Derwent had just increased the insurance cover to a cost that would rebuild the Hall. This however did not make up for the personal loss and inconvenience that was suffered. Chief Constable Basham's report stated it would cost £22,000 to rebuild the Hall and that £10,000 worth of personal effects had been lost. It also said that the brigade was claiming £23 10s from the Assurance Company.

As a reminder of the incident, on rebuilding of the Hall a pair of phoenix rising from the ashes was built on top of the gateposts.

A phoenix on one of the hall's gateposts

THE OLD GAS HOUSE

Gas Works had been built on Quay Street in 1834 by a private company, and had expanded over the years to take in parts of Long Greece Steps. When the Gas Company moved to new premises on Seamer Road in 1872, the vacated premises were used as stores for the local fishing industry.

At about 3.30 a.m. Thursday 1st September 1910, D Naylor, of the fishing trawler, 'Seal', was helping to berth the boat in the harbour when he saw smoke rising above the roofs of the old town. On investigation he found that the smoke was coming from the old gas works so he dashed to the Sandside police station to rouse police constable Stockdale who contacted the main police station who in turn alerted the fire station.

At 3.40 a.m. the call was taken and within five minutes there were a dozen firemen mobilised, who arrived at Quay Street with their hose carts by 3.50 a.m. They were soon followed by more firemen and sixteen policemen with yet more hose and the fire escape. Chief Constable Basham directed the firefighting efforts. He led his men and encouraged them to use modern firefighting techniques, (to get in close to the fire and not just to stand outside and throw water at the windows). Several jets were set up at both the back and front of the area.

Brogden & Wilsons – engineers, James Tweddill – local boat builder and P&J Sutherland – herring curers were in the part of the area that was burning the fiercest. The mixed trades involved meant that the fire was fed by a wide variety of combustible materials causing the fire to go through the roofs of the buildings by 4 o'clock.

Residents from the nine houses in Long Greece Steps and G Wray and S Smalley of 8 & 10 Quay Street, respectively, were evacuated.

Many horses housed in Messrs J Sellers & Sons were rescued by local men who risked their lives to do so, since most of the doors to the stables were locked and had to be smashed open.

Looters, as usual, used the confusion to help themselves to other people's property by pretending to help in the rescuing of personal effects. This situation was not helped by the fact that all the police were also firemen and, as such, were too busy with the firefighting duties to do their police work.

One thing in the firefighters' favour was the lack of wind, which gave them chance to contain the fire in the area, without it spreading rapidly. By 5.30 a.m. they had started to control the flames enough to take the refreshments that had been supplied by the local publicans.

Police sergeant Nalton twisted his knee and a horse that took fright lamed itself after rearing up, otherwise there were no injuries, which was surprising considering the size of the fire.

It was reported that the fire could be seen at sea by fishermen at Hayburn Wyke who, thinking that the whole of the town was ablaze, set sail for home in the belief that their families and homes were being razed to the ground.

Water pressure was very poor as the Water Company, then owned by the Corporation, turned down the pressure on the mains between 6 p.m. and 6 a.m. Chief Constable Basham was later to ask the Watch Committee for permission to approach the Water Company with complaints about the pressure. This was granted but the response from the company was minimal.

Fire Engineer Birkbeck was unable to attend this incident as he was confined to his home at the station after injuring himself the week before on the 24th August at Wrea Lane. This fire involved a fish curing warehouse owned by J Sampson, Hull and Scarborough. By the time the fire had been reported to the fire station and they had turned out, it had spread to the adjoining curers of J Spring & Company, but with the hose speedily connected and the water applied the fire was soon extinguished.

In August 1911 new wheeled and hand stretchers were purchased which were to be placed in sub-stations and brought from there if needed, and on 6th April 1912, Jowseys were ordered to vacate their premises which was the area in which the brigades hired horses were kept. Once again this brought the old problem of the supply of horses for the brigade.

Two alternatives were discussed by the Watch Committee, one being to obtain tenders for a motor fire engine and the other to obtain tenders to buy a horse which would pull the steamer or escape carriage when required and which could be used as a police horse at other times.

On 15th July 1912 Councillor Gambert Baines (owner of a local waxworks) offered to provide, free of charge, a motorised fire engine for the town.

Eventually this offer was taken up and an up to date Thornycroft motorised fire engine was purchased from John Morris & Sons, fire engineers of Manchester; the specifications of which included 80 horse power chain driven engine, solid tyres, secondary electric lighting, 50 foot Ajax escape ladder and a 500gpm centrifugal water pump.

RESIGNATION

At the Watch Committee meeting of February 1913, Chief Constable Basham tendered his resignation after 25 years police work. The post of Chief Constable was advertised and a short list was drawn up:

Inspector Blackburn	Tynemouth
Inspector Cromwell	Bradford
Sergeant Major Firth	Kildane
Chief Inspector Hughes	Liverpool
Inspector Ingrams	Southport
Inspector Windsor	Norwich

On 31st March Mr Henry Windsor (38) was appointed to start on the 8th April. However Mr Basham died after a short illness, aged 44, and his funeral was set for the 7th April. He was given a civic funeral and Norwich Constabulary released Mr Windsor a day early so he could head the police cortege. Six police sergeants were the coffin bearers, and after a service at St Mary's Church, a procession was formed to the cemetery on Dean Road where many old colleagues waited to say their last farewells, including Mr H Riches, ex-Chief Constable of Scarborough.

Sadly Mrs Basham died in the same month.

JESSIE

At a dedication ceremony for the new motorised fire engine Councillor Baines' wife christened the machine 'Jessie' (her own name) after which it went on a tour of the town and gave displays at Peasholm Lake and the Grand Hotel.

Chief Constable Windsor made his report on the running of the brigade and amongst the recommendations adopted was that Police sergeant Nalton be promoted, on a temporary basis, to Assistant Fire Engineer.

Councillor Gambert Baines next to 'Jessie'

SANDSIDE SUB-STATION

Other recommendations included the upgrading of Sandside sub-police station (now the location of Princess Restaurant, at the junction of Sandside/East Sandgate) to a sub-fire station. The sub-station to be equipped with a hand pump and other small items of firefighting gear. Another recommendation was that the serge jackets and tunics of the fire brigade were to incorporate a collar badge bearing the Borough crest. Possibly the most controversial of these recommendations was that the contracts of the remaining 'auxiliary' firemen be terminated at the end of the financial year and not renewed.

In 1913 an inspection took place of the fire brigade ladders that had been placed around the town after the Brooks' fire in 1898. All were found to be in poor condition and in need of major overhaul and painting. The ladder placed on the wall in St Johns Road was in such a bad state that it was beyond repair, so it was removed and not replaced.

March 1914 saw the Corporation Water Board request that if their presence was required out of ordinary working hours, the fire brigade should pay the fees of the man concerned. Therefore, the brigade decided to employ Mr Jefferson (a water board employee) as its own turncock. A turncock was the person responsible for the control of the town water mains by turning up the pressure of the water supply to an area when necessary for firefighting purposes, or to turn off one area so that another could receive an increased supply.

It was decided to advertise for an Assistant Engineer who was also a trained motor mechanic, but with the problems brought about by the Great War the idea was left in abeyance. Outbreak of the war caused the old problem of cover for outlying areas to come to the fore again, so the committee offered to attend fires for an annual retainer fee plus the cost incurred of the actual attendance at an incident. Once again this did not please the Rural District Councils who rejected the offer.

THE REMNANT WAREHOUSE

Nos 43, 44 & 45 Queen Street,
Nos 1, 2, 3, 4 & 5 Market Street,
Wesleyan Chapel – Queen Street,
Royal Vaults – Market Street,
Premises No's 15, 18, 19, 20 & 21 Market Street

All the above premises were destroyed in a fire whilst the following premises were damaged in the same fire.

Wesleyan Hall – Queen Street,
Premises No's 3,4,5,6,7,8,9,10,11,12,42,46,47& 48 Queen St,
Premises No's 6,7,8,12,13&14 Market Street,
Stables – Market Street,
Premises No 12 Chapel Lane,

Scarborough's worst fire since the introduction of a fire brigade occurred on 26th February 1915. This was during the First World War, but was not due to any enemy activity unlike the damage of weeks before when Scarborough endured the notorious bombardment by German battleships in the South Bay (16th December 1914).

Jessie and the escape ladder at Newborough/Queen Street Junction

Mr Daniels, a whitesmith of Hoxton Road, was on his way to work in King Street at a few minutes before 7 a.m. when, as he approached the Remnant Warehouse (now known as Boyes Store) on Queen Street, he heard a loud explosion.

He ran to the corner of Market Street with the intention of seeing if he could get into the store by the side entrance. When he reached the corner he could not get any further due to the amount of glass that was flying through the air, so instead, he ran off to the police station on Castle Road and reported the incident to them. The alarm was sounded at the fire station and the motor pump was mobilised straight away, followed shortly after by the steamer and every other appliance the brigade had available.

Jessie with the 'Rem' store blaze behind

When the motor pump arrived at the scene the fire had spread *'with alarming rapidity.'* The building was on fire for the full length and the heat being radiated was such that the driver of the pump stopped outside Queen Street Chapel before he plucked up the nerve to drive past the store. Even then the crew of the engine were scorched with the heat transmitting from the store.

A hydrant at the corner of Queen Street and Newborough was set into the pump. Hose was quickly laid out and within a short time the steam fire engine was set into a hydrant on the corner of

Newborough and St Nicholas Street, there were jets of water being directed at the fire from all quarters. None the less, the fire had such a good hold that the firemen could not restrain the spread.

People living in Market Street and the lower end of Queen Street had to be rapidly evacuated, as the heat was so intense. Residents in Market Street had to leave their houses by the back windows, climbing over walls and through other people's houses to escape, as it was impossible for them to leave through the front entrances because of the extreme heat.

On Queen Street, Mr Jackson was hurriedly getting his wife and four children ready to escape through the back door of their house, which was located opposite the Remnant Store, when the entire front of his shop burst into flames. The family managed to escape in various states of undress but unhurt, though there was much damage to his shop.

Neighbouring shops to Mr Jackson's were also subject to various forms of devastation as heat broke the windows. Water was sprayed on those shops

Damping down, Cryer's Boot shop can be seen on the right

continually by the firemen to stop them suffering the same fate as Mr Jackson's premises.

By 7.30 the fire had reached its height, the conflagration engulfed properties on the other side of Market Street and the

Queen Street Wesleyan Chapel. The Remnant Store was by now totally engulfed from end to end with flames through the roof, reaching high into the sky.

It was not until the holocaust had run its course, with total destruction of the store and Queen Street Chapel, devouring all that was capable of being burnt, that the firefighters were able to start controlling the fire spread to any extent.

Help of special constables, who were many in number due to the fact it was wartime, was enlisted to hold back the crowds of people who came to watch the spectacle. The Yeomanry and men of the RFA who were based temporarily in Scarborough also provided assistance. In addition there were also about 200 men from the Yorkshire Dragoons stationed in the town, who assisted with both the policing and the firefighting efforts. They helped protect the fire ravaged properties from looters, sightseers and any other unauthorised persons, and worked a rota basis until mid-day on the Saturday.

The public are allowed to view the remains, Market Street is on the right

Both the private fire brigades of Messrs Rowntrees and Marshall & Snelgroves were in attendance and gave great assistance. St Johns Ambulance Brigade, who were also there in great numbers, provided treatment to many firemen and others giving help in the firefighting efforts, for scorches, burns and cuts. Other helpers included the Boy Scouts who, along with women from near-by houses, supplied a constant stream of tea for the volunteer and professional workers.

Cryer's Boot shop, at the other corner of Market Street and Queen Street, was totally gutted. It was reported that someone escaped from inside the building by being pulled through the pavement grill in the footpath. Some of the houses in Market Street collapsed, followed by the clock tower of the Remnant Store, which fell to the ground with an almighty crash.

Firefighters, under extremely difficult circumstances, managed to prevent the fire spreading from Market Street into the houses backing onto Newborough and St Helens Square. Luckily there was a good gap between the buildings in Queen Street and the Queen Street Chapel, which made the job of stopping the fire spread in that direction much easier, although there was damage done to the row of houses on Chapel Lane.

Some of the armed forces that lent a hand pose for a photograph in front of the 'Rem'

It was 4.30 p.m. before the pumps on the motor engine and steamer could be turned off, although even then there were still lines of hose laid out direct from the hydrants, playing water into the basement area of the store. Water was used right through the night and well into Saturday. It was mid-day on the Saturday before Chief Constable Windsor thought it was safe to allow people to pass along Queen Street, St Helens Square and the lower parts of

Cross Street again, permitting the Dragoons to return to their
barracks. Crowds came from far and wide on the afternoon just to
walk past and look at the destruction. Remains of the store
amounted to a pile of rubble with twisted girders sticking out of it.
Shops on the opposite side of Queen Street were in various states
of damage and disrepair. Mr Jackson's shop front had been
boarded up and, in true British spirit, which was to the fore during
the Great War, had a placard secured onto it saying *'Keep on keeping
on, for we are not downhearted'*.

According to witnesses of the blast that started the fire, it
appeared to emanate from the basement area, in or near to the boiler room. Gas was made in a suction gas apparatus and as most of the damage seemed to originate from the area where it was installed, it was presumed to be the cause of the fire.

Estimated loss due to the fire was put down as £70,000, but at Chief Constable Windsor's annual report the total amount of fire damage for the year was put down at £53,043, the damage caused at the Remnant Store fire being £52,203.

The Rem Store with the entrance to Queen Street Chapel on the left

At the time of the fire Mr William Boyes, the owner of the Remnant Store, was in London buying stock and was informed of the devastation by his son Mr R Boyes, and returned to Scarborough straight away. On return he held a meeting of his staff to inform them of how they stood, and promised to open temporary premises as soon as it was possible to do so, as his intention was to keep people out of work for the least time possible. Up until the fire, and despite the war, the firm had kept a full staff without having to put anyone on short time, or reduce their wages, which was quite unique and fully appreciated by all his staff.

Sunday service of Queen Street Chapel was held at St Nicholas Hall (the premises that had been the old Town Hall, until recently the site of Lloyds Bank and now waiting renovation.) on St Nicholas Street. There were many letters and telegrams of sympathy read out during the service from other churches and their ministers.

The Wesleyan Chapel's board of trustees had been negotiating a long term use of the Hall whilst the Chapel was being rebuilt, but withdrew their application when they discovered that Mr Boyes was considering leasing the premises as a temporary store. Employment of sixty to seventy people was considered to be more pressing. Thanks to the trustee's withdrawal, Boyes Store opened on the temporary site of St Nicholas Hall on the 11th March 1915. Scarborough Pictorial issued a souvenir edition priced at one penny.

On the Wednesday following the fire a Territorial Army soldier appeared in court charged with stealing jewellery from Mr Jackson's shop whilst the fire was going on. Police had noticed a number of soldiers in the shop, who appeared to be doing salvage work, but when Mr Jackson was allowed to re-enter his premises he discovered an amount of jewellery missing from his living quarters. A description of the missing items was circulated to the local pawnbrokers, and when the territorial soldier tried to pawn the stolen articles, he was detained whilst the police arrived and arrested him. He was bound over for two years for the sum of £25.

A young boy appeared in court, on the 12th March, for stealing a pair of boots from the pavement outside the Cash Boot Company. He said that a group of soldiers were clearing the shop out, after the water damage, when one of the soldiers told him he could take the boots. The magistrates showed no compassion, saying that it was just as much theft taking them from the footpath as if he had gone inside the shop and taken them. They also said his parents should be charged with receiving stolen property, as they had done nothing about it when he took them home; both the boy and his mother were bound over at £5 each.

The job of rebuilding Boyes Store was given to Plaxtons who, despite the war and restrictions on building materials, managed to have the store ready for re-opening on the 19th July 1916. This was less than seventeen months after the catastrophe, a feat that today, despite improved building methods and technology, seems impossible as the drawing up of plans and obtaining the necessary planning consent alone can take that length of time.

Mr W Boyes went on to become the Mayor of Scarborough in 1921 and again in 1924. Sadly, after his last term of office, which he put a lot of work into; he died on 30th December 1925.

QUEEN STREET CHAPEL RE-OPENS
Reconstruction of Queen Street Chapel was not so rapid, as it was not until 1921 that the building contract was awarded to Jerams & Son. Whilst not submitting the lowest tender for the job, Jerams were awarded the contract; because the committee thought it better that the work went to a local firm. The new chapel eventually re-opened in 1923 (the original chapel had been on the site since 1840.)

Two of the firemen who were injured at the fire later made a claim from the Friendly Society, which Scarborough fire brigade had been contributing to since 1903. The society in turn made a claim against the Borough Council. The council's response was to withdraw from the contract with the Friendly Society, feeling that as they were paying an annual premium to the Society, they were not responsible for any payments made by them. Anyone requiring insurance cover after this episode was told to make his own arrangements from then on.

MOTORISED AMBULANCE
There was a suggestion put forward, in August 1915, that the town needed a motorised ambulance and in April the following year Mr Yarbrough Anderson donated one to the town. This caused

some confusion at first as to who would drive it; until they got sufficient policemen trained who were called on to drive on a rota basis.

Mr Jefferson, the turncock, died in September 1916 and was replaced in the following January by Mr Shaw who demanded better payment for his services. His wage was finally set at 2s.6d for the first hour plus more for any further hours at the discretion of the Chief Constable.

Inspection of the street fire alarms was carried out in 1916 followed by a report from the original installers, Shaws, which stated that all the alarms were in poor condition. The one at the bottom of Eastborough was missing as it had been broken off some time earlier. The committee's decision was that the contractors should remove them from the streets altogether.

Police/Firemen, in 1917, felt that they were not being adequately recompensed for their duties and asked for a pay rise, the Corporation offered them 5 shillings for each fire attended, to be reduced to 1s.6d if it was a false alarm.

Methods of getting the steam fire engine to fires were reviewed in 1919 as it was felt that whilst the engine was not often required the trouble of obtaining the horses for it was not worthwhile. It was suggested that the steamer be adapted to hitch up to the corporation's motor tractor rather than to the horses. Different means of adaption were studied over a year, and in November the Borough Engineer was given the task to complete.

MR CLARKE

At the end of 1919 it was decided to re-advertise for an assistant Engineer, the position having been advertised before the war and then left in abeyance. Committee members travelled the country to interview the applicants, leading to Mr Albert Edward Clarke, Superintendent of the Chester fire brigade, being appointed. He moved to Scarborough in January 1920 and was employed as a police constable seconded to the fire brigade with a weekly wage of £4.10s. At the time of his appointment a new Pompier escape ladder was purchased from Morris of Manchester.

In June there was a Home Office recommendation of a minimum wage for professional firemen, which the Corporation ignored, and the firemen later lobbied the committee for the recommended increase, but to no avail.

In July 1920 a long running disagreement between Fire Engineer Birkbeck and the committee came to a head and he was asked to resign, which he duly did, receiving one month's pay with a rateable reduction. As the decision was sudden, he was unable to find alternative accommodation immediately, so Chief Constable Windsor recommended that his month's wages be retained for the

Mr Clarke

inconvenience. In September, Mr Birkbeck wrote to the committee asking them to reconsider their actions on the withholding of his wages – the outcome was that he lost his wages but was paid £50 of the rateable reduction.

Mr Clarke was immediately promoted to Sergeant and Fire Engineer, with a new salary of £5 per week.

FIRE BRIGADE STRIKE

Pay was the cause of a dispute between the Filey fire brigade and the council as they were given a pay increase to 3 shillings an hour, but their 10 shilling minimum call out fee was discontinued. The disagreement went on until, on 1st November 1921 lead by Captain Wright, they went on strike refusing to respond to any calls. The council tried to ignore this, but eventually gave in and, on 7th November, an agreement was reached where the men would receive a minimum fee of 7s 6d, the same as for a drill period.

QUAY STREET

The final quarter of 1921 saw a large loss of life due to fires. This was no reflection on the firemen who, in every incident, did their utmost.

On 12th August, at just after midnight, Mr Cook, the proprietor, discovered a fire at 2 Quay Street, a boarding house. He tried to get upstairs to raise the occupants but was barred by the heat and smoke, so he shouted to them to keep the doors closed and try to escape through the windows. He then went to the front room, which was his bedroom, and moved his wife and baby to safety.

The police/fire sub-station on Sandside was

No 2 Quay Street – the bay window that was used for the rescue from the second floor can be clearly seen

informed and from there the central fire station was alerted and proceeded to the incident.

Mr T Flynn, a fisherman, made attempts to get upstairs to help, but was beaten back by the flames; he tried again helped by another fisherman, Mr C Harwood. The two assisted two guests, Mr and Mrs Greenwood, from their first floor bedroom, which they entered through the window. Whilst in there they heard someone move across the floor upstairs and open the window so they climbed outside onto the bay window top and grabbed the feet of a struggling guest, Mr Highley, as he lowered himself from his window. They eventually lowered him to the ground floor where he was attended to by other helpers. The two fishermen re-entered the house but were unable to go any further up the stairs.

As the brigade arrived, the appliances from the sub-station were being put into use, and it was discovered that there were two people still inside the building on the upper floors. The narrowness of the passageway meant it was impossible to get the wheeled fire escape in.

Attempts were made to gain access through the inside of the building by the firemen; eventually Fire Engineer Clarke and Police Constable Allen climbed the stairs whilst jets of water were directed over them. Fire Engineer Clarke first located a body in a bed on the top floor, and Police Constable Allan carried it downstairs, once outside he realised it was a young man.

Police Constable Allan quickly re-entered the building, as he knew Fire Engineer Clarke was near to collapse due to the smoke. Going back upstairs he found a door, which would not easily open, on forcing this he discovered a girl's body behind the door. The two men brought that body outside and artificial respiration was applied until a doctor arrived, who pronounced both the casualties dead. They were Ivy (aged 17) and Leslie (aged 20) Greenwood, brother and sister, on holiday with their parents from Halifax.

There had been twelve people in the house and the cause of the fire was thought to be a dropped candle in the linen cupboard on the staircase. The speed the fire spread and the intensity of the heat was due to the house having been modernised by having all the internal walls covered with matchboard.

Fire Engineer Clarke paid great tribute to the civilian helpers efforts, both before and after the arrival of the brigade. The inquest coroner who paid special tribute to Fire Engineer Clarke and Police Constable Allan reiterated this.

WEST BANK

The following October 21st saw a house fire at West Bank, at just after 6 a.m. the brigade was told that an old lady was still inside the building.

The wheeled escape ladder from Falsgrave sub-station arrived moments before the motor engine; entries were made through the front door and a first floor window. A thorough search was made of the first floor, where they assumed anyone would be so early in the morning, which took some time due to the smoke and many obstacles.

Nothing was found and the search continued downstairs, where the living room door was forced open and the body of Miss Dale was discovered, too late for any resuscitation.

When the smoke cleared it became evident that the obstacles encountered were large amounts of furniture. Miss Dale (73) owned both this house and the house next door, which she had recently sold. She had stored furniture from the sold house in her own, overfilling most rooms, causing her to sleep on a camp bed in front of the fire in her living room where ashes had fallen onto the floor and bedding causing the blaze.

HUNTER'S BALCONY

Before the year was out another fatality occurred, just around the corner from the fire station, at 4 Hunter's Balcony, James Street.

The call came on 9th December at 10.45 p.m. The victim was Mrs Hogg (50) who had already been brought out by the time the brigade arrived; efforts were split between applying first aid to her and fighting the fire. Mrs Hogg was taken to hospital by motor ambulance, but died on Sunday 18th December. She had been ironing clothes near a gas ring connected by a tube to a point near the mantelpiece. Somehow the bottom of her flannelette gown had caught fire and set alight. She had gone to a cupboard where the sink was to throw water over herself when her husband, who had been asleep upstairs, entered the room to see his wife engulfed in flames. He tried to get her outside but she was holding onto the sink, so he went for help. A passer by, Mr Wallace went to her aid but he could not release her grip, though he tried until exhausted. Mr Harvey, from 1 George Street, heard the commotion and went to help, managing to bring Mrs Hogg outside.

The fact that she had been in a cupboard started the rumourmongers of the district talking, stories were rife about how Mr Hogg kept his wife locked in and bullied her. These stories were repeated until the official inquest when the truth emerged.

After this busy period of fatalities there was not another death caused by fire in the town until a little girl was killed in Eastborough in 1934.

A NEW MORRIS BELSIZE

A second motorised fire engine was purchased in June 1922 from Morris & Sons Ltd at a cost of £2040. The money having been borrowed from the Ministry of Health; it was a Morris Belsize with a 55hp engine, with a 500-600 gallon turbine, four cylinders with a 53-4" by 7" stroke and in looks was a replica of "Jessie".

Mr Clarke and an engineer from Morris, Mr Galloway, brought it to Scarborough via Huddersfield, Leeds and York where demonstrations were performed in each of the towns. Demonstrations for Scarborough people to watch were organised on 20th June at the fishpond in the Valley (the duck pond below the Valley Bridge) and on St Nicholas Cliff where six jets of water were directed at the Grand Hotel.

'Jessie 2' attending drills on the St Nicholas Cliff

GABRIEL WADE & ENGLISH

There was a fire at Brook Street on 25th July 1922 involving the sawmill owned by Richard Wade, which incorporated Gabriel Wade & English (now Jewsons). It had just gone 2.30 a.m. when Mr Watson Retty, the firm's caretaker and horses man, who lived over the firms offices at 26A Brook Street, was awakened by the incessant barking of his dog. On looking out of the window he could see flames and smoke emitting from the basement of the sawmill, a two storey building which ran along the back of the houses on Trafalgar Street West.

By the time the fire brigade arrived it was obvious that the building could not be saved. Two jets of water were put on the timber store across the yard whilst another jet was set up at the corner of Brook Street and Trafalgar Street West to protect that property. It took the firemen forty-five minutes to control the blaze and confine it to the main sawmill property and by 5.30a.m. it was well under control.

At the height of the fire there were many eyewitnesses consisting mainly of worried residents from Brook Street, Trafalgar Street West and Cambridge Street. Chief Constable Windsor attended the fire and supervised the firefighting from an early stage. Firefighting operations were greatly assisted by the fact that there was very little wind at the time.

It was found on entering the building that a large amount of slaters' lathes stored on the second floor had absorbed so much water that their combined weight had caused the floor to sag in the middle to drastic proportions.

Machinery suffered the most costly damage, mainly planes, circular saws, moulding machinery and a deal frame. It was under a planer or moulding machine the fire was thought to have started. Mr Petty said he had checked the area at 8.30 the previous evening, as usual, but found nothing out of place at that time.

SUB-STATION CLOSURE

A review of the police policies and finances in 1924 saw the police station on Sandside close down and along with it the sub-fire station. In January 1925 the Watch Committee came to the decision that a new quick system for reporting incidents to the fire station was needed. It was suggested that telephone boxes, with plates stating that ambulance, police and fire calls were free, should be fitted around the town, by the General Post Office, to give cover similar to that provided by the street fire alarms before the war.

After discussions with the General Post Office, who at that time ran the national telephone system, it was arranged that a further nine (to the four already in existence) boxes should be fitted around the wards. The council paid £15 for each box, in return for which they received all monies taken on local calls and 50 per cent of that taken for trunk calls.

In 1925 the motor ambulance needed to have a new chassis fitted. When the estimate for the work was found to be almost the cost of a new ambulance the Corporation decided to look for a donor to replace the old machine rather than repair it.

MARKET HALL

The Market Hall was involved in one of the most difficult fires that the fire brigade had to tackle. The caretaker, Mr Appleby, left the building at just after 7.30 p.m. 22nd January 1925, and all seemed to be normal. At about 9.30 that evening a fire was seen burning in the hall. It was already well alight by the time it was discovered, which set the fire brigade a difficult task when they arrived as flames were issuing from the windows along the north wall and from the roof.

A few people had reported the fire at the same time; amongst these were Councillor Jackson and a bus conductor, Mr Grimshaw, who saw the flames from a bus as it pulled into the bus stop in St Helens Square. He ran into 'The Dug Out' fish and chip shop, Market Side, to ring the fire brigade. The first call was received at the police station at 9.26 p.m. by Police Constable Grant who turned out the new motor engine and a full crew within minutes.

A line of hose was set in from a hydrant on Market Street whilst firemen forced an entry through the panels of the large doors, not an easy task because of the size and strength of them. When they eventually got through, the line of hose was split and one jet was aimed at the seat of the fire through the doors, whilst the other was used on the north wall through the windows. In those days there were houses built up to the Market wall along the north side (now Market Way) making access difficult.

News of the fire spread around the town and large crowds came to watch, making the job of the firefighters harder as the onlookers were in the way. Many spectators tried to get closer to the building to see inside and there were people who even risked their lives by entering the hall, wasting valuable firefighting time as they were evicted from the building. Most of the curiosity was because people could not believe that the building could have burnt so easily. At that time the roof was the biggest single span roof in the town and the height of it, whilst resting on solid brick walls, seemed to present a reasonably fire resistant structure.

All the firemen at the fire were made up from the Police force; this fact meant that there was little chance of crowd control being carried out. For this reason Fire Engineer Clarke sent a request to the 5th Armoured Car Company, who were based in the town for a short period, to help organise the crowds.

There was an immense build up of heat, which the firefighters had to contend with, and nearly every stall on the north side of the building was alight sending flames high into the roofing. At first sight the worst of the fire seemed to be coming from the toffee stall, which was located on the left immediately through the doors. The fire was like a blowtorch sending a jet of flame straight at the rafters and the wooden ventilation shafts running along the roof, which in turn fed the fire up to the very top pitch of the roof.

Early difficulties included getting sufficient pressure on the water to reach the rooftop. It was not until they set in another line of hose from the hydrant, on Queen Street – Newborough junction, to the motor fire engine, which boosted the pressure, that they could make progress in extinguishing the flames on the rooftop.

Jessie, the other pump, was sent for, then two escape ladders were set up to supply further jets to the roof, supplementing the jets hastily set up by men balanced on make-shift ramps and ladders, constructed out of fruit boxes and anything else readily to hand.

Amongst the main priorities was the protection of the nearby buildings. These included a tallow works outside the northwest corner of the hall, which was in danger because the wind was fanning the flames towards it and a bakery further towards Dumple Street (roughly in line with where Friars Way is now).

Potentially the most dangerous area of all was the Bonded Store, run by His Majesty's Customs and Excise, underneath the Market Hall (now known as the Market Vaults). This store was full of spirits and without the aid of the thick, well-constructed floor to the hall could have caught alight with devastating results.

People who lived in the vicinity of the hall were advised to move their curtaining from that side of their building nearest the hall as there was a danger of it bursting into flames from the convected heat.

Internally the greatest danger was glass, which was continually raining down from the large skylights running the length of both sides of the roof. New hose had to be continuously run out as falling glass pierced the hose on the hall floor. There was more than one case of the helmets saving the firemen from serious injury and Fire Engineer Clarke had to be taken to hospital with serious cuts to his hands.

It took the fire brigade until 11.30 p.m. to get the blaze under control and firemen stayed at the incident all night dousing the occasional outbreak of flames. Damage was mainly confined to the roof, and inside to the north and west end of the building, whilst the south side and the balcony at the east end escaped fire damage, but not water damage, as vast amounts of water were used.

NEW AMBULANCE

Old questions about housing the firemen close to the station were again causing concern and when the council suggested an improvement scheme for the area and road widening on North Marine Road, the committee made a request that the housing of the firemen should be taken into account when redeveloping.

As the workload of the original motor ambulance had caused it to need renewing and with no sponsors stepping forward it was decide to purchase a new Daimler Motor Ambulance, from Messrs Wilson & Stockdale. It was duly delivered and inspected by the committee on 30th March 1926.

Fire Engineer Clarke's workload was also increasing so it was decided to employ a full-time Assistant Fire Engineer. Police Constable Baker of the Nottingham Police Force took up the appointment. At the same time electric lighting was installed in the living quarters over the station.

The ambulance station just before its demolition in 1987

ATHLETIC GROUND

Whilst not one of the biggest fires to occur in Scarborough, one that was talked about for many years was the destruction of the Scarborough Football Club grandstand. This had a dramatic impact on the club as most of the assets and a lot of the club's recorded history went up in flames with the grandstand in a very short time.

At 5 p.m. Sunday 27th May 1927 a Mr Jubb, of Hinderwell Road, saw smoke issuing from the middle of the main stand. He ran over to investigate and on opening a door at the rear of the stand he found a fire blazing inside so he ran to the telephone box at the main entrance and alerted the fire brigade. By the time he returned to the ground the whole of the stand was ablaze from end to end, helped by the fact that the stand was mainly constructed of timber soaked with creosote, and there was a brisk wind blowing.

On arrival of the fire brigade the building was already almost totally destroyed with the girders twisted out of shape and the corrugated metal roof crumpled in the middle from the intense heat. This heat made it difficult for anyone to get anywhere near the stand. The first task was to set up a water supply, which had to be connected into a hydrant in Hinderwell Road and then about a quarter of a mile of hose was run out from it. Initially two jets of water were set up which, due to the poor water mains pressure and the intensity of the fire, had little if no effect on the fire.

Amongst the hazards encountered by the firemen were jets of steam gushing out of pipes as water boiled in the heating boiler tank from the heat of the fire. There was a constant barrage of falling metal from girders and the corrugated roof, and glass from windows that kept shattering from the heat. There were, for a period of time, loud explosions, which baffled the firefighters until it was discovered that these were caused by bottles of carbonated water exploding.

Hose was eventually moved to the rear of the stand but such was the power of the fire that within thirty minutes of the fire brigade arriving the fire burnt itself out as there was no more material left to burn.

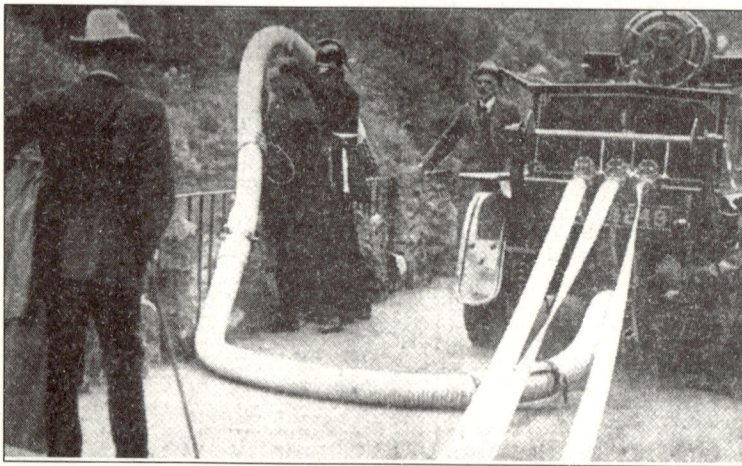

'Jessie 2' drilling at Valley Road 'fish pond'

Strong beliefs that the fire originated in the boiler house were dismissed by the fact that it was totally brick lined. The matter was put into the hands of the police, who surmised that children playing with matches started it.

Only having been built in 1922, the stand had cost a considerable amount of money along with other improvements to the ground. About half the playing turf was burnt by the fire as well as the stand, which contained the dressing rooms and offices as well as seating. In these rooms most of the clubs belongings were stored plus cricket gear belonging to the YMCA and Gas Board Cricket Club.

DUNOLLIE

At Dunollie on Filey Road, the north wing was being repainted externally on 23rd June 1927 when a painter, who had been burning off old paint along a guttering, noticed molten lead dripping onto his overalls. It was 10 a.m. when he realised that in his burning off the blow lamp had ignited an old bird's nest in the eaves, which in turn had set fire to the wooden joists in the loft area.

When the call was received at the fire station the new No 2 pump was dispatched. On arrival it was immediately set into the many hydrants in the area (this was next door to Willersley House, which in 1896 suffered badly due to the lack of water). Firemen then entered the roof void, which by this time was burning rapidly, fed by the plentiful supply of timber and bitumen felt which lined the roof. Heat was tremendous and the fire was spreading across the roof and entering other parts of the building. Ladders were used outside to set up two more water jets on the roof.

A large crowd had gathered on Filey Road and some of these helped direct the traffic off Filey Road and down Holbeck Road as the hose was by now blocking the road. At 11 o'clock a section of roof fell in, exposing the roaring flames inside, it seemed that once the air got to the fire it would spread through the rest of the roof area. More jets were brought to play through this open area, and when the flames were quelled, the crowd could see the heads of the firemen working inside the building.

The firemen took many risks as they manoeuvred themselves along the roof. At one point Assistant Fire Engineer Baker was seen to shin along a ridge that was only supported by the lead work, as he went further along he suddenly slid down the roof, causing a loud gasp to emerge from the crowd below. It was not until he stopped suddenly, they could see a rope tied around him and realised it was a deliberate act to gain him a better position from which to fight the fire.

A maid, who had re-entered the building to rescue her belongings, found herself in imminent danger when the fire cut off her escape route. She dropped a box of belongings down from a window and then had to be rescued by Chief Inspector Abbot, using a painter's ladder that hardly reached the window. As she stepped of the ladder she appeared very calm and unconcerned by her close brush with death; apparently unaware of the danger she had put herself and others in.

Firemen continued their battle using many jets and eventually brought it under control. Structural damage was confined to the roof space of the domestic wing but much damage was also caused throughout the building by the copious amounts of water used to extinguish the flames. The Scarborough Mercury bestowed much praise on the firemen for the risks they had taken, stating it was only the effort put in by them which had prevented the fire from taking the whole building.

Dunollie had already a gruesome reputation caused by the deaths of a maid and postman during the bombardment of Scarborough in the Great War. Today it has been converted to a private nursing home with a respectable reputation.

AMBULANCE STATION

The redevelopment of North Marine Road was to include shops from Castle Road corner up to the fire station property. It was requested that finance should be provided to build firemen's houses over the top of these shops. By December 1928 tenders amounting to £4,736 were accepted from Plaxtons and Messrs Smith & Biachi Ltd, for the building of these houses. These were to be built on the site occupied by the Merchant Seamen's Hospital, which had been there since 1752.

Chief Constable Windsor tendered his resignation after 31 years police service, the final sixteen as Scarborough's Chief Constable (he died on 27th January 1942). His position was filled on 1st April 1929 by Mr Walter Abbot (48) who had transferred to Scarborough Police Force in June 1919 as a Detective Inspector from the Sheffield Police.

DENNIS ENGINE

There was a new engine purchased which arrived in Scarborough on the evening of 9th June 1929. It was a 40-50hp Dennis, from Morris of Selford. It was capable of pumping 400 – 500 gallons of water per minute and carried a water supply of 40 gallons. It also carried four foam extinguishers giving a capacity of 64 gallons of foam. One thousand six hundred feet of hose could also be carried plus the escape ladder, which was already in service.

The cost of the new engine was £1070 and to help defray it 'Jessie' was sold to the manufacturers in part exchange. Also to defray the cost the steamer was sold for £25 to the Borough Engineer.

As there was a growing number of police, ambulance and weights & measures department vehicles being acquired e.g. utility vans and motor bikes, there were plans drawn up for a garage and a petrol tank was sunk into the station drill yard to supply them. Fire prevention work was carried out on the station, as the engine house ceiling and doors were lined with asbestos sheeting and the doors were made self-closing as an added precaution. Whilst all these alterations were under way the ambulance was altered to take a stretcher.

The Dennis fire engine seen drilling close to Scalby Mills Bridge

SUB-STATION CLOSURES

There were changes in the police and firemen's pension schemes at this time, which caused Mr Clarke to resign from the police force; he was then appointed as a civilian fire engineer. Permission was granted to employ a further fireman at the station on the same rate of pay as a police constable.

The Watch Committee studied a police box system; this was a number of contact points around the town linked direct to the police station. One asset of this system was that policemen could report for duty at the box on their beat instead of reporting direct to the police station and then marching (en masse as a squad) to their beats. The boxes made the sub-police stations obsolete and it was decided that money made from the sale of South Cliff and Falsgrave stations could supply eleven police boxes, plus help to finance the erection of the garage at the fire station to house the ambulance and police utility van.

Eleven police boxes were ordered at a cost of £1,259 12s 3d using a 'Carter-Micro' telephone system. They were erected and fixed by Jaram & Sons, and a tender of £695 was accepted from them in May 1930 for the building of a garage for the ambulance (the site is now the part of the fire station immediately adjoining the Mind Shop.)

MODERNISATION

On the recommendation of Fire Engineer Clarke a foam generator was purchased for use on petrol fires. He also recommended that a Salvus breathing apparatus (BA) set be purchased from Siebie Gorman, at the cost of £15 4s. (£15.20p)

Assistant Fire Engineer Baker resigned his post to transfer to Messrs J Players & Sons Ltd, Nottingham, on the 5th April 1932. There were three people short listed and interviewed to replace him, they were:

John George Jessop	of Rotherham
Cyril George Saxton	of Cambridge
Edward Taylor	of Glossop

Mr Saxton was selected.

There was a charge set at 1s 6d per mile for the use of the ambulance outside the borough boundary, in response to the requests from the suburbs.

An estimate of £10 15s from Plaxtons was accepted to enclose the ambulance driver's cab. The police also ordered an 8 horse power, Brough Superior motorcycle and sidecar costing £75 on 8th September 1932.

The National School next door to the police station, on Castle Road – Granby Place junction sought confirmation that with all the alterations the children would still be able to use the fire station yard as the school playground.

A W Sinclairs, builders, were building a new house for the council on Sandybed Lane, to house Chief Constable Windsor. At the same time, 1933, the new police dwellings, over the new shops in North Marine Road, were put into use. These new houses all had call-out facilities run off the town electrical current. There was also a large gong in the drill yard in case of electricity failure.

Continuation to the building programme saw Plaxtons awarded a contract to build more police dwellings and a weights and measures office incorporating an electricity board sub-station, on Castle Road (now the location of the fire brigades advice and education department) on the 14th November 1933, at a cost of £3,338.

FIRST USE OF BREATHING APPARATUS

On 16th February 1934 at 8 a.m. a fire was reported in Castle Road at the painting and decorating premises of Messrs J Knowles (now The Paint People). Fire started in the second floor store room where there was a large quantity of wallpaper being stored as a sale was in progress. The first machine was sent, and the attendance of the second was requested. The escape ladder was placed at the front windows, but due to the density of the smoke the firemen were unable to find the seat of the fire, so self-contained breathing apparatus sets were used. Whilst no rescues were performed, this appears to be the first recorded use of a breathing apparatus set at an incident, in Scarborough.

There was a demonstration at the fire station by St John's Ambulance, police and fire brigade, on 16th March 1934, using a Novox resuscitation set and the Lowmoor Jacket (a stretcher for lifting people in a vertical position). St John's Ambulance then presented the Lowmoor to Scarborough fire brigade on permanent loan.

LEYLAND FIRE ENGINE

On 11th June a new fire engine arrived in town at a little after 8 p.m. it was received from Messrs Leyland Motors Ltd, of Chorley, and was delivered by Mr Woodcock. Leyland's demonstrator. It was a 6 cylinder 'FK1' with a 27.3 horse power engine, capable of pumping 400 – 600gpm, at a cost of £1,128 7s 10d. It had two rows of seats, one behind the other allowing protection from the weather. Also included were a hose reel and a 40 gallon water tank. Features were pneumatic tyres and a searchlight, which had a 100 foot cable enabling it to be taken into buildings or down passages.

An advanced attribute for the time was a Caldwell heater and charger, a patent device for starting up the engine from the watch room so that by the time the crew was ready to mount the machine it was already running. This type of device was to cause many problems throughout the country as machines were often parked in gear, sending them smashing into appliance room door when they started up.

There was at least one incident, at Scarborough, caused by this device, it occurred during the war, when a call was received and the crew set off as usual. On arrival at the incident it was found that the wire and plug from the charger, which were plugged into the rear of the machine and were supposed to pull clear on drawing out of the station, had not for some reason. Instead it pulled up part of the wood block flooring of the engine house and proceeded to drag it along behind, all the way to the incident.

The Leyland fire engine outside the Chorley works

The old No 2, Morris Belsize fire engine was sold to Filey fire brigade for £60, to help recover some of the costs. This was Filey's first motorised engine as they had managed until that time with their old hand pump. It was a number of weeks before Filey brigade drilled with the machine, and when they tried to connect the engines hose to the Filey hydrants it was discovered that they had different connections. If there had been a fire in the meantime they would have been unable to obtain water.

On seeing the advantages of pneumatic tyres on the new machine it was decided to convert the Dennis pump to them also; it cost £70 from County Garages, St Thomas Street.

RACECOURSE GRANDSTAND

On Sunday 24th February 1935, the racecourse caretaker found the grandstand to be burning, only the day before he had chased children away. Firemen, as they turned onto Stepney Road, could see the fire blazing on the hilltop and knew they were in for a long stay.

Obtaining water was the first task on arrival, which due to the location was not an easy task. First supplies came from a water tank, supplying the defunct grandstand's domestic and commercial supply. To gain access to this supply the corrugated roof had to be removed exposing the contents.

Whilst this supply was being used a search of the area produced, a quarter of a mile away, a pond frozen over with three-quarters of an inch of ice. When the initial supply was exhausted, the not too easy task of getting the pump to the new supply was carried out, and the extra hose run out to the fire.

The Grandstand blaze

Chief Constable Abbot attended the blaze and his main concern was that the firemen took no risks in their firefighting, as there was no life risk involved.

In the afternoon a relay of men was set up, both to give cover to Scarborough in case of any other outbreaks of fire and also to obtain dry clothing. This relay was made more necessary by the fact that the fire had burned down the telephone lines to the town and this was their only means of communication with the firemen.

Fire Engineer Clarke said, after the fire, that the conditions were the worst the brigade had dealt with since the Hackness Hall blaze, (referring to the poor water supplies). He also said had the fire occurred just a short time before the fire brigade could not have dealt with it, as the racecourse had only just been brought into the borough boundary and their jurisdiction.

The grandstand had not been in use for racing since 1893 when the last race had been run (the first was run in 1789), but it was used regularly as a camp for the army who also used it to store rations and equipment in the basement. It has never been used since and there is now very little evidence of its existence, apart from the name of Racecourse Road, that it ever did.

ARTHUR ROBINSON

At this time it was decided to employ an additional wholetime fireman. Arthur Robinson who had been employed as the police motor mechanic was transferred to the fire brigade in December 1936.

SINCLAIR'S

At 6-30 p.m. 14th December 1936 Mr Armstrong, of Commercial Street, noticed a fire at a downstairs window of Sinclair Builders, on Commercial Street (now the premises of 3P Design) and went to get assistance from a Sinclair's worker, who lived on Wykeham Street. When the fire brigade arrived, at 6.45, the flames had spread into a builder's yard and his house, which backed onto the premises from St Johns Road and also that of the adjoining house of Mr C Nendick, 59 St Johns Road.

Fire Engineer Clarke, in charge of the first pump, found the building well alight on arrival and spreading fast, so he arranged for the No 2 pump to be sent immediately. Due to the building having been constructed from timber Fire Engineer Clarke decided it was too dangerous to enter the building and concentrated on stopping the fire from spreading.

Even when the roof eventually collapsed the flames were not easily extinguished as the corrugated sheeting covered the burning timbers preventing the water penetrating to the fire.

Large amounts of timber stored made the smoke very dense which in turn made the firemen's task excessively hazardous as breathing became difficult and visibility was reduced to zero. Just how fast the fire spread can be judged by the fact that only 45 minutes before the fire was discovered there had been people working in the premises and there was no sign of fire then.

At the height of the blaze flames were seen to be bellowing up 70 feet into the air, and there was concern caused by the fact that there was an underground petrol tank in Sinclair's yard. Firefighters poured water onto the tank throughout the incident to prevent the risk of explosion.

A lady pushing a pram was so engrossed in watching the firemen that she pushed it into one of the standpipes connected into a hydrant and broke the connection. As a result one poor fireman had to spend his time sat on the standpipe to keep it in place, not only did he get drenched and cold but he missed out on the excitement of the fire for the rest of the evening.

There was some concern for Park Laundry, the neighbouring site on Commercial Street, but covering jets played many gallons of water onto it and prevented the fire spreading to it. So successful was the protection of the laundry that it became possible to use its roof to set up jets on, from which to fight the fire in the yard. There were eight jets in all used. Chief Constable Abbott visited the fire and took over control.

Sinclair's stated that they were fortunate in that timber for their larger contracts had been removed that day, otherwise the loss would have been much greater. Chief Constable Abbott thanked the many residents and onlookers that supplied help. So much of an attraction was the fire that people arrived from as far away as Filey to observe it.

AUXILIARY FIRE SERVICE

In 1935 the government set up a working party, which sat in 1936, to discuss the fire brigades of Britain. This party was known as the Riverdale Committee, as it was lead by Lord Riverdale.

With the ever growing threats of aggression made by Germany it seemed almost inevitable that Britain was going to be involved in a war. Knowing the destruction that incendiary bombs had created in the Spanish Civil War and the capabilities that Germany had there was much thought given to home defence.

In February 1937 an act was passed in Parliament (the Air Raid Precautions Act, 1937) which amongst other things, required the local authorities to initiate, from 1st January 1938, improvements to their firefighting facilities. Up to 75 per cent of the cost of the improvements was to be funded from a central government grant. This grant also helped cover the cost of setting up, recruiting and training a volunteer fire force, to be known as the Auxiliary Fire Service (AFS) which was to supplement the services provided by the regular fire brigades.

The report from the Riverdale enquiry laid the foundation for the 1938 Fire Brigade Act, which made

Some of the early AFS recruits

many recommendations for the improvements of fire brigades. The insurance companies would no longer be billed for reimbursement of fire brigade expenses and authorities would be expected to assist each other. In the report firemens' clothing was reviewed and the first improvement that the men saw was the replacement of their leggings with a mackintosh material, helping to keep their legs drier.

Growing responsibilities of the ambulance section was becoming obvious as the Chief Constable asked for the St Johns Ambulance Brigade to provide an attendant on evenings to assist and instruct the police.

On March 19th 1938 the first six Auxiliary Fire Service firemen were enrolled, consisting of a bricklayer, a shop manager, a journalist, a fruiterer, a joiner and an engineer. By June there were 50 Auxiliary Fire Service members enrolled and Scarborough had been allocated two trailer pumps by the Home Office. In the meantime however, with both the developments in firefighting technology and the changing political climate due to the threat of war approaching, more and more responsibilities were being placed on fire authorities.

Standards of Scarborough fire brigade were high, but one of the main points in the Riverdale report was the reduction of police firefighting capabilities, with the Riverdale report stating:

> *"We have to remember that if a man is doing Police duty and fire duty, Either the police duty or the fire duty suffers."*

The Act required local authorities to make arrangements for establishing brigades independent of the police. Scarborough was by no means the only brigade run by the police, as there were in fact 63 police fire brigades, amongst which were many of the larger cities such as Manchester, Liverpool and closer to home, Leeds and Hull.

In response the Watch Committee later employed Auxiliary Fire Service members on a whole-time basis under the direction of Mr Clarke, the engineer and Mr Saxton, Assistant Engineer, but still responsible to the Chief Constable.

FALSGRAVE LAUNDRY

On the morning of 1st August 1938, people living in the Falsgrave area of town were woken by loud cracks that sounded like rifle fire. The noise occurred after a fire was discovered by Mr G Smith, boiler man, at Falsgrave Laundry, which was situated at the top end of Sitwell Street (now the turning area in the road). Mr Smith reported for work at his usual time of 5.30a.m. to make the premises ready for the rest of the staff who started work at 7 o'clock. When he opened the boiler house door he found the whole area ablaze, so he ran to the police box at the junction of Sitwell Street and Falsgrave Road, and informed Police Constable Collins, the duty policeman, who used the police telephone to alert the fire brigade.

As the engine raced up Victoria Road the firemen could hear the explosions coming from the laundry. On their arrival they immediately informed the

A group of AFS recruits waiting to undergo gas mask training at Plaxtons Coach Works – Seamer Road

station that the other machine was required. It was apparent that there was no chance of saving the building, therefore the main objective became the protection of the surrounding properties. The closest of these was Tyndale House and a garage, (now the Sitwell Enterprise Centre) which had just been taken over by the General Post Office for vehicle storage.

There was difficulty in getting water to the fire as the nearest hydrants were on St Johns Road and Falsgrave Road requiring a lot of hose, much of it being brought over the high walls that divided St Johns Road and Sitwell Street.

Fireman Dorsey was unfortunate enough to have burning embers fall into the top of his boots causing blisters on his feet and giving him a lot of pain. Afterwards Snowdrift Laundry on Scalby Road helped out by taking on the work of the Falsgrave Laundry.

THE GROWING AUXILIARY FIRE SERVICE
Locally, the Auxiliary Fire Service was still a little known section of the Air Raid Precautions so it was necessary to inform people of its

existence, in the hope that they would enlist. On 7th October 1938 there was a recruitment room set up in Huntriss Row, at Huntriss Hall (now the site of Laughtons night club). A display of equipment on show there included:

A Home Office hand pump (stirrup pump) at 22s-6d guaranteed to deal with any incendiary bombs and fires caused by molten metal from bombs.
A Home Office trailer pump.
The remains of an incendiary bomb that had been dealt with in a display by Scarborough firemen using knock out jets.
Two dummies, one dressed in full protection clothing with a general service respirator and the other in Auxiliary Fire Service training uniform.

Auxiliary Fire Service members were required to attend thirty, two hour, training sessions, plus an extra session for anti-gas instruction. The training was carried out on the trailer pumps at Scalby Mills Beck, on the seaward side of the road bridge and also at the Open Air Theatre off Burniston Road.

It was recommended that Scarborough Auxiliary Fire Service needed a minimum of 150 members, with 200 being the desired number. The campaign was a success with 130 men enlisted, including 35 who had enrolled and completed their training prior to the recruitment drive.

An incendiary bomb demonstration in the fire station yard

Overall responsibility for Air Raid Precautions fell on the County Council with Chief Constable Abbott being appointed as the co-ordinator for Scarborough.

In October 1938 Mr Abbott felt that the North Riding Council was doing Scarborough a dis-service with the amount of Air Raid Precautions cover it was getting, and as an objection to this, he publicly resigned his Air Raid Precautions post. He suggested that for administration purposes Scarborough should be classed as a County Borough, giving it powers to organise its own Air Raid Precautions. The idea and his resignation were rejected leaving the Chief Constable with a difficult administration problem.

AUXILIARY FIRE SERVICE ON STATION
E Hunters, builders, were entrusted with a £67 19s 6d contract to upgrade the fire station to accommodate the Auxiliary Fire Service. There was a further £50 set aside for furnishings. Lockers were installed in the station yard for the Auxiliary Fire Service clothing and equipment and the living quarters over the station were converted into training, reading and recreation rooms. Mr Nightingale, the mechanic, had to vacate the house over the station to allow for this and received 15 shillings a week rent allowance. Also the station yard was adapted, along with an area in the Corporation Yard, Dean Road, to take a fleet of trailer pumps supplied by the Home Office.

A delivery of trailer pumps supplied by the Home Office

A further whole-time fireman was employed in March 1939 to undertake Mr Robinson's duties as his time was totally taken in training and maintaining the Auxiliary Fire Service section. In the same month 19,000 sandbags were allocated to Scarborough for the use of protecting police buildings in the event of war. Whitby Urban District Council made a request, in April, for a Scarborough fire officer to instruct the Whitby fire brigade and Auxiliary Fire Service, which received a negative response from the Council. There soon followed a letter from the Home Office reminding them of the obligations owed to other authorities under the 1938 Act. By May, it had been decided to take six of the Auxiliary Fire Service firemen into the Scarborough fire brigade as retained firemen.

PROFESSIONAL FIRE BRIGADES ASSOCIATION

In 1939 the annual conference of the Professional Fire Brigades Association was held at the Spa. Members of Watch Committees attended it, along with Chief Constables, superintendents and many others with fire brigade connections. As part of the event, the

AFS firemen running out hose

Scarborough brigade personnel were involved in demonstrations of fire fighting techniques and equipment. A display held at Ravenscar, showed the use of foam. Another display, at the Children's Corner by the Spa, showed the use of asbestos clothing when two firemen sat in a burning structure. They suffered no ill effects from the fire due to the clothing and one of them even picked up some of the burning material in his hand and walked about in the flames much to the amazement of the onlookers.

NEW AMBULANCE

A brand new motor ambulance was bought from Messrs Lomas of Manchester, who built specialised ambulance bodies. It had a 27 horse power engine, mounted on a Vauxhall chassis and was finished in cream with pale blue waistline mouldings. It could carry two stretcher cases, or one stretcher and four seated. A Lomas stretcher device, for easy loading and unloading of stretchers, was fitted and there were concealed drawers lined in baize. It was designed to hold the Novox resuscitation machinery that the brigade already carried.

The Air Ministry, who had opened an experimental station on the top of Staxton Hill, made a request for the Scarborough fire brigade to provide fire cover for them. The Watch Committee reluctantly promised to attend.

WAR

By the 1st September 1939 war seemed inevitable as the German invasion of Poland began and the Auxiliary Fire Service was mobilised. On that evening 24 trucks, vans and cars were collected from their owners on an "on loan" basis, and taken to the fire station where they were kitted out before being allocated to the various 23 action stations around the town.

By the time war was declared two days later there were over 200 Auxiliary Fire Service personnel enlisted at Scarborough. The Auxiliary Fire Service volunteers were informed by mail that they had to attend the temporary action stations, which would be manned by them on a 12 hours on – 12 hours off rota basis. They were also instructed to attend the station in the event of an air raid warning being sounded.

Among the 23 stations covering the town from as far north as Scalby Mills garage to NALGO (now the site of Knipe Point, Osgodby,) in the south were: Dunollie, Filey Road, Sandside Garage, next to

An AFS Appliance and crew with Mr Saxton, in front of the Odeon (now Stephen Joseph Theatre)

Ivy House, North Bay Garage – North Marine Road (now Hollywood Plaza Cinema), Crown Garage – South Cliff, Miskin & Knaggs – Manor Road (now City Supplies), Woods Garage – Roscoe Street (now GNJ Metal Finishers), Vasey & Co Garage – Brook Street (awaiting conversion to Aldi Supermarket), Maltby & Co Garage – Falsgrave (now the Red Dragon Chinese Restaurant), Gallows Close Goods Yard (now Safeways car park), The old tram sheds – Scalby Road (now Harley Court), Cross Lane – Newby.

Despite the war there was still an unemployment problem in the town. In October, one councillor suggested at a meeting that the amount of hours put in by the wholetime Auxiliary Fire Service should be reduced from 12 hours a day, 7 days a week, to 8 hours a day to help relieve the unemployment figures. The Chief Constable informed him that as the Auxiliary Fire Service was Government postings the Council had no jurisdiction over them.

There were savings made later, however, as in April 1940, the police had their weekly 5 shilling retainer fee stopped as the Auxiliary Fire Service was undertaking their tasks.

WATER TENDERS

War started very slowly in firefighting terms and it became known as the phoney war, and the Auxiliary Fire Service was eventually stood down from their temporary stations in October. As nothing was happening, not only in Scarborough but also throughout the country, the Borough brigade used this period to consolidate their equipment and stations. The number of firemen was reduced by two thirds and the action stations reduced to eight.

The thirty quid brigade, Mr Robinson is seated in the centre

Arthur Robinson arranged for the brigade to purchase an old United, Leyland, 24-seater bus at a cost of £30. The back was cut away from the bus, the floors strengthened with timber and a large canvas bag (dam) within a steel framework was fitted to hold water. The pump was a Standard Gwyn, towed at the rear.

When all the conversion work had been completed, firemen climbed aboard and stood around the dam, and the bus set off down the yard. When the brakes were applied, the water slopped forward and drenched everyone, almost drowning the driver and officer-in-charge. This meant that it was back to the drawing board, but it did not take long to redesign the machine. This time the dam had planks running across it to act as baffles, to cut down on the turbulence, an idea still used in the modern water tenders of today.

It was given the title of SCU (Self Contained Unit) and was the first machine to incorporate water tank, pump and ladder all on the same chassis; it was in fact, the forerunner of the Water Tender and Mr Robinson was credited as one of its pioneers.

The Home Office Regional Inspector was requested to come and view the machine, after which he gave permission for local authorities to adapt more of this type of unit. Scarborough bought and adapted a further two of these buses and because of this the Scarborough Auxiliary Fire Service got the nickname of the "thirty quid brigade".

The "new" tenders were found to be especially useful on forest and rural area fires and were kitted out with two ladders, racks of flaked hose and had a covered crew compartment for five men.

SUB-STATIONS

More permanent stations around the town were opened, these being (as well as Scarborough Central):

Scalby Road, Tram Sheds –

> (Now the location of Harley Close) along with a house on Wykeham Street – Manor House, which was used as a watch room and sleeping accommodation.

Avenue Victoria Back Road, Saville & Ezard's Garage –

> (Was last the location of Proudfoots warehouse and is now housing) plus billets in the Albion Hotel, West Street.

Harcourt Place, Royal Garage –

> (Accessible via what is now Bar 2B, and located at the rear of what is now Bonnet's sweet shop on Huntriss Row.)

The three machines designed by Mr Robinson were based at these stations.

There were also stations at Newby East – in the grounds of Cross Lane Hospital, Hackness – at the estate office, Seamer – on the site of the farm at the roundabout in the village, and Burniston – Woods Garage, plus Scalby fire brigade and their Auxiliary Fire Service crews.

A trailer pump was bought from Dennis Brothers Limited, in April 1940, for £350 less a 20 per cent discount; it was a 350/500 gallons per minute pump and intended for rural area fires.

Mr Clarke leads a procession of AFS firemen, in front of the Pavilion Hotel

BURNISTON BOMBED

It was not until 26th June 1940 that the Scarborough area suffered any serious enemy activity when HX bombs were dropped at Burniston. An observer witnessed the incident from the top of the fire station tower; an officer in a car and a SCU from the old tram shed station were sent to attend. They were met with the sight of the top half of Boundary House, which had been devastated by the bombing, blocking the road. A man was seen to stagger out with only cuts and bruises whilst the lady of the house was rescued and given a piggyback to a neighbour's house.

The fire brigade vehicles then made their way to a cabin on fire at Cloughton railway station, which the firefighters soon had under control. A moor fire on Silpho Moor also resulted from the bombing, and due to the fear of enemy planes using it as a beacon to mark Scarborough, it had to be dealt with, this was the first time the Scarborough fire brigade had ever dealt with moor fires.

These incidents were followed by others around the town known as "Tip and Run Raids" such as oil bombs being dropped at Cloughton Bank top on 31st August. The crews attending these types of incidents were issued with revolvers, as it was feared that enemy parachutists could be lurking in the area and might attempt to commandeer the appliances. In the town itself the raids were restricted to land mines being dropped, and as there was no fire involved the fire brigade attendance was as a precautionary measure only. The worst of these early Tip and Run Raids was on 10th October 1940 when four people were killed and over 500 houses damaged at Potters Lane (now Castle Gardens).

On 12th November four part-time firemen enlisted from the Auxiliary Fire Service increased the Scarborough Fire Brigade in strength.

SCARBOROUGH HIT

The first incendiary bombs to be dropped, actually in the town, were observed from the fire station tower on 12th December at a little after 8.20 in the evening. There were many emergency calls received and dealt with that night, some of which included medium sized fires in St Johns Church on St Sepulchre Street (which at the time held a large amount of furniture, stored from the bomb damaged houses of Potters Lane) Blands Cliff, Longwestgate, the rear of the George Hotel, King Street, Cliff Bridge Terrace, Ramshill Road, West Street, and the Wheatlands Hotel. One incendiary dropped on the roof of St Mary's Church and was extinguished before it fell

AFS drills using ground monitors

through the roof which was fortuitous, as if it had not, it could have developed into a much larger incident because of the size and strength of the doors, they were unable to be opened.

It was whilst dealing with these incidents that the first SCU, designed at Scarborough, hit a telegraph pole and was deemed to be damaged beyond repair.

Just before 9.45 in the evening of 12th March 1941 Scarborough once again bore the brunt of the enemy forces, with fire incidents at 53 Scalby Road, and Saville & Ezards Garage on Falconers Rd.

By the early part of 1941, there were 61 whole-time (when required) Auxiliary Fire Service firemen, 105 part-time Auxiliary Fire Service firemen and 95 stand-by part-time firemen (who gave cover three nights in fourteen). They were under the command of three section officers and one patrol officer. In addition, there was also a telephonist and clerk employed.

The equipment supplied consisted of seven large trailer pumps, 24 light trailer pumps, three 1,000 gallon mobile dams, seven 500 gallon mobile dams, three permanently fixed 5,000 gallon dams, 14 towing vehicles, (three of which carried 1,000 gallons of water and three carrying 500 gallons.) Mr and Mrs Fitzroy Clayton of Osgodby donated a further Vauxhall/Lomas ambulance to the town on 30th January 1941.

THE MARCH BLITZ

Scarborough had begun the war relatively quietly, whilst London was taking the brunt of the bombing raids. This can be witnessed by the fact that the Evening News had to remind the local householders of their obligations to leave a bucket of sand and two buckets of water outside their front doors whether they were in or not.

On Tuesday 18th March 1941 the council again decided to increase the strength of the Scarborough fire brigade. That night, just a few weeks after the newspapers timely reminder about fire precautions, the whole of the north eastern area of England took the full force of the German raids. Luckily, this turned out to be the worst night Scarborough was to suffer, and it became known locally as "The March Blitz". The way it was reported in the Scarborough Evening News was intended to cause as much confusion to enemy informers as possible (also causing confusion to anyone trying to research the period!) The report went:

'BLITZ ON A COASTAL TOWN

During an attack on the North East Coast area on Tuesday night a coastal town was subjected by waves of enemy aircraft to a prolonged blitz. Incendiary bombs were showered in various parts of the town followed shortly afterwards to completely indiscriminate bombing with high explosives, some of which were of heavy type. In some instances bombs were dropped amongst fire fighters.

A number of houses were destroyed and many people were injured.

Firewatchers and ARP workers and civilians dealt successfully with most of the incendiary bombs, several fell on the hospital, without being allowed to cause damage. A theatre and dance hall were also struck, many houses suffered minor damage. A fire occurred at a printing works and a furniture repository was destroyed but all the fires were quickly put out. Some Auxiliary Fire Service workers were injured.

Places of worship were also struck by incendiary bombs.

Later the attack became less intense but there was desultory dropping of incendiaries and occasional high explosive bombs for some hours.

Most of the occupants of a row of seven small houses, which were destroyed by one high explosive bomb, were trapped among the debris.

Two of them were fatally injured and several injured people were rescued. Squads worked throughout the night in an attempt to release three others. A woman and two children. After working for some hours they were able to communicate with the victims who were uninjured and they were able to supply drinks to them.

A considerable number of people were removed from the damaged homes and were cared for at a rest shelter.

A number of delayed action bombs were dropped during the raid and some of these exploded later.

NUNS HELPED TO FIGHT FIRE

Nuns quickly put out one of three incendiary bombs, which fell on a convent and with the help of police and wardens prevented others doing much damage.

An incendiary bomb, which fell through the roof of a theatre soon after the audience had left, lodged in a grille. And set woodwork alight. The stage became involved but the fire curtains saved the auditorium and Auxiliary Fire Service men prevented the fire spreading to the dressing rooms.

The management of the theatre contrived to continue the performance the following night. Glass at another place of entertainment was pierced but other damage caused was only to a number of seats. A small café near was also damaged.

Praise for the local defence services – especially the Auxiliary Fire Service – was voiced in all quarters."

In fact that evening every appliance in the north east of England was in use handling the twenty one air raids in the area. Reinforcements were drafted in from Scalby, Whitby, Pickering and Malton. Middlesbrough and Northallerton pumps were also sent, but not used, and 15 pumps were standing-by at Leeds.

The alert was sounded at 9.40 p.m. and by 10 o'clock there were 22 incidents to respond to, with a further sixteen calls before 11 o'clock.

Dennis the printers silhouetted against the blaze

The dance hall referred to was the Olympia, whilst the theatre was the Opera House.

At the Opera House, a fireman shinned up the flys to train water on an incendiary bomb which was trapped in what was left of the roof. Whilst he was up there, the other firemen dealt with the fire it had created on the stage area. Little was left amongst the burnt framework of the scenery except a charred piano dripping in the water from the firefighting. Suddenly a man appeared amongst the firemen, he headed for the dressing rooms and, after a few minutes, reappeared, excitedly shaking hands with the fire crew for saving his props. He then waded through the water to what remained of the piano, lifted the lid and began to play. At this point the crew were ordered to attend a fire on the roof of Boots the Chemist, at the corner of St Nicholas Street and Newborough (now the Lloyds / TSB Bank). It was not until they were leaving the theatre that they heard the cries of their forgotten colleague stranded in the flys.

Dennis the printers the morning after

The old adage of the show must go on was carried out, as there was a show using make shift props put on the following evening.

ETW Dennis the printers, between Columbus Ravine and Melrose Street had been working until 9 p.m. and had only just closed when the bombing started. The building took direct hits and was totally gutted by fire. An Auxiliary Fire Service fireman was badly injured at this incident when he fell from a wall, breaking both of his legs. The firm went out of production for four months. ETW Dennis also went out of production totally in 2000.

Tonks was the furniture repository mentioned, temporarily based in the building belonging to Quartons, on Seamer Road (which had been Waddington's piano factory and is now the site of B&Q). The places of worship referred to were St Peters Church, St Columbus Church and Queen Street Chapel, all of which were damaged, although not seriously. The cafe in Alexandra Gardens was destroyed by fire, caused by the bombing. Amongst the many rows of houses which were destroyed or suffered damage were Commercial Street, Moorland Road, New Queen Street, North Marine Road, Queen's Terrace, Seamer Moor Road, Trafalgar Road, Tennyson Avenue, Victoria Park Avenue and Woodall Avenue. Even though fire was not involved at all the incidents, an Auxiliary Fire Service presence was still required for rescue work, to help people trapped amongst the rubble.

The air raid started at 9.40 p.m. and it was after 4.30 the next morning before the all clear was sounded. It had taken its toll on 1378 buildings locally and cost the lives of 27 people, injuring a further 45.

It became the firemen's job the next day to collect the unexploded incendiary bombs from around the town and take them to the Central Fire Station where they were disarmed. Until that time the incendiary bombs, which were being dropped around the country, were easy to extinguish, and people became quite blasé, saying Boy Scouts could handle the job. Unfortunately for the Scarborough firemen, the incendiaries that were dropped were of a new type, designed with a small explosive, which went off on a delayed detonator, exploding when the men were dealing with them, causing a great many injuries.

MR ABBOTT RETIRES

As stated the Watch Committee decided, in March, to recruit six more part-time firemen. They were to receive a rationing fee of two shillings and six pence a week and four shillings for the first hour, or part thereof, attended at fires, two shillings for the second hour or part thereof, and one shilling for each subsequent hour.

After this, there was some concern from committee members that, whilst it was saving money employing Auxiliary Fire Service trained personnel; the force was becoming a civilian brigade and not a police brigade.

Sadly Chief Constable Abbott suffered the loss of his wife on 3rd April 1941 and this was followed by a deterioration of his own health, so Mr Noakes, the Assistant Chief Constable, was appointed Acting Chief Constable. One of the first tasks he was ordered to do was to cost a turntable ladder and the covering of the fire station yard with a roof. He was also instructed to look into the feasibility of opening a combined control room, with Home Office funding.

On 4th May there was a heavy bombardment of HX bombs but, luckily, they missed the town, landing between Harwood Dale and the Flask Inn, on the Whitby Moors. The only incident was at Kirklees Farm, but there was a ten day battle by the Scarborough, Hackness and Burniston fire crews plus the military to contain and quell the ensuing moor fire.

Another spate of fires caused by bombs occurred on the 10th May. These were at the Londesborough Theatre, the Salvation Army Citadel,

Happier times – an AFS fireman marries and uses the Dennis to taxi the happy couple

the Esplanade Cafe, Somerset Cafe, York Place, the Chatsworth and Flowerdean Hotels, private houses in Alma Square, Albermarle Crescent and at the Falconers Road Flats and the Art School (now the site of Boothbys Garage showroom) which sustained a direct hit.

Hull was also receiving a hard time at the hands of Hitler and following this spate of bombing pumps from Scarborough were dispatched to help with their efforts. The machines carried an emergency supply kit, which contained essential items for the men, including shaving and washing equipment. There were two pumps from Scarborough and one from Scalby in this dispatch and the crews who manned them left home on the morning for work and did not return until three weeks later.

After this volunteers were sought to go to Coventry and assist with their firefighting; they were to man the pumps provided by Coventry City fire brigade – these volunteers became classed as industrial firefighters, earning £8 per week instead of the £3 Auxiliary Fire Service firemen were earning.

At the Watch Committee meeting of 13th May 1941 the members were informed that the Scarborough and Auxiliary Fire Service brigades were now under the general control of the Secretary of State.

By September Mr Abbott's health had worsened and the Watch Committee asked for his resignation, which took effect from 12th September 1941. His place was taken by Mr G F Goodman (42), the Chief Constable of Newark-on-Trent.

The qualifications Mr Goodman held in firefighting helped influence the selection committee, but by the time he took the appointment the Scarborough fire brigade no longer existed. The Home Office took over the responsibility of running the fire brigades on a national basis, this being the formation of the National Fire Service (NFS).

Not only was this the end of the police involvement with the fire brigade it also saw the end of the fire brigades involvement with the ambulance service, other than supplying petrol to them – a service which continued until they moved to their premises on Seamer Road in the 1970s.

Responsibility for the ambulance service, however, remained with the police until the end of the war, when it was organised on a county basis and moved premises to Dean Road, at the side of St Mary's Hospital, where it remained until the move to the depot on Seamer Road. (now Arundales). The ambulance service is now based on St Margaret's industrial estate.

Mr Noakes had applied for the job of Chief Constable, but was unsuccessful. When he complained about not even being short-listed for the job he was accused of canvassing the committee (even though the appointment had already been made), and he was given a reduction in rank, to night sergeant, as a punishment. Mr Noakes then brought an action through the courts against eight of the Watch Committee for unfair treatment.

By the time the case came to court in December 1942 Mr Noakes had been seconded to the National Fire Service as a column officer based in Stockton. The Judge found no case for complaint against the committee. The Home Office then pressed the committee to recover the costs of about £400, for the court proceedings, from Mr Noakes. There were members of the council who thought this unjust as there had been some indiscretions on the part of some committee members and even the previous Chief Constable. The dispute continued between the council and Mr Noaks until November 1944 when he ended up in the bankruptcy court. Mr Noakes died at Northallerton in 1978, aged 82, having left the fire brigade after the war.

The station bell (still used today) being presented at an AFS dinner, it was designed around the style of a wheeled escape trunion mounting. The Acting Chief Constable Mr Noakes can just be seen at the extreme right of the photo

NATIONAL FIRE SERVICE

The only sign the general public had of the takeover was that, in September 1941, a report of a small fire in the Scarborough Evening News mentioned that the Auxiliary Fire Service was using the new name of National Fire Service.

It was found, after the heavy bombing that London and the larger cities and ports endured in the early part of 1941, how inadequate the fire brigades were. The London blitz had stretched the resources of the London fire brigades to the limit, and supplemented as they were by the Auxiliary Fire Service, they still found it hard to cope.

Commander Firebrace

Orders were sent out to the County and Borough brigades to come to their aid, but, as there was no legislation making provision for this, some brigades only sent crews when they felt like it and some totally ignored the pleas for help. Many brigades would not release the men to London, as they could have been needed in their own locality if the bombings were to continue with the same ferocity.

Crews which did turn up to help were either poorly trained or trained in such a way that they could not work with crews from other brigades. The equipment they brought with them varied and was often incompatible with the London facilities i.e. the standpipes would not fit the hydrants, or the hose had different connections. It was found that the terminology varied from brigade to brigade for some items of equipment or tasks undertaken.

Mr Herbert Morrison, The Home Secretary, called a meeting with Fire Brigade and Home Office representatives on 18th April 1941 to discuss methods of dealing with the problems encountered. From the meeting came the concept of a National Fire Service (NFS) and it was decided to put before the House of Commons the Fire Service (Emergency Provisions) Bill, 1941, which would allow for the nationalisation of the Fire Brigade.

Commander Aylmer Firebrace was appointed as Chief of Fire Staff and Inspector in Chief of the National Fire Service. Previous to this he had been the Chief Officer of the London Fire Brigade and on declaration of war his powers were widened to take control of 67 fire brigades, including all the Auxiliary Fire Service personnel, which surrounded London. At the outset of war the country was split into twelve regions, each having a Regional Commissioner who had wide powers. In the event of the country being invaded he was to have become the authority for the area, carrying all the powers that Government normally had. In the northern region, Sir Arthur

NFS fireman damping down after a fire

Lambert was appointed Commissioner.

The National Fire Service also worked on these twelve regions, with each region having a Senior Regional Fire Officer. The regions were sub-divided into fire forces, with each having a Fire Force Commander in charge. Costs of setting up the National Fire Service and thereafter a quarter of the normal annual costs of the professional fire brigade was to be covered by the Government.

There came about a standard national uniform and rank structure. The hours worked were standardised with a 48 hour on duty – 24 hours off duty, routine being adopted. The pay for firemen was set at £3.10s a week.

Training was also standardised throughout the country; the basic means of adopting this policy was by a Fire Brigade Drill Book. An empty hotel, The Ocean, at Saltdean, near Brighton was requisitioned and turned into a Training College. Fire service members throughout the country were invited to attend and help set the standard drills etc.

Section Officer F Stephenson represented the Scarborough area. On return to the area he had the task of re-training the personnel, including his superiors, on how to carry out drills. Up until this time Scarborough had drilled to the whistle, i.e. one blast – get to work, two blasts – stop; the new system was totally different in that the orders were shouted out.

The new drill book along with, slightly later, (between 1942 & 1946) a set of Fire Brigade Manuals, were set to become the basis of the fire brigade structure. Whilst altered and modernised over the years, they are still, surprisingly, very similar, and form the same basic training structure of the brigades throughout the country today.

Mr Morrison also promised that at the end of hostilities management of the fire brigades would be returned to individual local authorities, to be run and financed by them.

Transfer to National Fire Service took place over a thirteen week period and on the 18th August 1941 the National Fire Service came into existence. To the general public there were no changes and no announcement was made for another month after the date. The idea of this was to give Germany no advantage in their war effort by catching our cities in a changeover period when they might be in disarray.

The fire brigade magazine 'FIRE' recorded at the time: –

'Excluding the London region, Great Britain, for the purposes of fire defence, is now divided into 39 Fire Force areas. Each with a Division, comprising of 2 Columns, 10 Companies, and 20 Sections. There may

be more than one Division in each Fire Force, the latter under a Fire Force Commander, responsible to the Regional Commissioner, and the Senior Regional Fire Officer.

The Fire Force Commander will have wide powers. He will be empowered to transfer full-time officers and men from district to district within his area. But that the transfers to be kept low and within local requirements.'

SCARBOROUGH AND THE NATIONAL FIRE SERVICE

To Scarborough this meant that the Scarborough Fire Brigade no longer existed and that Scarborough was now part of the No 1 region, under Senior Regional Fire Officer T Varley; in the No 2 Fire Force. The No 1 region covered the area from Berwick to Scarborough including Northumberland, Newcastle, Durham and the North Riding with the regional headquarters situated at Gosforth. The No 1 Fire Force covered Berwick to Hart, (near Hartlepool), their headquarters was Gosforth whilst No 2 Fire Force covered Hartlepool to Scarborough with this headquarters being Stockton-on-Tees, under Fire Force Commander Norwood.

Scarborough became the sub-division headquarters for D Division covering an area of 860 square miles, taking in Scarborough, Easingwold, Huntington, Malton and Whitby. The vicarage for St Marks Church, at 28 Stepney Grove, was commandeered to become the administrative offices for the division.

Mr Robinson, as the area co-ordinator of the Auxiliary Fire Service activities, was given the job of looking after the division as Divisional Officer, whilst Mr Clarke was appointed Senior Column Officer in charge of Scarborough. Mr W Gill was appointed Company Officer and was in charge of the control room at Scarborough.

Local branches of the Brigade at the divisional headquarters included:

Finance department,
Building and maintenance department – run by tradesmen employed by the National Fire Service as firemen,
Catering store department – which grew their own vegetables and bred rabbits,
Tailors department – housed in a shed in what was then a field across the road from headquarters.

A modern view of Stepney Grove Divisional headquarters, now converted into flats

A training school was opened at Scalby Manor, with ex-Sergeant Major Jim Metcalf appointed as the physical training instructor.

Ezards Garage on Falsgrave Road (now the location of The Red Dragon restaurant) was taken over and used as the maintenance workshops for service vehicles.

The borough was split into five wards, the same as the Auxiliary Fire Service system. The stations were allocated identification letters and were referred to by them from then on. Harcourt Place became W station, Avenue Victoria Back Road was X station, the Tram Sheds Y station and Scarborough Central Z station.

The shop next door to the fire station (now The Mind Shop) was taken over and used as an area control, manned 24 hours a day by firewomen. There was also a sandbag and timber construction at the top of the station yard, which was used as an emergency area control. One of the police houses in the fire station yard was adapted for mess, recreation and living accommodation for the firewomen.

The first two firewomen to be employed at Scarborough were L Machin and D Newham, starting on 22nd September 1941; many others followed them before the war was over. Many of the firewomen found themselves trained as full firefighters (Firewoman Machin, for instance, at a fire in the Grand Restaurant, found herself on her own, manning a pump which was relaying water from the duck pond on Valley Road to the incident).

Machines allocated to Scarborough were six brand new 2-ton Ford Austin Tenders, three 5-ton Ford Mobile Water Tank Carriers, a Mobile Canteen and a Salvage Van.

Water supplies around the town included five static basins (50000-gallon steel tanks), three 22000-gallon circular steel tanks, two 11000-gallon circular steel tanks and five pipelines. These were to supplement the town's water supply in the event of a blitz or in case of the water supplies being damaged by bombs.

Stations had to be patrolled on a regular basis in case of German infiltration and because of this there were patrol duties of two hour duration, undertaken on a rota basis by the on-duty firemen, who were issued with a Webley revolver and bullets. At the change of guard the revolvers were unloaded, the bullets counted by the officer-in-charge and the gun finally reloaded by the oncoming guard.

JACONELLI'S CAFE
One of the first fires tackled by the National Fire Service was in September and was a nasty reminder of why the old style brass helmets used by some brigades were rejected in favour of the more

modern leather helmets. The National Fire Service uniform consisted of round 'tin' helmets and at a fire in the rear attic of Jaconelli's Café (now

Some of Scarborough's NFS firewomen

Tricolos), 37 Newborough, Senior Company Officer (ex-Chief Engineer) Clarke, received an electric shock when his helmet touched a live wire. Two others, Leading Fireman Russell and Fireman Maw, who went to his aid, also suffered a similar fate, but they managed to drag the unconscious officer downstairs and out into the open air through a window. Mr Clarke was taken to hospital and was released later.

SAVED BY BREATHING APPARATUS

What was recorded, by the Scarborough Evening News, as the first lives to be saved from fire by the use of self-contained breathing apparatus in Scarborough occurred at 47 Queen Street. The incident was reported at just after 8a.m. and three units and a salvage van were turned out. On arrival, firemen were informed that there was still an elderly couple inside the premises, which had smoke issuing from every window.

NFS firemen with breathing apparatus

Leading Fireman Ridge put on the breathing apparatus and started to make a search of the premises; he eventually found Mr Eden (87) collapsed on the second floor, Ridge managed to drag him down to the first floor, where Leading Fireman Robson took over and carried Mr Eden outside.

A thorough search of the upper floors never revealed the whereabouts of Mrs Eden (82) and she was not discovered until the small understairs cupboard was opened to turn off the gas supply. Mrs Eden was unconscious inside, she was taken into the open air where firemen administered artificial respiration to which, after several minutes, she responded. The couple was removed to hospital in the police ambulance where, by the afternoon, they were sat up in bed none the worse for their ordeal.

The fire, which was in the under-drawing of the ceiling on the ground floor shop level, was soon extinguished. It seems likely that without the use of the breathing apparatus the couple would not have been found until the fire was out, by which time it would have been too late.

Eden's shop was next door to where the Brooks' disaster had occurred; though it emerged unscathed through that episode, and yet again escaped damage during the devastating fire at the Rem Store when the building on the other side suffered considerable damage.

THE GRAND RESTAURANT

It was the early hours of the 30th March 1942 when two policemen, who were on duty in the town centre, smelt smoke and burning.

It took some time before they located the source of the smell to the Grand Restaurant, on the Foreshore Road.

When they arrived at the site flames were leaping out of the windows. There were still workmen

A crew of women firefighters tackle the blaze at the Grand Restaurant

asleep on the site, totally oblivious to the fire, who had to be roused by the police before the arrival of the fire brigade. The alarm call was received at 4.40am and by the time the brigade arrived; fire was blazing rapidly all the way across the first floor of the building.

There was a waxworks display in the building at the time and this fuelled the fire. The firemen had the added problem of finding "dead and disfigured bodies" only to realise they were the exhibits which had become distorted with the heat.

Water was drawn from three static supplies some distance from the fire and supplemented by the town's water mains. There was some difficulty in reaching the seat of the fire due to the premises being used for storage during the war period.

Despite the efforts of the firemen, the contents were totally destroyed and, after the fire, the building was declared unsafe. It lay derelict for some years and became an eyesore until the Corporation purchased it in 1949 for £65000, and then demolished it. The site has lain untouched till the present day (though there was speculation that it was to have been developed after the Olympia fire in 1975, but this did not materialise).

OPEN AIR DISPLAY

The National Fire Service personnel put on a fire service display at the Open Air Theatre on the evening of 14th August, 1942 at which 1822 people were entertained with demonstrations on ancient manual pumps, horse drawn steamers, a 1914 appliance and modern appliances from Malton, Lythe and Whitby. Canoe and other water-based races were run and the highlight of the evening was when the brigade set up a giant V for Victory symbol out of water jets. The proceeds of £45 11s were given to Scarborough Hospital.

On 11th December 1942 Reverend Newman, of Queen Street Central Hall was appointed National Fire Service Honorary Chaplain for D Division and given the rank of Company Officer; this was the first appointment of its type.

GABRIEL WADE & ENGLISH

On Saturday 24th April 1943, just after 1 p.m., a resident of Trafalgar Street West entered his house from the back yard, which adjoined Gabriel Wade & English sawmill on Brook Street (now Jewsons). He was astonished to look out of his house onto a sea of flames as only minutes before he had noticed nothing amiss.

The fire was reported from all parts of town as, within seconds, a huge cloud of smoke rose, visible from all areas. The National

The remains of Gabriel Wades after the fire

Fire Service took the first call to the fire at 1.18 p.m. and the smoke from the fire could be seen by the firemen as they left the fire station.

There was a considerable amount of manpower needed to relay the water and, for this reason eight pumps, supplying 17 water jets, were brought into use. Pumps were brought in from Whitby, Malton and Filey to cover the area whilst the local pumps were busy.

Many people came forward to help and one of the water jets in use on the boiler house area was manned totally by civilians. There were also many sailors and RAF personnel lending a hand with the firefighting efforts.

All the frontage of the premises on Brook Street was described as *'a crimson wall of flames'*. The houses on Trafalgar Street West and Cambridge Street, which backed onto the sawmills, were hurriedly evacuated and the contents of these laid in piles in the middle of the road. Furniture was lowered from the upper floor windows; a feather mattress, which was dropped, provided a storm of feathers, which went flying everywhere. Not related to these feathers, but flying around, were a number of hens and chickens that had been rescued from a back yard in Trafalgar Street West.

The buses from the West Yorkshire Bus Company, sited at the corner of Trafalgar Street West and Northway (now Jewson's showrooms) were also hurriedly removed and parked along Northway.

The roof of the main building was asbestos and due to the heat this started to pop; a noise which was described by many people who were not even in the vicinity of the fire but could hear it, as machine gun fire. West Yorkshire Bus Company employees treated fireman J Russell for a head injury, after part of the main roof fell on him. He was later transferred to hospital where he was detained.

Mobilisation procedure and the amount of equipment available due to the National Fire Service system were described as first class and it was only this that enabled the fire to be brought under control by 1.55 p.m. Immediately after the fire a special team of National Fire Service salvage workers began their work. They managed to save a large quantity of timber and they cleaned and oiled the woodworking machinery making much of it reusable though the main part of the sawmill was gutted.

When the fire was subdued most of the evacuees were allowed to return home, despite the damage sustained by the external woodwork such as windows, doors and guttering. A few of the houses were not habitable due to water damage as hoses were lead through the houses to fight the fire from all angles; the occupants of these were taken to other houses by Air Raid Patrol vans.

A cause of fire was not determined but it was thought to be accidental and not malicious. The fire must have been burning some considerable time before the alarm was raised, but the Fire Watch had not noticed it.

Rebuilding plans were submitted to the Council, but at a Planning Committee meeting it was thought that the site of the sawmill was totally inappropriate and that it should be relocated on the outskirts of town. The full council meeting however took the view that the location of the mill was not their concern as it had been operating from its present site for many years.

Plaxtons were awarded the contract for rebuilding. Unfortunately, whilst the fire never claimed any lives the building site was the scene of a fatal accident when one of the construction workers fell from a scaffold and was killed.

TURNTABLE LADDER

On 12th May 1943 the town was supplied with its first turntable ladder (TL), it was a 100 foot Merryweather ladder on a Leyland Beaver Chassis. There was a spotlight, speaker and telephone system (to allow communication with the top of the ladder) attached. It was acquired as a direct result of enquiries held by the Borough Watch Committee prior to nationalisation and whilst the National Fire Service took full credit for supplying it, it would never have come about without the committee's earlier interest. It was put on public display at Scalby Manor, on Saturday 22nd May.

Scarborough was extremely lucky to receive a turntable ladder, as prior to the war either Metz or Magiras made the majority of turntable ladders being supplied to the brigades around the country. Both of these firms were German and, naturally, with the hostilities, the machines were no longer available. Merryweather, who had made a few turntable ladders in the past, only made six for this country in the war. Somehow, fortunately, Scarborough managed to take delivery of one by 1943.

Scarborough's first turntable ladder

MR CLARKE RETIRES

Senior Column Officer Clarke retired from the fire brigade at the end of August 1943 after 41 years of firefighting. His retirement was early due to the fact that he had never fully recovered from the electric shock he had received at the fire in 1941, at Jaconelli's cafe. Mr Clarke died on the 16th December 1944 and, because of the great respect that he had earned over the years, he was given a full fire brigade funeral. His body was taken from St Mary's Church to Manor Road Cemetery by the Leyland wheeled escape pump, where a large contingent of National Fire Service personnel paid their last respects.

Mr Clarke's funeral outside St Mary's Church

PLAXTON'S

What was Scarborough's most spectacular wartime night blaze (but not caused by enemy activity) occurred on the evening of Tuesday 5th October 1943 at the Seamer Road works of Plaxtons (now the location of the Seamer Road Trading Estate containing B&Q through to MFI). This disrupted the blackout procedure and lit up a vast area of the town, luckily to no advantage to the Germans as no attacks took place that evening. At the height of the fire it was said that blackout torches were rendered unnecessary as far away as Ayton and Scalby due to the illumination from the fire.

Plaxtons was already a coach works before the war, but these activities were curtailed with the onset of hostilities and it became a munitions factory, manufacturing boxes for ammunition. They came under the control of the Ministry of Aircraft Production and, as well as boxes, they produced flares and engine casings for Rolls Royce and Bristol aero-engines.

There were 17 people employed at the works as a fire watch when the outbreak occurred. One of them alerted the fire brigade whilst others set in hose to fire hydrants, but these were of little use as the flames spread rapidly. A bus body and several car bodies were recovered from the fire, along with Plaxton's fire pump which was supposed to be set into the Mere in the event of fire. As the

National Fire Service was on its way it was decided to await its arrival instead of setting the pump up.

Police Constable Smith also reported the fire. As he was cycling past he saw a glow of light coming from the building. He went to investigate when the windows in the northwest corner suddenly burst into flames and tongues of fire leapt out. It was said that the building was blazing from end to end within six minutes.

The first call which the fire brigade received was at 10.32 p.m. and within ten minutes of the call there were eight pumps at the scene. There then followed what must have been the most intensive firefighting activities ever to take place at a fire in Scarborough. Six pumps were set into the Mere and a further four pumps were brought in to help man the 32 water jets that were played onto the fire.

Operations were under the control of Divisional Officer Robinson and Column Officer Smith. Company Officer Gill

A NFS, ATV seen in the later North Riding Livery

sustained injuries to his hand and, after first-aid treatment failed to help, he was taken to hospital where he was detained.

By midnight the blaze was eventually brought under control, the firefighters having managed to save a number of the buildings on the site, along with stacks of timber and the sawmill. There was at least £70000 worth of damage done, and 600 people were temporarily put out of work, although Quartons, the local market gardeners and high street fruit and vegetable shop owners made premises available.

Fortunately, the working of night shifts had ceased the month before, otherwise many people could have been trapped in the fire because of the rapid rate of spread.

DEAN ROAD

In February 1944 the authorities were ordered to refill the static water supplies as the public were beginning to use them as rubbish dumps. They had been allowed to dry up due to the lack of enemy activity.

Also in February, on the 4th, at a little before 5 a.m. Mrs Butler, who had stayed the night at her sister's flat, above 10 Dean Road, entered the kitchen to find a fire burning out of control. She informed her sister, Mrs Dawson, who told her to go and get help whilst she moved the children out. When she returned she could not find her sister anywhere.

A NFS Fire crew

The fire brigade arrived in a matter of minutes and found the upper floors burning well; three firemen were detailed to search for the occupants whilst the rest set about fighting the fire. Leading fireman C Spavin found Mrs Dawson on the top floor, unconscious, clutching her youngest child. She and her three children were removed from the building and were in an ambulance on their way to hospital within ten minutes of the firemen arriving at the scene. Unfortunately, all four were found to be dead on arrival at the hospital. They were:

> Mrs Gwendolene Dawson
> Geoffrey Dawson   aged 8
> Malcolm Dawson   aged 3
> John Bryan Dawson   aged 18 months

Mr Dawson was in the RAF and away from home at the time of the fire, which is why Mrs Butler had stayed the night. It was discovered that socks drying on a copper wire over the fireplace had been the cause of the fire, as one of the socks had caught fire and fallen onto the carpet.

UNWANTED HELP

It was in June of the same year that another fire occurred, which could have had similar consequences, due to the so-called help of bystanders. At number 3 Westborough, a fire had started in the second floor sitting room; the lady of the house, Mrs Todd, ran up the stairs in the sitting room, which gave access to the third floor bedroom, to rescue the children. Mr Todd tried to fight the fire using buckets of water, but due to the poor water supply, the bucket was taking a long time to fill, and it was not long before the staircase was blazing ferociously and became unusable.

On arrival the fire brigade found that the only access was via a passageway, so it was decided to place a ladder up to the back window to effect the rescue of Mrs Todd and the children. A large crowd had gathered and they tried to prevent the firemen gaining access from the passage, wanting them to direct their firefighting efforts to the front of the building. A group of off-duty soldiers grabbed the ladder and wrestled it from the firemen's hands, then tried to erect it, but were unable to, as they had placed it upside down.

Firemen were allowed to recover the ladder and take it to the rear of the building, from where Fireman Witty in breathing apparatus entered the building and passed the children to Leading Fireman McCullum, who carried them to safety. Mrs Todd was then helped to safety down the ladder.

FINDING WORK

Because of the lessening of enemy activity in this country the fire brigade was over-manned; as a temporary measure the men were given various other jobs to do on the home front, such as helping with the harvesting in the countryside. The station underwent alterations as the tradesmen amongst the firemen fitted the pole drop at the station, for a quicker departure. They also knocked windows into the drying tower so that it was capable of being used to drill on, allowing hook ladders to be hung from the windowsills for scaling. Doors were knocked through in the living quarters to make access between kitchen and mess deck more easy, etc.

Planning permission to make the alterations was applied for, but work commenced before the approval was given. When the application came before the planning committee in June 1944 there was no

Firemen seen helping with the harvest

objection to the plans but the council were upset that there had been no consultation by the National Fire Service before the work had started.

ILLEGAL FIRE BRIGADE

It was not just at local level the National Fire Service was in trouble because in June it was realised that, through an oversight, the Act of Parliament which had brought about the National Fire Service had never been properly laid before Parliament for approval, which made it invalid. Mr Morrison apologised to the House of Commons and put through an Indemnity Bill, which legalised the fire service.

In 1945 the war drew to a close and the number of firemen and stations were reduced, the sub-stations were closed and only the Central Station was manned. The old Leyland and Dennis pumps again covered the station plus a Thames front mounted pump. The old foam tender was also kept on the station.

Divisional staff seen at the rear of the Stepney Grove Headquarters

A system of part-time retained firemen was set up to provide back up cover for the whole-time firemen. They would respond to a siren (similar to the old air raid one) on top of the station tower and permission was sought to test it, for one minute, at a set time every week. The Council replied that there were no objections to the test providing they were done silently; this was obviously impossible and the tests went ahead with the siren sounding each Monday at a 12.45 p.m.

OLDE TYME CAFE

A fire, which took place at Rowntree's Olde Tyme Cafe, Westborough, in 1946 whilst not being devastating, is worthy of notice. It started as a chip pan fire on the ground floor of the building, then spread to a wood-lined flue and caused a great deal of smoke. The firemen were tackling the fire without much difficulty when screams for help were heard coming from the upper floors of the building. Firemen hurriedly donned breathing apparatus and made their way to the upper floors where the screams were becoming more urgent. They eventually reached the top floor only to discover that their "damsel in distress" was a parrot, which, on hearing the commotion going on downstairs decided to join in the noise being made. It was rescued without coming to any harm.

Sadly, though, the parrot suffered its demise only a few months later, ironically in another fire at the restaurant, when the fire started in the stillroom on the first floor and spread to the top three floors of the building. The entire station was turned out to this incident and Scalby firemen were brought to stand by at Scarborough Station in case of any more calls. The only casualty of the fire was the parrot, which suffocated.

A NFS crew in front of the turntable ladder

In 1946 the control room next door to the station became redundant as the fire brigade operations were capable of being handled on the station itself. The police transport section took it over, along with the house above it, which had been used as the firewomen's quarters. Also in June that year the National Fire Service asked the Watch Committee if they had any objections to the old Dennis pump being disposed of as it had, by now, reached the end of its useful days. There were no objections and it was transferred north to National Fire Service headquarters from where it was disposed of. In its place a Thames front mounted pump, capable of pumping 700 to 900 gallons of water per minute was issued.

After the brigade had nationalised to assist the larger cities, the bombing of London never reached the same proportions it did in early 1941. It seems, in retrospect, that the old brigades and the Auxiliary Fire Service could have handled the firefighting cover for the rest of the war.

Scarborough's NFS contingent take the salute in front of the Town Hall on Castle Road, the present day fire safety offices can be seen across the road

NFS crew in front of Scarborough Fire Station.
Note the arches removed in 1954

North Riding County Fire Brigade

After the war, a new Labour Government was elected and, with their policies towards nationalisation, it took some time before they considered de-nationalising the National Fire Service, as Herbert Morrison had promised. They used the excuse that there was much work to be done by the service, such as selling off or mothballing the excess machines brought into commission for the war. Also, there were the emergency pipelines to be dismantled and stored.

Eventually though, on the 1st February 1947, a bill was put before Parliament passing the 1947 Fire Brigade Act which required that the National Fire Service be placed back into the hands of the local County and County Borough Authorities. This bill meant that the management of the fire brigades would be by 147 authorities and not the 1,440 that were running them before the war. The idea was that it would be more efficient for the brigades to be divided up into larger areas.

Scarborough area, as far as the fire brigade was concerned, was to come under the authority of the North Riding of Yorkshire County Council. The Scarborough police force had already been taken over by them in 1947, whilst the ambulance service was also in the process of being adopted by them through the Health Authority, as part of the National Health Service Act 1946. Eventually the ambulance service was taken over on 5th July 1948 under the command of the County Ambulance officer, Mr Hole, the former Superintendent of the Medway Ambulance Service, Kent. Scarborough had an ambulance depot opened at Dean Road at the side of St Mary's Hospital. Station Officer Frank Welburn, of the old Scarborough Fire Brigade, was in charge of the 18 driver/attendants, many of whom were ex-wartime firemen. There were five ambulances and one staff car stationed at Scarborough.

The local authorities put up opposition to losing control of their police, fire and ambulance services, on the grounds that Scarborough's geographical situation did not lend itself to being run from such a great distance away (Northallerton). These complaints fell upon deaf ears. At the time of the merger of the Scarborough Police into the North Riding Force it consisted of one Chief Constable, Mr Browne (who became Deputy Chief Constable of the North Riding Constabulary in charge of the Scarborough Division), one chief inspector, four inspectors, ten sergeants and 62 police constables.

North Riding Council formed its first ever Fire Brigade Committee, as even before the war City, Borough, Rural or Urban councils had handled the whole of the county's firefighting arrangements. The first meeting of the committee was on 24th October 1947, and it consisted of Aldermen, county councillors and representatives from borough and district councillors who were all under the guidance of the clerk of the council.

There were some comments from the Scarborough Watch Committee about the North Riding being able to compulsory take over the station and the firemen's houses, without any reimbursement to the Borough, but they found themselves powerless to do anything about it.

CHIEF FIRE OFFICER CORBRICK

The new committee's first job was to appoint a Chief Fire Officer Designate who, with Home Office approval, was Mr Lawrence Corbrick, the Senior Staff Officer at the National Fire Service, No 1 region headquarters, Newcastle.

The headquarters were to be at Northallerton in the old police headquarters, which after being vacant for some years needed much structural work to bring it up to standard. There were communication systems to install which required post office engineers to fit a ten-plug switchboard. A stores area

CFO Corbrick

had to be developed and the place needed to be cleaned and totally redecorated.

Part of the agreement of the de-nationalisation of the National Fire Service was that any serving member who wanted to return to their home town had a right to do so. There was also a large number of firemen who did not come up to the standards required by a non-wartime fire brigade in that they were too small, short-sighted etc. and they were either discharged or kept on as temporary firemen until it was possible to fill their places.

Also in the Fire Service Act were some strict criteria that the new authorities had to meet, such as the standardisation of equipment, so that a member of one station could move onto any other and basically know how the equipment worked and how to use it.

It was decided the new brigade would consist of three divisions, namely:

A1 Grangetown	B1 Scarborough	C1 Northallerton
A2 Redcar	B2 Malton	C2 Richmond
A3 Saltburn	B3 Whitby	C3 Reeth
A4 Skelton	B4 Danby	C4 Hawes
A5 Guisborough	B5 Lythe	C5 Leyburn
A6 Loftus	B6 Robin Hoods Bay	C6 Masham
A7 Thornaby	B7 Scalby	C7 Bedale
A8 Yarm	B8 Snainton	C8 Thirsk
A9 Stokesley	B9 Pickering	C9 Easingwold
	B10 Kirbkymoorside	
	B11 Hovingham	
	B12 Helmsley	

There was a national decision made, in January 1948 that the rank structure would be different to that of the National Fire Service and this caused some confusion amongst the members for some time. At Scarborough, the divisional officer (DO) would be Mr A Robinson. The officer in charge of Scarborough station would be Station Officer (StnO) Mr J Gill. There would be two sub-officers (SubO), four leading firemen (Lfm), 28 firemen and two temporary firemen.

There were to be two whole-time pumps and one part-time retained pump based at Scarborough, plus the turntable ladder (TL). The pumps were unchanged from the National Fire Service ones – the old 1934 Leyland that was based there before the war, the converted front mounted Austin towing vehicle, a Fordson, the salvage van and of course the turntable ladder which had been delivered in 1943. They were all eventually painted red instead of the National Fire Service grey livery.

RADIO CONTROL ROOM

A wireless system was installed, giving radio contact between brigade headquarters and divisional headquarters plus five mobile contact points, which were the chief fire officer, the assistant chief fire officer plus the divisional officers. The system was rented on an annual maintenance fee, plus installation expenses, from the Secretary of State. It was run in conjunction with, and the co-operation of, the police.

Scarborough was responsible for mobilising pumps for its own area and also that of Scalby and Snainton; there was one control room operator employed, being made up later to six (these posts were filled by people who were registered disabled). The control room men or, when needed, firemen, therefore manned the control room, or watch room as it was known, 24 hours a day.

Two pumps and the turntable ladder attend an incident at the Pavilion Hotel

999

It was about this time that the larger towns in the country adopted the 999 system of dialling, but this had little effect in Scarborough where calls were still connected by the operator. It was to be some years before the local exchange was made automatic. The 999 system had first been introduced in London in 1937 and spread through some of the larger cities before the war delayed further adoption.

This page sponsored by:

GREG'S PLAICE

72 Castle Road – Scarborough – Telephone 01723 353531

NORTH RIDING FIRE BRIGADE

Scarborough station adopted and worked with the new structure for some time before the change over, so that when, on Friday 1st April 1948, the change did occur it made very little difference to the members who carried on very much as before. The station was the same, as were the pumps (the exception in the whole brigade being one self designed pump on a Ford chassis, which had been constructed by firemen). The only notable change in routine was the visit of the Chairman of the Fire Brigade Committee, County Councillor G Cruddas, who paid a visit to all the whole-time stations in the brigade, to wish them well.

1950 Home Office inspection. Note the tin helmets and the Land Rover appliance at the rear left

By December, the new brigade emblem used on cap badges, buttons etc. was adopted; it was to be the Yorkshire rose. There were also a thousand surplus stock uniforms purchased from the Home Office.

The first Christmas served by the brigade was a busy one, as a fire broke out at Wykeham Abbey timber store on Christmas Day. At first the Abbey staff tried to contain it, but eventually conceded defeat and called for the fire brigade. There were two pumps sent from Scarborough and one from Snainton; the crews of the machines said that the flames could be seen as they got to the top of Racecourse Road. One thousand pounds worth of damage was caused to the building and the timber inside it. Only four minutes after the Scarborough pumps had left the station another call was received to a chimney fire, which the retained crew had to handle.

In the first twelve months of the North Riding Fire Brigade, Scarborough handled 191 calls of which 33 were special service calls, that is incidents not involving fire, and 27 false alarms. By the time Chief Fire Officer Corbrick made his first annual report to the council, Scarborough had been awarded a trophy for being the most efficient whole-time and part-time station in the Brigade, an award that was to return to Scarborough on many occasions throughout the North Riding lifetime.

POST WAR AFS
The government realised that it would be prudent to retain the firefighting knowledge and abilities gained throughout the war, as they looked to the post-war structure of the fire brigade, especially in light of the growing cold war with Russia and the fears of nuclear war.

An enlistment campaign was held throughout the country to provide a civilian emergency protection group, with the first local enrolments taking place on the 1st December 1949. The funding was as before, with 75 per cent of costs to be provided for by the government. This time, however, the AFS was not to be involved in local fire brigade activities and were treated as a completely independent section.

UPDATING EQUIPMENT
There were, over the next few years, many changes made to the pumps throughout the county, as old war-time appliances were brought up to standard, many by using surplus Home Office equipment and with grants supplied by them. The Scarborough turntable ladder was fitted with a medium pump unit supplied by the Home Office.

In 1950, the brigade took possession of three Land Rover chassis from the manufacturer and these were adapted to become light fire appliances. One of these was fitted with a 60-gallon tank and coupled to a Scamell Wheelbarrow Pump and hose reel. This machine was then used on many occasions at Olivers Mount motorcycle races and other shows held around the vicinity.

PLAXTONS FIRE ENGINE

It was not until May 1951 that the finances of the brigade would run to buying new purpose built engines. To this end the brigade turned to Scarborough, and it was Plaxtons (the works had been rebuilt after the fire in 1943) who supplied two water tenders with 400 to 500 gallons per minute pumps, built on a Commer chassis. Not surprisingly, the shape of the front of the tenders resembled the Plaxton's 1948 Avenger Coach.

Scarborough station was to receive one of these pumps, in October 1952, with the intention of it moving on to Whitby as soon as a new pump escape could be obtained for Scarborough. In turn the old Leyland pump was moved to Malton.

The Plaxton / Commer water tender

For some reason Plaxtons never went on to become one of the classic fire engine designers, although, with a bit of effort in that direction, they probably could have done so. However, this was not the end of the fire engine building days of Plaxtons as between 1953 and 1959, they produced in excess of 400 Green Goddess fire engines used by the new AFS. Many of these were mothballed in 1969 on the disbanding of the AFS and are still on stand-by, in hangers, in the event of a full-scale civil emergency.

The Home Office stopped supplying uniforms and the North Riding Fire Brigade went into a share scheme with the Durham County and Northumberland Fire Brigades, whereby they could bulk purchase equipment and clothing to gain discounts.

Old style metal helmets used by the National Fire Service were replaced. The new style helmet took on the shape of the original leather and brass helmets popular up to the war; the material they were made from was described as shock proof 'plastic'.

Memories of the disaster that had occurred at Gabriel Wade sawmills during the war were revived when a call was made at noon on 10th October 1951 to the same premises. But with good work by the men involved in the firefighting efforts the damage was confined to the boiler house and the rest of the building hardly suffered.

SPORTS ARENA

In 1949 Ebenezer Baptist Church moved to its present location on Columbus Ravine, leaving behind the site it had occupied on Longwestgate (just past the bottom of Tollergate) since 1776, with the building in question having been built in 1826. Mr T Boothby had converted the former church into a sports arena, where the spectator sport of wrestling had become popular.

On the evening of 20th March 1952, 700 people had enjoyed an evening of wrestling and, at the end of the contests, had left the premises. A few minutes later, whilst

1952 Home Office inspection. Note the 'plastic' helmets

a large number of the audience were still outside talking, it was noticed that the upper windows of the building, where the wrestling had taken place, were totally engulfed in flames.

On the arrival of the fire brigade, entry was made into the building where it was found to be so hot, due to the amount of timber wall and ceiling panels which had burnt readily, that the firefighters were driven back. A request was put in to make pumps five, to include three Scarborough pumps, one Scalby and one Snainton pump, whilst a Malton pump was brought to Scarborough to cover the area in case of any further fire calls.

Divisional Officer Robinson commented to the local *Evening News* '*The fire is roaring around the top storey like a furnace*'. As a result of this eight water jets were set up, including jets covering the roofs of other properties surrounding the fire, in an effort to reduce the risk of fire spread.

Firemen were only allowed to man the jets for five minutes at a time in case they suffered from the effects of the heat which was excessive because the internal timber walls had been coated in highly flammable varnish, which also helped the rapid fire spread. Firefighters on the inside had to use makeshift screens, made out of doors and other items they could find. A further hazard occurred when the roof began to collapse in small sections, showering the men with slates and debris, this proved to be a good indication to the reliability of the new style helmets the men had, as the slates simply bounced off. By the time the fire was brought under control there was little of the old sports arena left, though there was only a minimal amount of damage to the surrounding properties.

BEREAVEMENT
On 20th June 1952 there was the sad loss, from natural causes, of one of the firemen, Mr J Russell, who was a serving fireman and had been part of the Scarborough National Fire Service. He was given a fire brigade funeral on the 25th June.

Fireman Russell's funeral moves along Northway. Alma Terrace can be seen in the background

Towards the end of the year also proved a time of high fatalities, as at 2.25 a.m. on 21st October a night porter at St Mary's Hospital on Dean Road (now the temporary car park) saw smoke coming from the direction of Lower Hope Street, (now part of William Street coach park). The fire brigade was informed and arrived at the incident within a minute of the call, as it was only in the street opposite the station.

When they arrived, they found the corner property of 4A Lower Hope Street well alight; a Mr Batty had already jumped to safety from a first floor window. The firemen were informed that there were three ladies still inside the building. It was difficult to obtain entry as the windows were boarded up due to the fact that the property was awaiting demolition and the fire was seen to be burning on every floor. Entry was eventually forced but the stairway was completely burnt away causing difficulty in gaining access to the upper floors. Fireman Tomblin located a body on the top floor, Divisional Officer Robinson and Sub-Officer Hunt discovering two more bodies, one in another room on the top floor and the other in a first floor room, soon after. All were declared dead at the scene of the fire. They were Mrs E Ward (63), Mrs W Fenton (67) and Miss H Eden (48).

Two pumps had been mobilised initially with a further two following on, but the fire took until 5.15 a.m. to extinguish. At one point, rumours spread that there were two children unaccounted for but Mr Batty confirmed that there had been no children inside allaying these fears.

The premises had been condemned in 1938 as part of the ongoing improvements to the area that were taking place pre-war and were purchased by the council in 1950; Mr Batty who had lived there for 22 years was awaiting the council to re-house him. The property at one time had been the Wheatsheaf public house and then the Oxford Club. The council demolished the premises soon after the fire due to their dangerous state. It was presumed that children storing rubbish against the back door in preparation for Bonfire Night was the main cause of the fire.

These deaths were followed in November by Mr F Postill (63) at Brook Street, found dead due to burns. Mrs R Beaumont (67) at Filey Road died in a fire. Mr G Hirst was rescued from a fire in Garfield Road, only to die a few weeks later on the 3rd December.

On the same day another fire claimed a life in Auborough Street where Fireman Newton recovered the body of Miss Howe (70) and Leading-Fireman Dawson rescued Mr J Roberts, a partly deaf and blind man, from a fire started by a gas stove.

In a 44 day period eight deaths had occurred in Scarborough due to fire.

GREAT GALES

The weekend of 31st January and 1st February 1953 saw some of the worst gales to hit Great Britain in living memory with over 300 lives lost in collapses or floods. In Scarborough, firemen were called to numerous occurrences including one to the burnt out shell of the Sports Arena on Longwestgate, when the walls collapsed into the roadway, shaking houses around the vicinity and causing the premises of number 10 to be evacuated for the occupiers' safety. Other calls were to make safe television aerials, chimney pots and stacks, and the pumping out of basements in both domestic and commercial properties. There was over £50,000 worth of damage caused and the council alone needed £35,000 from its private insurance fund, set up in 1921, to carry out repairs, which included repairs to 600 corporation houses.

VOLUNTEERS

Lincolnshire, being flatter, had suffered far more from the gales than Yorkshire and the services were finding it difficult to cope; volunteers were requested to help out in that location. Two pumping crews from Scarborough were raised and on the 11th February joined a convoy of support formed from the North Riding and other brigades at

The Land Rover appliance leads the convoy to Lincoln

Scotch Corner. Snow blizzards were sweeping the north by then and many small accidents occurred en route.

On arrival, the North Riding contingent was based at Lincoln, and two watches were set up to allow pumping to take place 24 hours a day; they then moved onto Mablethorpe on the 17th. When it was time for the convoy to return home, it was discovered that the Land Rover appliance used by North Riding was extremely beneficial as the heavier wagons were bogged down and needed to be extracted from the mud by the smaller appliance. Much embarrassment was caused to crews from the larger machines, who had at first belittled the North Riding appliance. The volunteers returned home late on the evening of 19th February.

NEW CHIEF

1954 got off to a bad start for the brigade when Chief Fire Officer Corbrick, who, after building up the brigade on a shoestring budget, found the pressure too great and suffered a heart attack and died on 3rd January. The Deputy Chief Fire Officer Mr C Outhwaite, replaced him officially on the 1st March.

Later the same year, the first new machine to be officially allocated to Scarborough by the North Riding Fire Brigade was delivered; it was a Dennis F8 Pump Escape (PE) at a cost of £3,270. The Plaxtons built machine then moved to Whitby.

The station had to undergo alterations as the doorways to the appliance rooms were widened to allow easier access for the bigger appliances: this meant that the characteristic archways at the front of the building disappeared. The watch-room was also altered at this time – the gas burner that had been kept alight since the opening of the station (to provide ignition for the steam fire engine) was put out and removed. Also, to improve the facilities for the AFS in 1956, two rooms over Scalby fire station were adapted into lecture and recreation rooms.

CFO Outhwaite

BEST IN BRITAIN

A quiz team lead by Leading Fireman J Cowen was slowly progressing through various stages of the national fire brigade quiz, until, on 29th March 1958, they were in the final at the Fire Service College, Dorking. The event was organised by the Fire Service Research and Training Trust. Four teams made the final where Scarborough obtained 39 points; easily beating second placed Norfolk, and also Bristol and Manchester.

Scarborough's team of Leading Fireman Cowen and Firemen K Andrews, L Russell, W Locke and C Waggitt were the first northern team ever to win the contest.

NEW DEPUTY & DIVISONAL OFFICER

Divisional Officer Arthur Robinson was promoted to Deputy Chief Fire Officer, on 1st May 1958, and Mr Fred Stephenson filled his place.

Mr Stephenson had joined the AFS at Scarborough in 1938 and, on formation of the National Fire Service, he was posted as a member of the overseas firefighting contingent. Eventually, on the formation of the County Brigades in 1948, he joined the Middlesbrough County Borough Brigade, and was promoted to Assistant Divisional Officer in Sheffield Fire Brigade before returning to Middlesbrough as Deputy Chief Fire Officer.

In 1959, Scarborough was yet again issued with another machine which, whilst new to the brigade, was in fact a second hand 1951 Dennis F7 Pump Escape which had just been purchased from ICI Wilton for £1,904.

The Dennis tender outside Throxenby Hall

By April 1960, the workload for the officer-in-charge of the station was increased to such an extent that another Station Officer was set on to work along side Station Officer Gill, this being Station Officer J Cowen who had worked his way through the ranks at Scarborough.

THE BALMORAL

November 5th for the duty watch in 1963 certainly meant that there were plenty of fires to watch. At the Balmoral Hotel in Westborough (now the site of the Balmoral Centre) a lady who was residing at the hotel, whilst attending an hotelier's convention in Scarborough, was woken by the smell of burning at about 4 a.m. On investigation she found that the staircase was brightly lit by fire and the fire brigade was called. As the firemen left the station the fire could be clearly seen and the officer-in-charge asked for four pumps to be sent, as well as the turntable ladder. These were Scarborough's three pumps plus one from Snainton. Later, another pump was sent from Filey, whilst fire crews from Malton stood by at Scarborough station.

Every available ladder was used to remove the 54 people who were trapped and unable to get out of the building because of the thick smoke. It actually took fifteen minutes to evacuate the building. The fire was mainly confined to a newly refurbished bar that had only been reopened earlier that year (the opening being conducted by Freddy Trueman, the famous cricketer).

Pumps and the turntable ladder outside the Balmoral Hotel – Westborough

Policemen drove cars out of the hotel car park, which was accessed by a tunnel that ran through the centre of the hotel at ground floor level. The position of the bar was also at ground floor with a central atrium extending up through the centre of the building, this was the cause of the severe amount of smoke spreading. After the fire was put out it only took a further hour to clear the building of smoke and then re-house the visitors in other rooms that had not been touched by the fire or smoke. Damage amounted to around £10,000. Ironically, part of the theme of the hoteliers' convention was fire prevention, or lack of it, in hotels.

ALTERATIONS TO STATION

At the end of January 1964, Deputy Chief Fire Officer Robinson retired (he died in 1971). Divisional Officer Stephenson was promoted to Deputy Chief Fire Officer whilst Station Officer Gill superseded him, in turn his position being filled by Mr W Boyle, from West Riding Fire Brigade.

The fire station was altered in 1964 with £19,540 being spent on the refurbishment. Two pump bays, with a dormitory over, were created in the area next door to the station, which had only been used for parking and as an entrance to Simpson's Garage.

The station also received a new Bedford J5 HCB Angus water tender costing £3000. This was the first of the Bedford pumps, which the brigade had been buying since 1955, to come to Scarborough.

The shell of the new extension to the fire station

The extension to the station allowed more space for the fire prevention section to be handled at a local level and another station officer post was created for this. Station Officer Pepper was promoted internally to this position. Also Station Officer Cowen transferred to the Staffordshire Fire Brigade, his place being filled by Station Officer Copley, from Wakefield. Because of increased workload, a new post was created in each division that of assistant divisional officer, Mr Steeples from Lincolnshire becoming the first of this rank in B Division.

CLUB AND INSTITUTE

At 12.30 a.m. on 22nd September 1966, someone ran into the cafe in the railway shops, (now Burger House) Westborough to raise the alarm of a fire in the Working Men's Club opposite. The proprietor rang for the fire brigade, then, armed with an extinguisher, ran to the blaze. He saw the staircase was alight, and he could see the steward, Mr Joe Burke, shouting from the top window. As he tried to enter the building he was beaten back by the intense heat and could see no way of rescuing the steward.

As the fire brigade arrived the entire roof collapsed, showering sparks and flames everywhere. The firemen's first action was to raise an escape ladder to where the steward had been last seen. Before the ladder was in position, Mr Burke came staggering out of the passage dividing the club from the Victoria Hotel (now The Old Vic). Somehow he had managed to reach an external fire escape at the rear of the club and make good his escape.

A Bedford water tender at drills on the harbour

Flames were belching through the open area that was once the roof and, as a precaution, the residents in surrounding properties were evacuated. Divisional Officer Gill said that it took over an hour before the fire was under control. After three hours of firefighting, the turntable ladder and one pump returned to the station, whilst the other two pumps stayed on the fire ground all night. A happier side to the job was that the firemen managed to rescue a spaniel that had been trapped on the top floor, and whilst it was in a bad state, it did recover.

The building was classed as a write-off as the entire staircase and the top two floors were gutted, but, with some sensitive design and building work, the whole of the interior was removed, leaving the shell intact, before a brand new interior was rebuilt. The facade was cleaned to its original state; the interior was now a well designed entertainment complex.

SALISBURY HOTEL

Just three weeks later, on 14th October, at the Salisbury Hotel, Huntriss Row (now the Salisbury Arcade), another incident occurred when, half an hour after closing, a fire was discovered. The entire ground floor was ablaze and the building was heavily smoke-logged. When the firemen arrived they were told of a mother and son still inside the building. Firemen wearing breathing apparatus went in to search and eventually brought them out to safety.

One tale from this incident is that a fireman who could not find a breathing apparatus partner (policy is that a minimum of two men work together in breathing apparatus) tied a rope around himself and told another fireman to pull him out if he thought he was in trouble. After he had been inside for a few minutes the fireman on the outside felt the rope being continually tugged (a distress signal) so he started to pull on the rope, enlisting others to help. The fireman inside knew nothing of this until he was pulled off his feet and dragged backwards at a rapid rate. In his desperation he clung onto anything to steady himself, emerging from the fire holding on tightly to a table and chair. The resulting damage caused by the conflagration came to £4,000.

Mr Gill

AFS DISBANDED

The 31st March 1968 saw the disbanding of the AFS, as the Government saw no need for a peacetime civil defence force. In Scarborough, this meant 1 AFS sub-officer, 2 AFS leading firemen, 12 AFS firemen, 1 AFS leading firewoman, 2 AFS firewomen leaving the service. The next day saw the formulation of the Teeside

Fire Brigade as Middlesbrough and surrounding areas amalgamated. This left the North Riding without Grangetown, Redcar, Thornaby, and Stokesley. This period also saw the adoption of the North Riding Fire Brigade committee into the Civil Protection Committee.

Part of the changeover saw the return to Scarborough of its former pump, but not to be on the run. The old steam engine was returned along with a manual pump. The steamer was cleaned and put on display before being donated to the Council who displayed it at a museum in St Thomas's Church (now the Sea Cadets headquarters). When the museum closed, the pump was taken to Londesborough Lodge, dismantled and stored, where it remains today.

A new turntable ladder was delivered in 1968 to replace the old one, which had now seen better days. The new one was an AEC Mercury/Merryweather 100 foot ladder costing £13900. Two new pumps were also delivered, both Bedford TK – HCB Angus, one pump escape costing £6500 and one water tender costing £5000. The turntable ladder was the last fire appliance to be issued to Scarborough with a fire bell, as the new two-tone sirens were becoming popular and more effective.

CHANGES
There was a change of policy in the management of the station in 1969 as Assistant Divisional Officer Steeples was appointed officer-in-charge of the station in conjunction with his other existing duties. Station Officer Copley transferred to Barnsley Fire Brigade and Station Officer Pepper went to Teeside, their places being taken by Mr C Cowie, from South Shields Fire Brigade, and Mr D Christian respectively.

Station Officer Cowie had a warm initiation to Scarborough on Sunday 16th March with a fire at the newly refurbished Rowntrees' Grocers, corner of Westborough and Vernon Road (now the Card Store). At 11.48 a.m, flames were seen to be issuing from the first floor windows, so three pumps and the turntable ladder were dispatched from Scarborough Station.

Due to a very strong wind feeding the fire sending the flames spreading up through a central stairwell like a chimney, two more pumps were needed. These were brought in from Snainton and Filey; the brigade remained at the fire for nine hours before it was extinguished. The building was completely rebuilt after the fire (the upper part of the original building was the site of Scarborough's first telephone exchange, from 1899 to 1910. The rear part of the building was the site of an early fire engine house).

The 1st April 1969 saw the retirement of Chief Fire Officer Outhwaite, replaced by Deputy Chief Fire Officer Stephenson.

Rowntrees blaze seen from Vernon Road

Further moves followed in November, when Divisional Officer Gill retired, being replaced by Assistant Divisional Officer Steeples and in turn his place filled by Mr R Mohun, from Staffordshire Fire Brigade. 1970 saw Fire Prevention Station Officer Christian transfer to Cardiff City Fire Brigade, being replaced by Mr G Jones from Warwickshire Fire Brigade. In October, Divisional Officer Steeples transferred to Bath City Fire Brigade as Chief Fire Officer. Mr P Hooper from Warwickshire Fire Brigade filled his post.

The restructuring of North Riding Fire Brigade proceeded as Assistant Divisional Officer Mohun was promoted to headquarters at Northallerton and Mr G Mepham, from A Division, became assistant divisional officer in 1971. The fire prevention department was expanding and in 1972 Station Officer Jones transferred to Bath City Fire Brigade and was replaced by Station Officer D Deaves, from Northallerton headquarters, who became assistant divisional officer in charge of fire prevention when his position was upgraded two months later.

The brigade reformed the call out facilities and, in January 1972, Scarborough became the last station in the brigade to transfer over to the VFA system 'A' call-out. This meant that calls were handled at Northallerton, who were then responsible for turning out the Scarborough pumps, and the demise of the need for local watch-

A Bedford escape pump, Scarborough's last wheeled escape

room men. The retained firefighters could also be called out by means of personal alerters activated at Northallerton. This brought to an end the need for the public fire sirens, which had previously called them to the station when needed, (this also saw an end to the sirens public testing every Monday lunch time).

Two further Bedford pumps were purchased a pump escape and a water tender, in 1971 and 1972 respectively, costing £6000 and £7000. After service in Scarborough, the 1972 purchase moved to Malton, then Pickering and ended in the reserve fleet. It was then donated to Addis Ababa in 1989 in a 'Fire Aid' appeal, when fire authorities were asked to contribute to third world countries. Addis Ababa gifted a set of chairs and a carpet (now in Scarborough Library) in appreciation of the donation.

SILVER GRID
A similar incident to the Salisbury Hotel fire occurred in the premises next door, the Silver Grid (now the Pizza Hut), on 22nd November 1972. From his beat in Westborough, Police Constable Robinson saw smoke issuing from the upper floors of the building and radioed for the fire brigade before ringing the doorbell, to which one person responded.

On arrival, the firemen were informed that a woman and child were still inside; the turntable ladder was set up and a rescue of the two was easily made. The location of the seat of the fire proved more difficult as it took 45 minutes to discover. The fire, which had started in the basement, had spread through four floors and out through the roof of the building.

The licensee was on holiday at the time and it was his parents, Mr and Mrs Metherham, from Doncaster, who were in the premises with their granddaughter. They stated that there was no sign of fire when they retired to bed at 12.30 a.m.

NEW CHIEF
As county boundaries were changing, county, borough and city brigades were to disappear, merging into larger county brigades. With this in mind Chief Fire Officer Stephenson retired (he died in 1996) giving the new Chief Fire Officer, Mr P Brennan (from West Riding Fire Brigade) a chance to settle into the job before the changes came into effect.

The AEC – Merryweather turntable ladder

NORTH YORKSHIRE FIRE BRIGADE

Reorganisation of political boundaries and rationalisation of fire brigades throughout Great Britain saw the 147 county and county borough brigades for England and Wales decreased to 54. North Riding Fire Brigade ceased to exist on 1st April 1974 replaced by the larger North Yorkshire Fire Brigade (NYFB). This new brigade took in all of the old North Riding, parts of the East and West Riding Brigades and the York City Fire Brigade. Mr Brennan the Chief Fire Officer of the old brigade took the helm of the new one.

There were four divisions, A, B, C and D, with Scarborough, as the headquarters of B division, directly responsible for the running of Filey, Sherburn and Snainton stations.

The stations and their allocated numbers were:

A1 Harrogate	B1 Scarborough	C1 Richmond
A2 Bentham	B2 Danby	C2 Bedale
A3 Boroughbridge	B3 Filey	C3 Hawes
A4 Knaresborough	B4 Helmsley	C4 Leyburn
A5 Masham	B5 Kirkbymoorside	C5 Northallerton
A6 Ripon	B6 Lythe	C6 Reeth
A7 Settle	B7 Malton	C7 Stokesley
A8 Skipton	B8 Pickering	C8 Thirsk
A9 Summerbridge	B9 Robin Hoods Bay	
	B10 Sherburn	
	B11 Snainton	
	B12 Whitby	

D1 York
D2 Easingwold
D3*
D4 Selby
D5 Tadcaster

* D3 was allocated to Acomb Fire Station opened in 1979

Divisional Officer Hooper remained the divisional officer at Scarborough, with his assistant Assistant Divisional Officer Mepham. Station Officer Cowie, however, was promoted to assistant divisional officer, in charge of Scarborough Fire Station, whilst Station Officer Boyle was transferred to Whitby as station officer in charge.

There were still three shifts on station but the working hours were soon to be reduced from 56 to 48 hours a week as soon as manning would allow. The officers-in-charge of the shifts, Red Watch – Des Ware, White Watch – Pete Atkinson and Blue Watch – Derek Oldcorn were promoted to station officers. There was one sub-officer, one leading fireman and eleven firemen to each shift, with the intention of raising the number of firemen to thirteen to cover the reduction in hours.

One of the earlier incidents to be handled by the North Yorkshire Fire Brigade was a sign of the new type of techniques firemen were having to adopt. A routine turn out was made to a job at McCains, frozen foods factory, Havers Hill, Eastfield, on 6th January 1975, where a pipe carrying ammonia had sprung a leak. Fire brigade personnel were required to go in and turn off a valve, they wore full firefighting kit and breathing apparatus, and carried a hose reel to spray water, to which the ammonia is attracted. Fireman Colin Haycock was unlucky enough to get the ammonia over his legs and whilst it was not immediately obvious to him, he suffered ammonia burns. By the time he removed his clothes he was in agony, and the accident resulted in a twelve month period off work whilst he recovered from the burns. As a direct result of this chemical splash suits, which cover the whole body, were issued for use at any such incidents, followed soon after by the type of gas-tight suits worn today.

THE OLYMPIA

North Yorkshire Fire Brigade's first large fire at Scarborough was the Olympia on Foreshore Road, it was discovered at 11.40 p.m. on 28th July 1975. Two pumps and the turntable ladder were sent out. Sub-Officer Ian Wilkie was in charge of the first pump and Leading Fireman William Crawford in charge of the second. Whilst proceeding to the incident, a bright glow could be seen through the gap in Merchants Row, and by the time they had turned the corner onto Foreshore Road, flames were extending high into the night sky. Sub-Officer Wilkie made pumps three, followed soon after, by making pumps four.

It was evident that the main part of the building, leased to Henry Marshall as a children's indoor entertainment complex, was already lost. Therefore the

The Olympia blaze

priority was to protect the surrounding properties, including the Grand Hotel to the rear, the Windmill amusement arcade to one side and, across the gardens on the other side, the Futurist buildings. To facilitate this, the first pumps to arrive were put into running out hose from the hydrants along the Foreshore.

Divisional Officer Hooper arrived and took charge of the job and made pumps six. Two Filey pumps and the Snainton pump were set into hydrants on St Nicholas Cliff and St Nicholas Street area and attacked the fire from behind. One of the Filey crew remarked that as they were leaving Filey their officer-in-charge asked if anyone knew where the Olympia was. He was told to look towards

Firemen Coopland, Shannon and Westwood close in on the Olympia

Scarborough and just follow the glow that they could see.

At the foot of McBeans Steps was the old rocket station tower, built as the original call out system for the local lifeboat. A team of firemen were put on saving this historic building and spent many hours covering it with water. Much to their chagrin, only a few days later, the council on cleaning up the site had the tower demolished without a second thought.

Some shops facading the building were saved sufficiently to allow the owners in to recover any valuables salvageable on the following day, but these were also demolished soon after; these included gift shops owned by Councillor Charles Hall, Mr Messenger and Pacitto's ice cream parlour. At the other side of the building was a block of public toilets which were saved and many years after they were revamped into a set of super-loos.

Luckily, on the night, it was quite calm and what wind there was, was not blowing towards the Grand Hotel, which was one of the main concerns of the firemen. At the Futurist buildings, their staff had been set-to with hose reels dousing the walls down, as the heat was so intense that they were afraid of convected combustion.

Control of the fire was eventually gained at 3 a.m. and it was almost out by 6 a.m., though there were firemen present on the site all that day and throughout the following night. At the height

The burnt out shell of the Olympia the morning after

of the fire, there were pumps from Sherburn and Robin Hoods Bay on stand-by at Scarborough station in case of any other emergency calls being received.

Though the start of the fire was never attributed to any definite cause it is believed that the fire started inside the cafe area of the building. Estimated cost of the fire was placed at £750,000 and the council used the money recovered through insurance towards the redevelopment of the Spa complex. They then sold off the Olympia site for private development into the present Olympia Complex.

Originally, the building had been erected in 1895 as a fisheries and marine exhibition, in the gardens of J W Woodall, the founder of the old Volunteer Fire Brigade and member of the fire sub-committee of which he became chairman in the mid to late 1800's. At the time it was built, it was the largest covered hall in the town, and over the years had many uses including being a production area for Plaxtons in World War One, where they manufactured munition boxes. It holds fond memories for many local people as a dance hall, and people still remember the Dancing Waters show held there, along with various exhibitions. In the years prior to its destruction, it had been used as an amusement arcade and cinema.

LONG HOT SUMMER

Divisional Officer Hooper retired in 1976 (his death occurred in September 1991) and was replaced by Divisional Officer Stowe. His first major job in the division was in the summer of 1976 when the extremely dry weather took its toll on the moors around Rosedale. There was a fire which necessitated a continual presence of firemen, forestry workers, National Park wardens and even the military (at the worst of the blaze) for many months, as it stubbornly refused to go out, due to it being deep set into the peat-type ground. In this period, there was a 24 hours a day presence of Scarborough firemen, both full- and part-time, along with firemen from as far afield as York and Harrogate, all under the overall control of Divisional Officer Stowe. At one point the shortage of machinery resulted in two of the Home Office reserve 'Green Goddess' fire engines being brought into use.

On 1st October 1977 Chief Fire Officer Brennan retired and was replaced by Mr RT Ford (45), previously deputy chief fire officer of Staffordshire Fire Brigade. The following ten years can arguably be described as the most progressive years in the change of firefighting in Scarborough since the turn of the century when the station was built, a steam engine introduced and a whole-time engineer employed.

There were three new Bedford tenders placed on the station at Scarborough, whilst the old ones were sent out to the surrounding retained area. Before any of the new policies could be brought into existence there was a threat of a national strike looming. After continual enquiries into the running of the fire brigades, all of which came out in favour of substantial pay rises for firemen, the Labour government of the day placed a pay restriction on the country after promising the fire brigade a good pay deal. Threat of strike locally was met with mixed feelings because the firemen believed there was no way the government could let the fire brigade go on strike.

CFO Ford

COOPLANDS

On 9th November 1977, only five days before the strike was to begin, a fire occurred at Cooplands Bakery on Londesborough Road (now the site of individual units on the Londesborough Road Trading Estate). Most of the complex was destroyed in an all night battle which required four pumps to quell the flames. Sub-Officer Summers was the first officer at the incident followed by Assistant Divisional Officer Deaves who took overall responsibility. There was an estimated £50,000 worth of damage, £30,000 being in foodstuffs. In an adjacent building there was £100,000 worth of machinery, and whilst the flames did breach the wall, the fire was kept away from this.

There were six jets of water used on the fire, which was fought from both ends of the building, and it took the firemen forty minutes to bring the fire under control, but even then there was a danger of it erupting again. By

An Angus water tender

3.30 a.m. it seemed the fire was almost out and the firefighters could start to relax when another fire call came through, sending the Scarborough crews racing to McCain frozen foods factory at Eastfield, where a store keeper had seen smoke coming from the dry store.

By the time they arrived the 150 strong night shift workforce had been evacuated and the sprinkler system was activated, the McCains private fire brigade were in action using their own breathing apparatus and containing the flames until the regular firemen could get at the fire. An estimated £20,000 worth of damage was caused. The fact that two large fires could occur so close to each other was proving ominous signs of warning for the strike, which was looming.

FIREMEN'S NATIONAL STRIKE

At 9 a.m. on 14th November 1977 White Watch finished their tour of duty and, after a parade where there was no on-coming watch to take over duty from them, they walked to the bottom of the fire station yard. There they were joined by members from the other two shifts on the car park, at the site of the old police station, as a show of strength against the Government.

They left behind an empty fire station, the first time in over 75 years that the station had not been the hub of firefighting operations for Scarborough. The only people to defy the call out were a handful of officers all above the rank of station officer and one leading fireman, Walter Leeman, who found his conscience would not let him strike so he decided to take early retirement in this period.

The officers changed their place of work to the Burniston Road Army Barracks (now the site of a housing development) where there was an Army Green Goddess fire engine and a truck with a trailer pump sited. These fire appliances were supplied by the Home Office from the stocks of equipment mothballed throughout the country after the disbanding of the post war Auxiliary Fire Service, the purpose of which was to ensure availability in the event of civil disturbance or war. To man these appliances, there was a team of twenty inexperienced firefighters made up of soldiers from the 7th Royal Horse Artillery under the command of Major I Fowler. They were to be advised at fires by the officers who had not gone on strike.

The soldiers handled numerous calls to small fires as the strike continued, until, on the evening of 15th December, a fire broke out at Alexandra Laundry, in Printing House Square, just off Columbus Ravine. Mr R Cox, a mechanic from the adjoining Grand Garage, saw flames at Alexander Laundry from his home in Columbus Ravine

A green goddess fire appliance in use at Scarborough

and raised the alarm. Initially, the Green Goddess and the truck with a trailer pump were mobilised, these were followed by the pumps from Filey, Sherburn and Snainton manned by part-time firemen who were not supporting the strike.

There were a large number of onlookers, many giving a hand to man the hoses and remove items from the building. Vehicles, including two Red Cross Ambulances, ten cars and a caravan were removed from the lock up garages belonging to the laundry and rented by the Grand Garage. Mr T Martin, a director of the garage, had a lucky escape when he was rescuing documents from part of the building that was directly linked to the laundry. A large section of roof fell in, close to where he was standing, bringing down the door and frame and bursting hose that was laid throughout the area.

Amongst the onlookers were a number of striking firemen with very mixed emotions, to whom the obvious inexperience of the army firefighters was apparent, as their method of fighting fire was to stand outside and throw water at it. At the height of the fire one of the striking firemen went through the lines, much to the annoyance of the officer in charge, to advise an army fire team with a hose that they were in danger of a wall collapsing on them. They pulled back and a matter of minutes later, the wall collapsed where they had been standing, causing a moment of panic as two of the army crew were unaccounted for. The soldiers were eventually found in another area of the fireground. Sergeant G Cheesman suffered the only injury at the job, when a falling brick hit him on the leg.

It was an hour before the blaze was brought under control and it was feared at one point that it might spread into Dennis's printers on the other side of the square. A convoy of three Green Goddesses, a truck and a Land Rover were dispatched from York, arriving in Scarborough at 9 a.m. but by this time their services were not required.

Over 20,000 articles of clothing were lost in the fire, with the total damage being estimated at £300,000. The building, which had originally opened in 1913, remained derelict until it was totally destroyed some time later in yet another fire. After this incident, Scarborough was supplied with another Green Goddess, from Topcliffe Barracks, and an extra 24 soldiers.

It was not until 16th January 1978, after nine weeks of strike, that the firemen returned to work when, ironically, White Watch, who were the last watch on duty before the strike, were the first watch back on duty at 9 a.m. By lunchtime, the turntable ladder and one of the pumps were back on the run after undergoing tests and by the end of the day shift, the whole of the turn out facilities were back in the hands of the firemen.

Major Fowler went on to become a Brigadier, and the British Attaché in Washington.

SCARBOROUGH'S EMERGENCY TENDER

One of the first effects of Chief Fire Officer Ford's policies was the introduction, in 1978, of Scarborough's first Emergency Tender (ET). This type of machine is used mainly for attendance at road traffic accidents, chemical incidents, when additional lighting is required and/or large amounts of breathing apparatus needed.

Scarborough's first emergency tender, an unusual feature of it was its yellow livery

Scarborough received an old emergency tender that had done much duty elsewhere in the brigade (it had originally been the first emergency tender bought by the North Riding Fire Brigade and stationed at Northallerton in 1968). However this was a great improvement on not having one at all. The turn out area of the machine was as far north as Scaling Dam, south past the Dotterel Inn and inland to Malton.

Divisional Officer Stowe moved to York for promotion to be replaced, for a short while, by Divisional Officer Howcroft. The uniforms and firefighting kit were vastly improved over this period, the most noticeable difference to the general public being the change of colour from black to yellow of

The emergency tender at an incident in Roscoe Street

the fire helmets and wet legs (the waterproof over trousers worn at incidents) and new NATO type pullovers were introduced.

As a direct result of the strike, there was a reduction in working hours to 42 hours per week, so to accommodate this system, a whole new shift had to be introduced and sufficient men trained to make the numbers up. Chief Fire Officer Ford's reaction to this was to create North Yorkshire Fire Brigade's own training school at Ripon as, in the past, the brigade had paid other brigades (mainly Durham and West Yorkshire) to do the training. The knock on effect of this was that, once the school was founded, many other courses were run from there.

GREEN WATCH

On 1st April 1979 Green Watch was born, the Officer in Charge being Station Officer Wilkie with Sub-Officer Temple as his assistant, plus three Leading Firemen and eleven firemen. Divisional Officer Howcroft moved on to Northallerton (he died in October 1993) and was replaced by Divisional Officer John Simpson.

The 1971 Fire Prevention Act was starting to take effect at station level with the first phase affecting hotels, boarding houses and any other fire-certificated buildings which all had now to be inspected on an annual basis by the Fire Brigade. This put a heavy workload on the

1982 Home Office inspection. Members of Green Watch receiving commendations

station due to there being so many hotels and boarding houses in the town.

There were further replacements of the Scarborough machines and the first of the engines designed to the brigade's own specification was delivered. The specifications included reinforcement of the cabs. One of the machines was soon transferred to service in Whitby because of the design of a narrower wheelbase made it ideal for their many small and narrow streets. In 1980, the old emergency tender was replaced with a new Ford Transit emergency tender.

Green Watch encountered one of its first difficult jobs on 30th April 1982, when they were called to a house fire in Hoxton Road. A small child was still in the house

Two Scarborough Water Ladders

and, with great difficulty, the crew managed to make entries at the front and rear of the building. At one point two firemen manhandled a ladder (one which needs four men to carry and erect it) around a small passage and erected it themselves, and this was the means by which the child was rescued. This action resulted in the shift being awarded a written commendation from Chief Fire Officer Ford.

YORK MINSTER

A fire of some significance to the North Yorkshire Fire Brigade was the York Minster fire which occurred at 2.30 a.m. on 9th July 1984, and, whilst not a Scarborough fire, it was attended by Scarborough's turntable ladder with Leading Fireman K Hudson and Fireman K Morgan. Scarborough fire engines were transferred to York to stand-by for any other calls which might be made in that area, whilst the Scarborough and Filey retained stood-by at Scarborough. There were twenty pumps utilised at the job, three turntable ladders, an emergency tender, one foam/salvage tender and a control unit.

Due to the dry timbers in the roof void the fire soon had a good hold, before the arrival of the fire brigade. Firemen had great difficulty in reaching the blaze due to the tight internal winding staircases up to the roof void. Turntable ladders were used to get several water jets to work on the roof, whilst one turntable ladder provided a continual curtain of water on the famous Rose Window. At the height of the fire, the roof of the transept was allowed to collapse to prevent the fire spreading to the central tower and to enable the firefighting to be performed at floor level.

The fire was contained within this area and, in recognition of saving the rest of the Minster the Archbishop of York awarded the fire brigade the Cross of St William (replicas of this can now be seen on the jackets of all North Yorkshire Fire Brigade firefighters and officers). The brigade is one of only two brigades in the whole country that is allowed an addition to its uniform, Royal Berkshire being the other who wears a royal award.

Lightning storms over York were put down to be the most probable cause of the fire. Chief Fire Officer Ford was awarded the OBE in the New Years Honour's List of 1985 for his contribution to firefighting, and this incident must have had some bearing towards that.

From a picture displayed at all North Yorkshire fire stations that attended the York Minster fire

Chief Fire Officer Ford wanted to see Scarborough with a new station as the old one was antiquated and inadequate for modern firefighting means. To this end, he looked at various sites around the town, including Seamer Road at the junction with Queen Margaret's Road – now MKM Builders merchants, Columbus Ravine at the site of the old Central School entrance – now Kwikfit motor repairs, and Woodlands Drive – now the site of Quakers

Close. There were problems with the Borough Council at all of these sites and, after years of haggling, it became clear that the only way forward was to redevelop the existing site. This was a major project in as much that, since no other premises were available, the building work had to go on around the existing station, which had to remain fully operational at all times. The new development would include bays for six fire engines. Four bays could be accessed from the yard at the rear of the station therefore saving appliances from having to be backed into the station from North Marine Road, which with the increase of traffic over the years was becoming quite a hazardous task. There would be a proper lecture and demonstration room, a new tower away from the main building and a breathing apparatus training complex. Tenders were put out and Shepherd Construction Ltd of York won the contract, the cost being just short of three quarters of a million pounds.

In October 1986, Assistant Divisional Officer Cowie was transferred to Malton fire station and was replaced by Assistant Divisional Officer Holiday (his father had been part of the original Scarborough Fire Brigade just before the outbreak of war).

CASTLE HOTEL
At just past 6.30 on Bonfire Night 1986 a fire was reported at the Castle Hotel, Queen Street, a large hotel that was undergoing major repairs at the time, and two pumps and the turntable ladder were sent, with Station Officer Paul Lewis in charge. By the time the first machine arrived, flames were seen coming from all the windows along the first floor of the building. Station Officer Lewis made pumps four, (one pump from Scarborough retained and one pump from Filey were mobilised), meanwhile two firemen in breathing apparatus entered through the main doorway with hose, where they found the main staircase in front of them was well alight and burning furiously.

A further jet was taken through the archway to the rear of the building and a metal fire escape was utilised to reach the first floor. By this time Assistant Divisional Officer Homer had arrived and taken charge of the job. He made pumps six (being the three Scarborough pumps, two Filey and one Sherburn) and requested the emergency tender. There was also a control unit mobilised from Ripon for improved communications and a salvage tender from Tadcaster for better lighting of the area. The turntable ladder was set to work as a water tower as by this time the fire was spreading rapidly and further jets were put to work off ladders at first floor level.

Cottages through the arch to the rear of the premises were evacuated in case the fire spread. Later, the residents were allowed to return as the fire was contained to the main shell of the hotel building. Sixty per cent of the main building was destroyed before the fire was brought under control at 8.15; operations were stepped down around midnight, but firemen stayed on the site all night.

An interesting feature of the job was that whilst the firefighting was still going on, sufficient evidence was

Breathing Apparatus crews prepare to enter the Castle Hotel

obtained by using the salvage tender facilities to prove that the fire had been deliberately ignited. Later forensic evidence backed this up by showing that there were four seats of fire.

Arguments arose over who owned the premises at the time of the fire as contracts were still in the process of being signed, and the original owners, owners-to-be and the insurance companies all had a claim. The premises remained empty, boarded and shored up for a number of years after the incident, as there was some debate about the historic value of the building. It has now been redeveloped in to an apartment block and is known as Friars Buildings.

HURST

A major addition was added to the emergency tender in 1987, when it was kitted out with Hurst equipment. This is hydraulic cutting, lifting and spreading equipment, which was supplied by Dales of Gristhorpe (now called Genergy). Dales had introduced it to the UK from America, where it is known as the Jaws of Life. Dales had been running an Emergency Production Division as part of their company since 1977, and amongst other things they supplied to fire brigades was the Stem-Light (Storable Tubular Extendible Member) which the North Yorkshire Fire Brigade appliances had been carrying for some years.

Scarborough Crews attend a railway incident at Seamer Railway Station

Hurst gear comprised of cutting jaws, spreaders and rams, adding a whole new dimension to the extrication of people trapped in road traffic accidents. It was not long before the firefighters were being advised not to refer to the equipment as 'Hurst' as it was somewhat alarming for anyone trapped, hearing the Hurst being asked for (thinking they might be about to die and a hearse was required). Dales Emergency Products Division was discontinued in 1990.

BUILDERS START

Shepherds started their contract on the 17th November 1986, and one of the first signs that the job of refurbishing the fire station had begun was the removal of one of the town's most famous landmarks, the fire station tower.

Chief Fire Officer Ford retired in June 1987, before completion of the refurbishment of the fire station. Mr Colin Jones (46), who had been the Deputy Chief Fire Officer of East Sussex Fire Brigade, was appointed Chief Fire Officer. Divisional Officer Simpson retired and was replaced by Divisional Officer Ian Westmoreland. Assistant Divisional Officer Holiday also retired in December 1988 to be replaced by Assistant Divisional Officer David Hall, from Northallerton.

NEW FROM OLD STATION

Rebuilding went on until March 1988, when the builders finally left the site, followed in June by the

CFO Jones

official opening of the, all but, new station by Councillor Mrs Eva Mullineaux, the Mayor of Scarborough.

Mr Jones reviewed the brigade's layout and revised it in 1989; the brigade was now split into three divisions, not the original four. Scarborough was the headquarters for the new 'East Division' and Scarborough station became a district in its own right, with no overall responsibilities for other stations. The training programme for the brigade was also revised and a much more rigorous programme was introduced, both in practical and theoretical work, to help prepare the firefighters (the title firemen was no longer used) for the more modern equipment and technology that would be encountered in the future.

A new turntable ladder replaced the 1968 one in 1987 at a cost of £180,000. It was a Volvo/Metz/Angloco, which had cage operation facilities that allowed more than one man at a time to be hoisted aloft, and could be controlled from within the cage as well as from the base of the ladder. The ladder was also capable of being lowered below horizontal level, which meant that it could be used in such places as over the Marine Drive.

At Scarborough part of the new training programme included a group of firefighters trained as vertical rescue workers, competent in carrying out rescues on cliff faces, bridges, cranes, pylons etc. Mountaineering experts initially trained them, and then they passed on the skills to others. The Vertical Rescue Team (VRT) was eventually put on the run in a Land Rover (with the call sign Scarborough 6) which had been adapted to carry the team and specialist gear required.

The first machine at Scarborough was replaced in 1987 with a Carmichael water tender type 'B' on a Volvo chassis. Two years later, yet another Volvo of the same type was brought onto the station. These machines cost over £65,000 each. Also replaced, in 1988, was the emergency tender for a larger, more powerful, Dennis HCB Angus, at a cost of £55,000.

The old and new – Leading fireman Tony Brown stands between the two turntable ladders

North Yorkshire

FIRE & RESCUE SERVICE

Ever increasing calls to incidents classed as special service (jobs not involving firefighting i.e. extrication from road traffic accidents, removal of chemicals, etc.) were accounting for a third of all calls handled by fire personnel. The result of which saw the brigade change its name on 1st January 1990 from North Yorkshire Fire Brigade to North Yorkshire Fire & Rescue Service.

BT

At 4 a.m. on the 14th November 1990 residents of Lower Prospect Road smelt smoke and, on investigation, discovered that there was a fire in the telephone exchange, which backed onto Prospect Road. They tried to dial 999 but found the phones were

The remains of a mini car involved in a RTA at Cayton bay. Scarborough's emergency tender and the Flying Doctor's (Nick Morton) car can be seen in the photo

not working due to the fire so someone had to run down to the fire station and report the fire in person. Two pumps were sent out with Acting Sub-Officer Moment in charge of the first machine and when they arrived they found the whole of the switch room well alight.

The trouble was only just starting as the fire brigade central control at Northallerton discovered when they tried to mobilise the retained firefighters, by activating their alerters. There was no response as these also work through the telephone network system. Men had to be sent in cars to the homes of the officers and firefighters to alert them to the fact that their presence was required. Assistant Divisional Officer Cowie eventually took charge of the incident and made pumps four. This meant all the Scarborough pumps attended the incident plus one from Filey.

It was found that the whole town and surrounding area as far as Filey and Hunmanby had been cut off from the rest of the world's telephone system. Due to the fact that there was no 999 system in the town, a control unit, with a radio system was brought in and set up in front of the fire station. Vans and cars, which were linked to the control unit by radio, were placed at strategic points around the town and manned 24 hours a day by Scarborough and Filey retained personnel (which still had to have enough members ready to act as crews in case of fires).

The whole-time personnel were keeping a high profile in all areas of the district by permanently circling the streets in the fire engines on a type of fire watch. This vigil went on, aided by police and council workers, for over five days in different parts of town, whilst British Telecom (BT) staff worked 24 hours a day, first restoring the 999 system to the public telephone boxes and eventually to business and private lines.

The cost of the damage was £4,500,000, plus 20,000 homes and businesses were stranded without telephone lines, many for more than a week. Costs to local businesses were unable to be estimated and BT refused to pay any individual compensation for any losses caused. However, they did give a gift to the town of £250,000 as a gesture of goodwill; this money was earmarked towards the conversion of the old Odeon Cinema into the new Stephen Joseph Theatre. It is now hard to imagine the chaos caused as if the same problem occurred now there would not be the same difficulties, due to the massive increase of the mobile phone network.

LUNA PARK

Another well known landmark was hit by fire on 12th June 1991. At 5.45 a.m. the Harbour Master noticed that there was smoke coming from the Luna Park amusement arcade at the end of the

Marine Drive. He alerted the fire brigade and two pumps were dispatched with Sub-Officer Silversides in charge of the first machine, (he had been in charge of the second machine to respond to the York Minster fire as a Leading Fireman at York in 1984.)

On arrival, it was found that thick smoke was seeping from the roof and it was obvious that a large build up of fire was occurring inside, but access was difficult as the property was secured with roller shutter doors. Pumps were made up to three and a request for the emergency tender to attend, to assist with forcing an entry, was made. The Hurst (hydraulic lifting and cutting equipment) gear was used to this end. Assistant Divisional Officer John Watson arrived and took charge, making pumps four and requesting the turntable ladder. There was extreme danger from the amount of electricity supplying the many slot machines and amusement games present at the park and from the fact that the mains would not fuse out. This hazard carried on until the electricity board dug a hole in the road and cut off the supply

The turntable ladder seen in action over Luna Park

(also cutting off the supply to many parts of town).

The whole complex was built on wooden legs protruding from the harbour bed, with wooden beams and slat type wooden floors which allowed the air to rush through, feeding the fire with oxygen in the same way as a fire grate acts, causing the fire to burn fiercely and fast. The main priority was in protecting the surrounding area and in stopping the wooden stilt-type construction that the park was built on from catching fire. It took two hours to bring the fire under control and a crew remained until 4 p.m. It was hard to see evidence of the cause of the fire due to the severe amount of damage that had occurred, but it was believed that it was the result of an electrical fault in a fridge.

FURTHER PROMOTIONS

Mr Hall was promoted to divisional officer (operations) as deputy to the divisional commander in March 1992, his previous post being filled by Assistant Divisional Officer Dean McQue from Northallerton. By April 1993, Mr Hall sidestepped to divisional officer (advice and education) on the retirement of Mr Atkinson, whilst Mr McQue took up the vacant Divisional Officers post, whose place in turn was taken by Mr Neville Smith, promoted from division headquarters. Chief Fire Officer Jones retired in 1994 and his

CFO Clark

post being filled by the Deputy Mr Clark, Mr Smith also retired due to bad health, his post being filled by Assistant Divisional Officer Tony Dyer.

RICHMOND HOTEL

As social ideas moved away from council house estates in the early 1990's, more families, without the means to purchase their own homes, were being accommodated in multi-occupancy buildings. In Scarborough, with its slow decline in the long-stay holiday trade, many of the hotels and boarding houses were converting to this type of use. The Richmond Hotel on North Marine Road was one of these buildings. An event took place there in the early hours of the 5th May 1994 which sent shock waves, not just in Scarborough, but around the country.

A call was received at the fire station alerting the firefighters to a fire at the Richmond Hotel, within a few hundred yards of the station. Within two minutes of the call there were two pumps and a turntable ladder at the scene of the incident. The firefighters were informed by a small crowd, outside the building, that there were still several people trapped inside and that there was a fire on the second floor. Within four minutes of the brigade's arrival a man was removed from a second floor window using the turntable ladder, further information lead to the turntable ladder then being placed at another window where it was believed two children were trapped inside. Two firefighters, Leading Firefighter J Conway and Firefighter D Sprintall made attempts to search the heavily smoke filled room and eventually found the two sisters, Natasha and Terri Anne Jones, 4 years and twenty months old respectively. They were given mouth-to-mouth resuscitation as they were carried down the ladder by Leading Firefighter Conway. Sadly Terri Anne was found to be dead on arrival at hospital.

Two men, Simon Barker and David Holly, living in the building also helped in rescuing people from the rear of the hotel, but there were still four people unaccounted for. Breathing apparatus crews searching at the rear of the building were alerted to a bedroom when a man jumped from the second floor, landed and went through the flat top roof of the kitchen at ground floor, luckily only sustaining cuts and a broken jaw. Firefighters R Riby, A White, J Broadley and N Bennett (from Scarborough 3 and Filey pumps which were by then at the scene) entered the room. They found, in the extreme heat and flames, electricity arcing and sparking dangerously. They then saw the shape of 33-year-old Katherine Harrison at the far end of the room and after various attempts to fight their way through the flames and electricity they managed to drag her to the fire escape outside. Sadly however, she too had died from the effects of the fire. By this time everyone had been accounted for.

As well as the three Scarborough pumps there were two pumps from Filey plus Scarborough's emergency tender, the control unit from Ripon and a foam / salvage tender from Tadcaster in attendance. Standby crews from Sherburn and Snainton covered Scarborough in case of any further fires.

The fact that a woman and child had died in these circumstances sent shock waves through the whole area of multi-occupancy buildings, causing many towns and cities to toughen up on their bed-sit policies and collate lists of how many and where they were.

PAVERS

It was only two weeks later on 26 May that another large fire struck in the town at Paver's shoe shop on Westborough, in the premises adjoining the site of the Rowntrees' fire of 1969. A window cleaner, Fred Theobald, doing his rounds just before 5 a.m. heard bangs and thuds; he made a closer investigation of the area and saw smoke issuing from the shoe shop.

Firefighters prepare to enter the Pavers blaze via the turntable ladder

The brigade was at the scene within minutes but by that time the fire was well alight on the top three floors. Successful efforts were made in containing the fire to the one building. However, the main fabric of the building was badly damaged and it was eventually demolished and rebuilt completely. It was believed that the fire started from an electrical fault in the storeroom and must have been burning for some considerable time before Mr Theobald heard what was probably one of the floors collapsing.

EQUALITY

For a number of years a woman firefighter had been attending incidents in Scarborough, this was Jane Barker a retained firefighter from Snainton fire station. She, along with the Snainton crew, provided cover in Scarborough at larger incidents or stood-by on Scarborough fire station to provided cover when the local pumps were busy on smaller incidents. Whilst it had been the brigade's policy for a long time to recruit female firefighters it was not until late December 1994 that Scarborough fire station received its first post-war, whole-time female firefighter. This was Joanna Funnell (25) who was allocated to Red Watch.

Firefighter Joanna Funnell

RETAINED FAREWELL

After two years of constant threats from government cuts to the County Council, Scarborough had its third (retained) machine removed from its strength in May 1995. It was a sad farewell from the whole-time crew members who had come to respect and value their retained fellow firefighters who were there to back them up whenever the need arose, invariably at the times of most danger to life and property.

Scarborough retained firefighters

Scarborough's first machine was due to be replaced by a Volvo pumping appliance which had only been on the run at Whitby for a relatively short time, as it in turn was been replaced by a rescue pump (RP). This is a pump which carries a smaller version of the hydraulic cutting gear than found on the emergency tenders, allowing quicker response by firefighters with cutting gear in outlying areas. However it was pressed into service at Scarborough more quickly than originally anticipated when, in April 1995, responding to what turned out to be a malicious false alarm the first machine ran into the rear of the second machine when it braked sharply. The resulting accident saw both machines off the run for many months and the J registered Volvo taking an early place as the new Scarborough one machine.

COMBINED FIRE AUTHORITY

In April 1996, government reorganisation meant that York became a unitary authority (a council in its own right), but it was decided that the firefighting arrangements should remain with the North Yorkshire Fire & Rescue Service. Therefore the firefighting responsibilities were removed from the Public Protection Committee and placed in the hands of North Yorkshire Fire & Rescue Service Combined Fire Authority, (comprising of representatives from North Yorkshire County Council and York Council). At this time the brigade saw the abolition of the division structure, replaced by eleven districts. Mr McQue was transferred to Northallerton in charge of fire safety for the whole brigade. The divisional headquarters were converted into fire safety and advice & education offices for the brigade and had no direct links to Scarborough fire station (the fire safety officers once again being seconded from Northallerton to Scarborough).

ST THOMAS STREET

The St Thomas Street area of the town suffered badly as two successive fires within the space of four months saw a large portion of it devastated by fire. The Opera House Theatre was the first to be damaged. It had laid empty for some time, and had became an

The turntable ladder in use at the Royal Opera House

unofficial haunt for the local homeless, glue sniffers and drug addicts, in fact there had been a number of calls to small fires started in the premises.

However at 3.10 on the morning of 1st October 1996 a fire was seen in the front part of the main building and the fire brigade was sent for. One of the Scarborough pumps was already providing cover at Whitby as their pumps were at a large fire in Tranmere. The remaining Scarborough pump and turntable ladder were called and attended along with pumps from Filey, Snainton, Sherburn, Pickering Malton and York.

The blaze had started in the first floor bar area and quickly spread to the second floor and through the roof. Once it was ascertained there was no one inside the building the main objective of confining the fire to the buildings' front part was achieved, thus preserving the main theatre auditorium. The building lay empty for years and was the subject of many further minor fires before being acquired by Shaw Amusement group. The reception and bar areas at the front have been demolished and permission is being sought to demolish the rest of the theatre before redevelopment.

Just four months later on the evening of 12th February 1997, whilst Scarborough fire engines were responding to an alert to a forest fire at Wrench Green, a 999 call was made stating there was a wheelie-bin on fire next to Lockwoods carpet store (now Calvert Carpets). A pump from Snainton was turned out to attend whilst a pump from Filey was also turned out to another report of a wheelie-bin on fire in Scarborough.

Minutes later control was receiving calls to Lockwoods stating that the fire had spread into the store. Scarborough's turntable ladder was mobilised to the incident where on arrival the crew requested the attendance of the emergency tender, purely for the initial man power they could supply in setting up firefighting facilities.

Eventually there were the Filey and Snainton pumps initially sent, followed by the two Scarborough pumps which were re-routed, plus two from Malton and one each from Pickering, Robin Hoods Bay and Bridlington (of the Humberside Fire Brigade). The Scarborough emergency tender and turntable ladder, plus a foam/salvage unit from Ripon, the mobile control unit and control room staff from Northallerton also were in attendance. The fire took three hours to bring under control and the various pumping crews were then relieved through the night by pumps from York, Sherburn and Kirbkymoorside.

The many shops fronting Lockwoods on St Thomas Street were badly affected by the fire, whilst Lockwoods itself had to be totally rebuilt due to the damage it received.

RESCUE PUMPS

To allow the emergency tender to give a more central coverage to the area the emergency tender was moved from Scarborough to Malton in March 1997 along with the 'Scarborough One' water tender. The rescue tender (RT) based at Malton was in turn transferred to Scarborough. This rescue tender was basically a water tender with additional quick response cutting gear for road traffic accidents and other similar incidents, its call sign became 'Scarborough Three'.

GREEN WAVE

With the improvements in computer technology the traffic light system in Scarborough was controlled from a central computer system at the Town Hall, this meant it was far easier to control the flow of traffic. It was therefore decided by the fire service to approach the council for a 'Green Wave' system which allowed firefighters to press a button at the station and all the traffic lights on a given route would change to green, allowing faster passage through the town centre for the fire engines. After a few years of negotiations the system was put on line in July 1997 making an immediate favourable impact with the responding crews.

The ex-Malton rescue tender was replaced in January 1998 for a new rescue tender followed in the June by a new water tender to replace the Scarborough Two.

PEASHOLM PARK

The kiosks in Peasholm Park had, in more recent years, been the targets of vandalism with many turnouts in the early hours of the morning to find them well alight. In the lead up to bonfire night of 1999, at 5 am on 30th October, a call was received to Peasholm Park. On arrival the crew found that the park's centrepiece, a forty foot high pagoda, topping the island in the centre of the lake, was totally engulfed in fire. Their main problem was getting water to the top of the island which was only accessible via a footbridge. They had to manhandle portable pumps over the bridge where they were set into the water and fed the crews at the top of the island. It took almost two hours to bring the blaze under control, by which time the pagoda was beyond saving. The pagoda was eventually demolished with the intention of a new (possibly improved) one being built.

MILLENNIUM

Throughout the period that the old millennium came to a close the fire service was undergoing major, but subtle, changes. The government of the day (Jack Straw, the Home Secretary) declared that the prime role of the fire service was no longer firefighting but more an educational fire preventative role.

In April 2000 a sign of these times was (literally) on the fire engines as North Yorkshire Fire and Rescue Service entered a major sponsorship deal with the Scarborough based chip company, McCains. Advertisements for McCains oven cooked chips were placed on the entire first line appliances throughout the North Yorkshire Fire Service. The idea was to persuade people not to use chip pans and hot fat but to use oven chips which are much safer to cook.

Many other partnerships were formed including one with Scarborough Council when a very active campaign was run encouraging people to have smoke alarms fitted in their homes. As an incentive the firefighters would come and install the alarms, a feature of which were long-life batteries that last ten years.

Another aspect of the changes occurring within the fire service was the steady demise of the fire service semi-military style of organisation and management. The undress uniform, the clothes worn when not at fires, changed. Ties and caps were withdrawn, whilst the jacket and blue or white shirts were changed for a more informal black shirt and, when needed, a bomber style jacket. Officers were no longer saluted and first names were used between officers and firefighters.

The new millennium saw the sideways move of Mr Dyer, officer-in-charge of Scarborough to officer-in-charge of Malton station and Mr Cluderay, to fire safety duties at Northallerton. Assistant Divisional Officers Chris Stark, from training school, and Keith Dobson, from York, filled their places respectively.

FLOODS

Whether or not due to global warming, the year ended up as being one of the wettest on record. November saw flooding, in line with that witnessed in the Lincoln area in 1953, with the North Yorkshire area being one of the worst affected in the country. They were however two different types of flooding, the 1953 floods were brought about by atmospheric, wind and sea conditions, whilst the 2000 floods were the result of the sheer volume of rainfall. The area surrounding Selby was so badly flooded that for a time it became the biggest lake in Britain. Scarborough pumps were mobilised to Malton, York and Selby areas for days on end.

CENTENARY

The 30th August 2001 saw one hundred years of Scarborough's firefighting activities being run from the fire station on North Marine Road, to commemorate this anniversary a reconstruction of the original opening day was attempted. The Mayor, Councillor Lucy Haycock arrived, but instead of pulling a rope to open the station doors, she unveiled a plaque commemorating the station's one hundred years of serving the community.

Then instead of the Mayoress naming the fire engine, three local school children, John Barker, Hannah Lickes and Christopher Baxter named the three Scarborough fire engines. They had won the right to name them by winning a fire safety poster competition. The turntable ladder was christened Chris's Crusader whilst the two pumps were called John

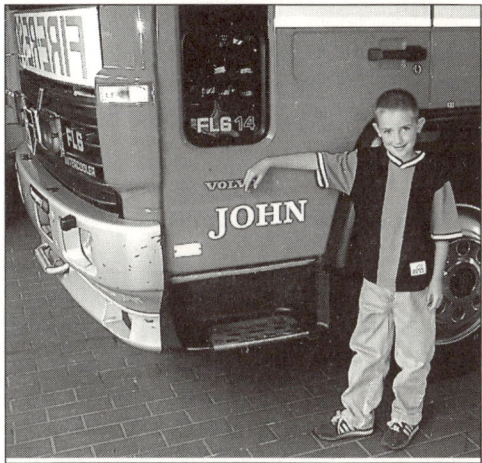

John Barker naming Scarborough Two

and Hotrod, the names the children had picked.

Firefighting drills were performed in the station yard, but instead of throwing water up the tower, a more modern role of the fire service was displayed by the use of hydraulic cutting equipment on a road traffic accident simulation. As part of the educational role, demonstrations were performed on how and how not to handle chip pan fires. As part of the partnership McCain supplied the brigade with a special mobile kitchen for these very effective demonstrations.

SEPTEMBER 11TH

September 11th 2001 saw the atrocities of the World Trade Towers in New York and at the Pentagon in Washington. Highjackers commandeered four passenger aeroplanes flying two into the Trade Towers, one into the Pentagon, whilst on the fourth the passengers fought with the terrorists but the plane crashed into the ground. In New York the fire service was in attendance when the towers collapsed and almost 350 firefighters were among the thousands killed.

The fraternity of the fire service was never stronger, as fire brigades throughout the world raised money for the families and dependents of the New York firefighters. Scarborough alone raised over £16,000. Following September 11th in America there was a spate of anthrax scares, as unknown person or persons were sending anthrax spores through the mail system to high profile media people and politicians. The anthrax scare spread wider as postal workers came into contact with it.

Scarborough was caught up in the scare when on October 17th a suspect package was received at Raflatac factory on Cayton Low Road Industrial Estate. When the package was opened powder and a note saying 'anthrax' was discovered. What followed was a major decontamination programme which eventually saw all the staff from the area where the package was discovered undergoing a full

Raflatac personnel get decontaminated after the anthrax scare

decontamination process. This was the first biological incident handled in the North Yorkshire area (although there had been many chemical incidents before).

It transpired that the package was nothing but a hoax. This cost all the emergency services a vast amount of wasted time. In addition it had put lives at risk due to the fact that the person opening the package suffered from a heart problem. One of the people put through the decontamination process, which included being hosed down with icy cold water in the cold open air, was pregnant.

RESTRUCTURING

Once again the fire brigade underwent changes to its structure when in April 2002 the brigade was split into four areas, roughly taking in political boundaries, Scarborough then fell into Eastern area which incorporated Scarborough and Rydale councils. There was no longer one person with overall responsibility for Scarborough Fire Station, instead the four watch officers were in charge of the station when they were on duty. Three assistant divisional officers were appointed as support officers to the district, Tony Dyer – human resources and training, Chris Stark – performance, best value and planning and Danny Westmoreland – health & safety and assets. In charge as area director was Colin Chadfield. Fire safety was split up, there was no longer an overall officer-in-charge and though still working from the Scarborough offices, the station officers were appointed to various parts of the Area, with Dave Grinstead as the Scarborough adviser.

WATER WATER EVERYWHERE

The summer of 2002 saw yet again the rain level records smashed as flash flooding hit Pickering in late July, and Scarborough pumps were sent to help out. By early August flash flooding was hitting Scalby, Burniston and Cloughton areas. The flooding was so bad that the inshore lifeboat was called to rescue stranded holidaymakers at a caravan site on Burniston Coast Road. One poor caravaner who had been rescued decided the next day to cut short his holiday and head home early, only to find that when he was towing the caravan up Staxton Hill the water damage to his car caused the engine to catch fire. There were long hold ups on the road whilst the Scarborough firefighters dealt with it.

Only a week later the flooding returned, smashing yet again the records for rain-fall set the previous week. All areas of the town were flooded but the worst affected areas were Eastfield and Cayton. Over 400 calls were received by control for Scarborough and Filey in less than two hours. The strength of the water cascading through Cayton Low Road area left many businesses and Pinder School out of use for several days. Pumps were sent to the area to assist with pumping out from as far away as Harrogate and Selby. In all, over one hundred properties had been badly affected and 80 people made temporarily homeless.

Further developments in equal opportunities were seen in September 2002 when Scarborough fire station had its first husband and wife firefighting team. Firefighter Chris King who had been at Scarborough for some time was joined by his wife, Louise, on transfer from Harrogate. They both went onto duty on Blue Watch.

NATIONAL STRIKE 2

At 6p.m. on the 13th November 2002, after 25 years industrial peace the fire service nationally went on strike, Scarborough fire station included. The tactics used this time were different to the 1977/8 all out strike, as a number of two and four day strikes were held. Scarborough was covered by a Green Goddess fire engine crewed by military personnel plus a breathing apparatus rescue team (BART) in a RAF appliance, both based at Coldyhill Lane Territorial Army Centre.

One incident attended by the military personnel on the 24th November involving a man trapped in a flat at the corner of Valley Bridge Road and Somerset Terrace. The striking firefighters crossed the picket line and took a Scarborough pump to the scene to assist. A breathing apparatus crew of Scarborough firefighters entered the building and rescued the man. That same evening the military answered a range of calls including a fire involving gas cylinders which presented great danger to them.

By January the government had obtained a number of so called 'Red Goddesses', these were mainly fire engines of the same standard as the ones used by the civilian fire services. Due to the number of incidents handled by the military personnel at Scarborough which was far more than anywhere else in North Yorkshire, one of these was allocated to the town.

As the Iraq conflict escalated, further short strikes were cancelled to release the military personnel for war duties. An agreement was eventually beaten out between the government and the union which involved a pay rise with many strings attached.

RESTRUCTURING CONTINUED

Scarborough got a second rescue tender in May 2003 replacing the water ladder. The continuing restructuring of the brigade saw Chris Stark promoted to DO as east area director.

COOPLANDS

At 6.30 a.m. on 23rd July 2003 staff at Cooplands Bakery on Claxton Way, Eastfield, were alerted to a fire in the factory where pie fillings were made. The workforce was immediately evacuated and firefighters from Scarborough, Filey, Sherburn and Snainton took part in an hour and a half battle to bring the flames under control. It was later discovered that new equipment being installed into the bakery had not yet been fully installed causing and helping the spread of the fire. Against all odds the production was up and running again by the following day.

NORTH YORK MOORS

Ironically as the strike of 1977 was preceded by a major battle on the North Yorkshire Moors and a fire at Cooplands Bakery (then in Londsborough Road) the strike of 2003 was followed by the fire at Cooplands and yet another major moors battle starting on 17th September, but this time it was closer to home and actually in Scarborough station's turn out area.

It is believed that the fire started in a rubbish bin at the Jugger Howe lay-by on the Scarborough side of the Flask Inn, off the Scarborough Whitby road. Due to the long, hot, dry spell of weather the moors were tinder dry and the fire spread was rapid. There followed the most intense firefighting operations to occur within Scarborough's turn out area since the Second World War. In addition to more than half the North Yorkshire Fire Service's resources (in terms of personnel and appliances drawn from across the whole of North Yorkshire) there were also pumps and firefighters from Cleveland and Humberside Fire Services, park rangers and workers of the North York Moors National Parks Authority were involved in the firefighting activities. Heavy earth moving equipment and a helicopter were drafted in and movements of equipment and personnel were felt as far away as West Yorkshire and Durham fire services.

With flames reaching up to forty feet high and the fire spreading towards the coast properties in the area had to be evacuated and special firefighting efforts were made around these properties. After almost two days a separate blaze broke out closer to the Robin Hoods Bay area which was thought to be the work of arsonists. Due to efforts of all involved plus a minor amount of luck, when the weather changed and provided rain cover, the fire was brought under control within a week. This was the first time a helicopter had been used at such an incident in North Yorkshire.

THE FUTURE

As there has been many changes in just a few years it would be surprising if the future is going to remain without any change. There are many ways the fire service can go, the following are just a few alternatives.

As government make more and more restrictions on the council's purse strings an amalgamation with other brigades is an option. Geographically it would be possible to unite North Yorkshire with Humberside Fire Service (East Yorkshire) and, on a grander scale, West Yorkshire could be considered. Having only one headquarters and control room would reduce the number of senior and control room staff necessary and costs.

It could just as easily go in the opposite direction as privatisation has been forced on many of the utility services such as water, gas, electric and telephones. It would not be beyond imagination to see towns again sponsoring their own local fire service, using a consortium of businesses to do this; there is already an indication of this when you look at the sponsorship supplied by McCain across the county.

A different alternative which the present government has taken into consideration is the combining of the fire and ambulance services, again only one headquarters and control room would be needed, firefighters and ambulance personnel could combine or cover each others job.

As history has proved events do not always take the expected course and none of the above may apply, whatever the future has in store the Scarborough Fire Station personnel will adopt it and continue to provide the town with the best possible fire cover and special service needs cover.

CONCLUSION ONE

In recent years society's attitudes have changed rapidly, none the less the fire service has managed to keep pace with these changes. When modern health and safety rules were introduced it was assumed that because of the nature of the work undertaken, the fire service would apply for exemptions. This was not the case.

Health and safety issues were met head on and addressed, so that when everyone else is heading away from an incident, the firefighters are heading in the opposite direction knowing full well they are working to health and safety standards.

When sexual and gender equality was asked for, the fire service adapted. More comments about firefighting being a man's job and should not be for women' are now heard from outside the service than from within the ranks. The firefighters have accepted their sisters and realise they play as important a role as anyone else. This is despite the fact that in many other walks of life women are still having to fight to gain their acceptance.

When the government introduced a national vocational qualification (NVQ) scheme to increase the skills of the national workforce the fire service adapted their training methods to fit the scheme. Every firefighter in North Yorkshire is working towards competency based achievement, the same as NVQs. In addition to this the service has been awarded the Investors in People quality standard. The fire service has proved time and time again that it can adapt effectively and quickly at all levels to meet the changes as necessary.

CONCLUSION TWO
The above conclusion was written before the national firefighters' strike of 2002/3, surprisingly some of the many strings the government want attaching to the pay deal include improvements in health and safety, equality and training, all of which have already been addressed by the North Yorkshire Fire & Rescue Service over the last few years. The government want firefighters, not just officers, to take a more active and varied role in fire safety matters. Scarborough, with their many hotels and boarding houses, have used firefighters to carry out fire safety inspections and for fitting smoke alarms in partnership with other agencies. The government have yet again been beaten off the mark by the North Yorkshire Fire Authorities, as they suggest that brigades should change their title to Rescue Service, a change made in North Yorkshire in January 1990.

Not only does Scarborough, as part of North Yorkshire Fire & Rescue Service, provide a first class rescue service to the community but is also ahead of the times in doing so.

Scarborough Three 'Hot Rod' Rescue tender

*Scarborough Two
Rescue Tender*

Scarborough Five "Chris's Crusader' Turntable Ladder

OTHER FIRE BRIGADES

The following is a short résumé of other fire brigades that have been formed in or around Scarborough and have provided cover in addition to the Scarborough Fire Brigade for the Scarborough area.

ARMED FORCES
As previously stated Scarborough Castle had a hand pump and the Captain of the regiment stationed at the castle would often dispatch a contingent of men and the pump to aid at large fires. This type of aid continued until the barracks were moved from the castle to Burniston Road and even then manpower was provided as seen at the Rem Store fire in 1915. The modern day army is still called upon at large moor fires and even to replace the local fire brigade, as seen in the two national firefighters' strikes.

PRIVATE FIRE BRIGADES
In the early 1880s it was common for businesses to provide fire cover for their own property, very much like modern day establishments provide fire extinguishers. As at that time fire extinguishers were still a thing of the future, the equipment they provided was varied, i.e. buckets of water, sand, fire hose etc. The larger organisations would also provide hand pumps, due to the limited amount of equipment and manpower in the early years of organised fire fighting it was not uncommon for these larger businesses to provide both of these to the fire service.

THE NORTH EASTERN RAILWAY opened Scarborough Railway Station in 1845. It no doubt had a number of minor fires brought about by flying embers from the steam trains and there was a handcart stacked with hose and standpipes in readiness. This was the responsibility of the Stationmaster. It was called on to attend large fires when necessary. The Spa fire in 1876 would have been much worse without the aid of both the forces and the railway helpers.

MARSHALL AND SNELGROVE, in the 1890's, was a large department store on the very fashionable St Nicholas Street. Due to the large amounts of flammable stock it was decided that good firefighting facilities should be available. They purchased a hose cart fully stocked with firefighting equipment and then trained a small number of men in firefighting. This became the Marshall and Snelgrove private fire brigade. Due to their location they started to attend fires with the Scarborough Fire Brigade, sometimes to the annoyance of the local brigade, as seen at the Butler's Optician – Huntriss Row fire in 1897. Their hose cart was stored in the yard at the rear of the store off King Street. They were still helping at fires in 1915 including the Rem Store.

ROWNTREES was another large department store sited at the junction of Westborough and York place (now the Brunswick Pavilion) in addition it had a large repository on Wooler Street. Rowntrees private fire brigade appear to have been formed

Rowntrees Fire Brigade undergoing an inspection by Merryweathers outside their Wooler Street repository

round about the same time as the Marshall and Snelgrove's brigade. They were also kitted out with a hose cart, which was supplied by Merryweathers. They wore uniforms and had annual inspections by Merryweather's fire inspector. Their presence was still to be seen at the Rem Store fire.

SCALBY FIRE BRIGADE

For many years Scarborough Fire Brigade attended fires outside the borough boundary, but it was often found that they received no compensation for it. They therefore approached the various rural and urban councils for some form of donation towards the upkeep of the local brigade. These requests were not only rejected but quite often totally ignored. The Watch Committee had to make it policy for the fire brigade to only attend fires outside the boundary if there was a firm offer of payment from the area authorities or the person whose property was on fire.

Scalby's fire engine and trailer pump

To overcome this problem a fire engine for Scalby was discussed at a Parish Council meeting in February 1922. It soon became clear that the £1562 and £1823 estimates for engines were beyond the finance of the committee. As an alternative thirty Minimax fire extinguishers were bought and placed around the area, also two ladders were sited in the area, one at Mr Allanson's Scalby and one at Mr Procter's Newby

It became quite common for dignitaries and speakers visiting Scalby to comment on the fact that the urban area should get together to form their own fire brigade. In late

Scalby Fire Station

November 1926 Chief Constable Abbott addressed a Rotarian meeting and suggested that the urban area should purchase a pump and hose reel.

Only a few days later, his suggestion was to prove provident when a steam train passing by caused a fire at a farm in Scalby. Sparks from the train ignited a haystack that was close to a barn. Villagers and the North Riding Police had to spend many hours working before they could contain the fire. Considering there was a fire brigade only a few miles away, this situation was not adequate.

Scalby crew drilling at Scalby beck close to Scalby Mills Bridge

In 1930 Scalby appointed an architect, Mr TE Dearmer as the surveyor and sanitary inspector to the council, he was concerned at the lack of firefighting facilities and he pestered the Urban District Council until they gave permission for an Urban Fire Brigade to be formed.

A new station was built in 1933 at Moor Lane, Newby, with the intention of sharing the facilities with the Urban Council, for storing of lorries, road rollers, etc. Scalby Urban District Fire Brigade came into existence on 1st January 1934. It affiliated itself to the

Scalby Pump and crew

National Fire Brigade Association (NFBA), Mr Dearmer was appointed Chief Fire Officer; Mr Marshall, Fire Engineer; L Appleby 2nd Engineer; plus six firemen - T Appleby, R Atkinson, D Lamb, H Lyons, W Thornton and J Swales, all employed on a part-time basis. Uniforms were styled on those recommended by the National Fire Brigades Association. A siren made the call outs.

Two months were spent drilling in both firefighting and St Johns Ambulance work in preparation for the arrival of an engine.

Sir William Wordsworth escorted by Mr Dearmer inspects the scalby crew

An Albion Merryweather motor fire engine and a Hatfield trailer pump were purchased from Messrs Merryweather & Sons, Greenwich, at a cost of £1,565. It consisted of a four cylinder, 65 horsepower petrol engine and pneumatic tyres whilst the rear wheels had a twin tyre, four-wheel brake system. It was finished in well-seasoned mahogany, with metal polished where appropriate, or painted in vermillion picked out in gold and white. There were twenty 75 foot lengths of canvas hose carried in the side-mounted boxes. First aid equipment (meaning hose reel) was supplied by a 40-gallon water tank. Also carried were a searchlight and a 35-foot 'Telescala' Merryweather ladder, plus resuscitation equipment, which had been donated.

The delivery date, 3rd February 1934, was also the official opening day of the fire station, when amidst visiting dignitaries Lady and Sir William Wordsworth declared the station operational. Fire Engineer Clarke of Scarborough Fire Brigade stated that Scalby Fire Brigade was amongst the best equipped in the country.

Scalby Fire Brigade was to attend its first fire on 6th May 1934, at Moor Field Farm, Ravenscar, (just after returning from drill competitions at Saltburn for the Fire Brigades Friendly Society where they took second prize.) The journey took twenty minutes and the firemen found garden sheds and poultry rearing houses ablaze. Their work was to stop the flames from spreading to the tool sheds and main building, a task they achieved well.

There was no doubting the firemen's enthusiasm, as in 1935 they used their own money from the social club to purchase hose to enter fire brigade competitions. They also adopted a motto for themselves,

> *'Progress to do our best for the community and to follow the traditions of the fire brigade service'.*

It seems there must have been some difficulties when calling them out, as in 1935 Chief Fire Officer Dearmer asked the public,

> *'When calling the Scalby Fire Brigade ask the operator for the fire brigade and not to give the number, as this causes confusion.'*

An unfortunate incident occurred on the afternoon of 5th February 1936, when a call was received to Wydale Farm. Somehow the address got mistaken for Wykeham Farm and Chief Fire Officer Dearmer, his men and pump arrived at Wykeham before the mistake was discovered. They had to turn around and go all the way back to Scalby. When they eventually arrived at Wydale Farm they discovered an oat stack burning ferociously. To get water to the farm they had to run out a quarter of a mile of hose from a pond which was frozen and had to smash the ice off the top before pumping could begin. It was seven hours before they could leave the fire ground.

Later that same month the brigade held its second Annual General Meeting, which was attended by, amongst others, Scarborough's Fire Engineer Clarke and Mr Stubington, a representative of Merryweather's fire appliance manufacturers. In the after dinner talk by Mr Clarke he predicted that the way forward was a national fire brigade due to the threat of war.

In 1938 Mr Clarke's prediction started to come true, as the threat of war grew more likely. The government organised the Auxiliary Fire Service, a group of volunteers who would, if required, be available for firefighting. Scalby fire station housed the Auxiliary Fire Service – Newby (sub-station to Scarborough) and was issued with a trailer pump and lorry. The two sections responded together to incidents and it appears that they formed a good team, as the newspapers of the day made many favourable comments about the way in which fires had been handled by the two Scalby fire engines.

An example of this was the fire at Wykeham Abbey, which the abbey fire brigade could not manage to control on their own, so help was sent for from the Scalby brigade. The newspaper reported that the two Scalby pumps set hose into use from their engines whilst the abbey fire brigade had hose working from the hydrants. With help they had the fire out in twenty minutes. Three thousand pounds worth of damage was done to the roof and furniture but without Scalby's help it could have been far more.

In 1939 along with Scarborough Fire Brigade they took part in demonstrations for the professional Fire Brigades Association, which was holding its annual conference locally.

They were to render much assistance to the Scarborough Fire Brigade and Auxiliary Fire Service in the 'March Blitz' and a pump was sent along with two from Scarborough to assist at Hull in the height of the bombings.

In 1941 Scalby Fire Brigade, like all other brigades, was taken over by the National Fire Service and run from Divisional headquarters, Scarborough, the part-time firemen became whole time (except for those who had been enlisted or called up), Fire Engineer Marshall became Officer in Charge.

In 1948 when the National Fire Service was handed back to the County and Borough authorities, Scalby, like Scarborough, fell under the North Riding's jurisdiction. It became station B7, had two Officers in Charge, Retained Leading Firemen F Cooper and S Cappleman and there was a complement of nine retained firemen.

In the first year of the North Riding Fire Brigade it was decided that the £190 needed to repair the 1934 Hatfield pump was too expensive. It was therefore replaced with an ex-Auxiliary Fire Service Austin Towing Vehicle, which was converted by the brigade, at Whitby, into a hose-reel tender using equipment supplied free by the Home Office.

By the end of the first full year of the North Riding Fire Brigade the Scalby station had handled eight calls, of which one was a house fire and one was a false alarm.

Mr Dearmer, whose connection with the Fire Brigade finished on the formation of the National Fire Service, retired from local office in October 1951 at which time he was presented, by Sir William Wordsworth, Chairman of the Council, with a canteen of cutlery. Sir William made comment about the fact that he was indebted to Mr Dearmer for forming the Fire Brigade as his wife had been saved by them in 1935. He also went on to mention the fact that Mr Dearmer had been responsible for designing and setting out the Highfield and Newby estates, and had been in charge of air raid precautions for the Scalby area in the war.

By 1959 it was decided that because of the few calls the Scalby station was handling and with the development of faster fire engines, Scalby could be adequately covered from the Scarborough fire station. On 30th April 1959 the station closed as a first line appliance station. Retained Sub-Officer Cappleman was reduced to the rank of Leading Fireman and transferred along with Retained Fireman Feeley to Scarborough, whilst Leading Fireman H Lyons and Firemen W Milow, G Appleby, L Sherwin, G Coomer and H Hewitt (all retained) were discharged from service.

The station building became an Auxiliary Fire Service base for training and storage until 1968 when the Government disbanded the Auxiliary Fire Service, it then lay empty until 1980 when it was sold and demolished and a housing development built in its place, now Havard Court.

BURNISTON FIRE BRIGADE

With the approach of war Mr Fred Wood of Whitby Road Garage, Burniston wondered what service he could perform for the community. As he came from a family with an old fire brigade tradition, (his father was a West Riding fireman) he thought that Burniston, being an urban district would not be supplied with any firefighting equipment, so he decided to supply and form his own brigade.

Experiments were carried out using old oil drums as water tanks, to which were added a hand rotary pump, lengths of hose, a few fire buckets, chemical extinguishers and an extension ladder. A trailer was then designed to take the equipment and to fit onto his car; this was achieved by fitting brackets to accommodate it. Other equipment included six buckets of sand, various tools such as saws, axes etc. All the equipment was painted red whilst the trailer was painted grey. It cost Mr Wood about £40 to put together.

He then supplied himself with a uniform to distinguish him as Chief Fire Officer. The next task was to enlist volunteer firemen; his first target was his son Tom. The Fire Brigade eventually consisted of; Fred Wood – Chief Fire Officer, Tom Wood – Leading Officer, Ossie Beadle, Fred Hill, George Coates, Henry Pearson, Lol Lyons, Walter Collier and Charles Bennett – all firemen.

Their headquarters was an old shop next door to the garage, which was equipped with a telephone. On the outbreak of war he organised a rota system whereby two or three men were on duty each night passing the time away by playing dominoes. The pumps were washed out in the pond near to the garage

Fred and Tom Wood with the Burniston fire engine

where it is reported there were often water battles going on. In 1941 his position was described in the local newspapers as Deputy Fire Officer for the Burniston area. At the time of the report he was attending a council meeting trying to obtain hose for the Burniston district, he recommended 300 yards of hose should be placed at various accessible points around the area for use in emergencies. The Council's reply was that supplying hose was the responsibility of the Auxiliary Fire Service which was run by the Home Office, therefore it was not their business.

The largest job they tackled was a fire at Kirkless, following a bombing. It needed four engines to handle the fire, and one of the firemen was blown into the beck from which he was pumping, when a bomb landed near him, but he was not badly injured.

On formation of the National Fire Service, in late 1941, the Burniston Fire Brigade was absorbed into it, and Mr Wood was appointed Section Officer. By the time war finished there was no longer a need for the smaller out-stations and along with the Scarborough sub-stations the station was closed.

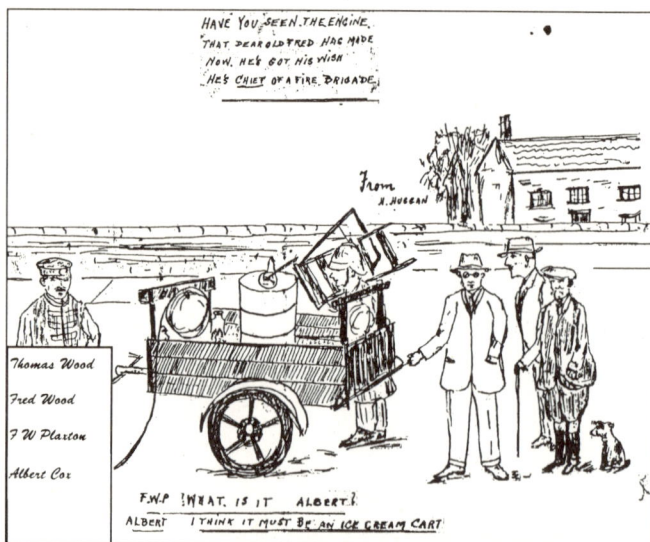

A cartoon depicting the Burniston Fire Brigade

STAXTON WOLD FIRE BRIGADE

Staxton Wold was opened just prior to the war; the purpose of the building was top secret. This caused much speculation, and many tales were told of what was happening in the vicinity. A death ray device was one of the most popular whilst there were even suggestions of alien connections being made. It was in fact the development of radar which was being carried out. The local fire brigade was asked to provide cover for this new site, which after much negotiation they did. Up to that time it had been the policy not to provide cover outside the Borough boundary, but as the government was subsidising the Auxiliary Fire Service by two thirds of its cost they felt they could demand that the Borough provided cover.

Radar became a major factor in the defence of Britain and in helping to win the war. After the war radar detection was just as important, due to the development of rockets and the deepening cold war with communist Russia. Staxton Wold grew as more emphasis was put on radar. The site was also a prime target for enemy action; it was therefore decided in the 1950's to place an Air Force Fire Fighting contingent at the base. This Air Force team would tackle any fire emergencies and give initial response until the local fire service could attend and assist if necessary.

In 1974 with the government reshuffle of the county boundaries, Sherburn came under the North Yorkshire Fire Service and they being closer than Scarborough provided the first support turn out to Staxton Wold. It was realised in the 1980's that the expertise held by the RAF could be put to good use in supporting the North Yorkshire Fire Brigade in the local area. Staxton Wold Brigade started to attend fires and more importantly road traffic accidents in an area they could get to a lot quicker than Sherburn or Scarborough. This had both the benefits of providing the support to the area and also allowing the Staxton Brigade experience at incidents. This arrangement continued until 1997 when an agreement was officially drawn up with Staxton Wold and the North Yorkshire Brigade. There was an alarm system installed at the base direct to Northallerton Control Room. However this did not last long as by the turn of the century modernisation was making its mark at the base and most of the operations carried out there could be either controlled automatically or remotely from another base. Personnel numbers were drastically cut along with the fire brigade on the site.

TREE WALK FIRE BRIGADE
What must be the most viewed and admired fire brigade in Scarborough never put out or even attended a fire, or even moved a wheel in all the time of its existence. It was the Tree Walk Fire Brigade, which was located in Peasholm Park. On the island in the centre of the park there was a display know as the 'Tree Walk' it consisted of various fibreglass characters lit internally. From the 1950's to the late 1980's it was a top tourist attraction and one of the displays centred on an old fire engine crewed by squirrels and rabbits.

The fire engine in actual fact was the second one made for the display in 1968, the original was made out of an old P4 car which was kitted out with a turntable ladder, hose, pump and blue lights. The council engineer, Len Wellock, who carried out the conversion used the registration number from his own car, PUB711G, to finish it off. Unfortunately whilst transporting it to the island on a raft the car rolled off and sank, on recovery it was declared a write off. Unperturbed Mr Wellock acquired a second P4 and set about converting this model which eventually made it to the island.

The attraction was discontinued in the late 1980's and the Tree Walk Fire Brigade ceased to exist. This was unfortunate as the squirrels and rabbits could have put on a brilliant display in 1999 when the pagoda was set on fire.

A sketch of the Peasholm fire engine

APPENDIX 1

SCARBOROUGH FIRE ENGINES

The following is a list of fire engines etc. that have been officially allocated to Scarborough. It must be remembered however that there has been many more fire engines used at Scarborough, which have provided cover on a temporary basis only.

BOROUGH CORPORATION & INSURANCE COMPANIES

	Manual Pump	
	Manual Pump	
1802	Manual Pump	
1855	Wheeled Escape	
	Wheeled Escape	
	Wheeled Escape	(South Cliff)
1903	Wheeled Escape	

SCARBOROUGH COUNCIL

1901	Steamer		Shand Mason	Shand Mason
1913	PE	AJ 1522	Thornycroft	J Morris
1922	P	AY 8249	Morris Belsize	J Morris
1929	PL	VN 282	Dennis HJ	J Morris
1934	PL	VN 5829	Leyland FK2 Cub	Leyland

AFS

1939   There were 25 temporary vehicles on loan from various local companies and Scarborough Corporation.

These included:

Bedford Lorry	from Plaxtons	VN 6230
Ford Truck	from Mariner	WX 8580
Ford Truck	from Rawlings	YG 1740
Bedford Lorry	from Andersons	VN 6284
Ford Lorry	from Lawty	
Chevrolet	from Clarks	
Ford Truck	from CWS	
Ford Lorry	UL 9943	
Morris Van	VN 4622	
Morris Oxford	PY 8099	
Ford	VN4828	

1940	SCU	VF 4180	{Second hand
1940	SCU	VF 7676	{conversions from
1940	SCU	VF 7681	{United Bus Company

NATIONAL FIRE SERVICE

1941	ATV	GLM 77	Austin 2 ton
1941	ATV	CYN 218	Austin 2 ton
1941	ATV	GLE 61	Austin 2 ton
1941	ATV	GLE 62	Austin 2 ton
1941	ATV	UM 4027	Austin 2 ton
1941	ATV	GLW 5	Austin 2 ton
1941	MDU	GLE 756	Ford 5 ton
1941	MDU	VN 4028	Ford 5 ton
1941	MDU	VO 8225	Ford 5 ton
1941	SU	UL 9943	Ford Tender
1941	CU	VN 4622	Morris
1943	TL	GXA 67	Leyland/Merryweather

NORTH RIDING COUNTY FIRE BRIGADE

1952	PE	HVN 778	Commer/Plaxton
1954	WT	KPY 666	Dennis F8
1959	PE	HPY 190	Dennis F7 (Second hand, 1951, from ICI)
1964	WT	AVN 934 B	Bedford J5
1967	TL	MAJ 921 F	AEC / Merryweather
1968	WT	PAJ 42 G	Bedford TK
1968	PE	PAJ 43 G	Bedford TK
1971	WT	XVN 277 K	Bedford TK
1972	WT	DAJ 538 L	Bedford TK

Transit ET

NORTH YORKSHIRE FIRE BRIGADE

1975	WrL	HVN 738 N	Bedford TK-HCB Angus
1975	WrL	HVN 739 N	Bedford TK-HCB Angus
1975	WrL	HVN 740 N	Bedford TK-HCB Angus
1977	ET	GAJ 421 D	Commer Davenport Vernon (bought as the brigades first ET in 1966)
1978	WrT	YVN 466 T	Bedford KG CFE
1979	WrL	DPY 592 V	Bedford TK (SWB) HCB Angus
1980	ET	JDC 471 T	Ford Angloco A0610
1983	WrL	A 78 GVN	Bedford KG Carmichael
1983	WrL	A 81 GVN	Bedford KG Carmichael
1986	TL	D 429 EHN	Volvo FL16 Angloco Metz
1987	WrL	E 474 KVN	Volvo FL14 Carmichael
1988	ET	F 304 VDC	Dennis DS153 HCB Angus
1989	LR	E 103 HEF	Land Rover 110 (1987 pvc)
1989	WrL	G 356 BDC	Volvo FL14 Carmichael
1990	WrL	H 476 JAJ	Volvo FL14 Carmichael
1995	WrL	J 574 RPY	Volvo FL14 Carmichael (1992 ex-Whitby)
1997	RT	M 657 RVN	Volvo FL14 Carmichael (1993 ex-Malton)
1998	RT	R 228 OHN	Volvo FL14 Carmichael
1998	WrL	R 227 OHN	Volvo FL14 Carmichael
2003	RT	NU52 RHA	Volvo FL14 Carmichael

Dennis ET

APPENDIX 2

<u>SCARBOROUGH'S FIRE CHIEFS</u>

SUPERINTENDENTS OF SCARBOROUGH FIRE BRIGADE

Ed Smith	1847 – 1850
James Thompson	1850 – 1862

CHIEF CONSTABLES & SUPERINTENDENTS

Richard Roberts	1862 – 1865
William Pattison	1865 – 1898
Henry Riches	1898 – 1902
William Basham	1902 – 1913
Henry Windsor	1913 – 1929
Walter Abbot	1929 – 1941

NATIONAL FIRE SERVICE (CHIEF OF FIRE STAFF) (LONDON)

Commander A Firebrace	1941 – 1947

NORTH RIDING FIRE BRIGADE CHIEF FIRE OFFICERS (NORTHALLERTON)

Lawrence Corbrick	1947 – 1954
Cyril Outhwaite	1954 – 1969
Fredrick Stephenson	1969 – 1973
Patrick Joseph Brennan	1973 – 1974

NORTH YORKSHIRE FIRE BRIGADE CHIEF FIRE OFFICERS (NORTHALLERTON)

Patrick Joseph Brennan	1974 – 1977
Ralph T Ford	1977 – 1987
Colin Jones	1987 – 1994
Eric Clark	1994 –

APPENDIX 3

OFFICERS IN CHARGE OF & BASED ON SCARBOROUGH FIRE STATION

SCARBOROUGH BOROUGH FIRE BRIGADE
1901 – 1920   Fire Engineer   W Birkbeck
1920 – 1942   Fire Engineer   A Clarke

NATIONAL FIRE SERVICE
1942 – 1948   Company Officer   W Gill

NORTH RIDING FIRE BRIGADE

1948 – 1964	Station Officers	W Gill	1960 – 1964	J Cowen *
1964 – 1974	Station Officers	W Boyle	1964 – 1969	Copley
			1969 – 1974	C Cowie

| 1968 – 1969 | ADO | Steeples ** |
| 1969 – 1974 | ADO | R Mohun |

NORTH YORKSHIRE FIRE BRIGADE

1974 – 1986	ADO	C Cowie	
1986 – 1988	ADO	B Holliday	1986 – 1988
			StnO I Hogg ***
			1988 – 1989
			StnO I Wilkie

1988 – 1992	ADO	D Hall
1992 – 1993	ADO	D McQue
1993 – 1994	ADO	N Smith
1994 – 2000	ADO	A Dyer
2000 – 2002	ADO	C Stark

In 2002 the brigade went through a restructuring process, at that time Scarborough no longer had any one individual designated as in charge of the station. The four watch officers assumed this responsibility when they were on duty.

*   In 1960 the position of officer in charge of Scarborough Fire Station became a shared role.

**   From 1968 to 1974 the Assistant to the Divisional Officer as part of his job description took on the responsibility of officer-in-charge Scarborough fire station.

***   From 1986 to 1989 the Assistant Divisional Officer took on a greater responsibility for a district and an assistant to him was appointed in charge of the station

Colin Cowie

Tony Dyer

APPENDIX 4

DIVISIONAL OFFICERS

In 1942 Scarborough Fire Brigade was absorbed into the National Fire Service. After the war it then passed into the North Riding and eventually the North Yorkshire fire brigades. Thus it became part of a larger set-up. Through these brigades Scarborough has been the headquarters for a Division. The following is a list of Divisional Officers who in their role took on responsibility for Scarborough Station.

NATIONAL FIRE SERVICE – STEPNEY GROVE
1942 – 1948   DO   A Robinson

NORTH RIDING FIRE BRIGADE – SCARBOROUGH FIRE STATION
1948 – 1958   DO   A Robinson
1958 – 1964   DO   F Stevenson
1964 – 1969   DO   W Gill
1969 – 1970   DO   Steeples
1970 – 1974   DO   P Hooper

NORTH YORKSHIRE FIRE BRIGADE – PREMISES AROUND THE FIRE STATION YARD
1974 – 1976   DO   P Hooper
1976 – 1978   DO   A Stowe
1978 – 1979   DO   L Howcroft
1979 – 1987   DO   B Simpson
1987 – 1996   DO   I Westmoreland

The Divisions were abolished in 1996 in favour of a District system. Under this system Scarborough became a District on its own.
2002 saw a restructuring of the Fire Service. Four Areas were defined around political boundaries. Scarborough became part of the East Area incorporating Scarborough and Ryedale. There were Area Directors appointed.

NORTH YORKSHIRE FIRE & RESCUE SERVICE – EAST AREA DIRECTORS.
2002 – 2003   DO C Chadfield
2003 –   DO C Stark

APPENDIX 5

FIRE PREVENTION – FIRE SAFETY – ADVICE & EDUCATION

Fire prevention or fire safety, as it is now known as, has been carried out around Scarborough since the 1880's when it was the Chief Constable's job to inspect theatres. This role applied right up until the formation of the North Riding Fire Brigade when the Divisional Officer took on this role. However as the workload increased and covered other types of premises i.e. offices, shops etc. it became a full-time job for at least one person. By the mid-sixties it was decided to employ an officer whose sole responsibility was fire prevention and whilst he was sited at Scarborough fire station he was seconded from Northallerton.

1964 – 1969	Station Officer	Pepper
1969 – 1970	Station Officer	D Christian
1970 – 1972	Station Officer	G Jones
1972 – 1972	Station Officer	D Deaves

In 1972 due to the heavy workload from the 1971 Fire Prevention Act (when hotel and boarding houses were included) and the number of officers required to carry out the duties, Scarborough became a department in its own right; with the officers attached to the Fire Prevention Offices Scarborough.

1972 – 1978	ADO	D Deaves
1978 – 1989	ADO	P Atkinson
1989 – 1993	DO	P Atkinson
1993 – 1994	DO	D Hall

With the abolition of the Divisions and the centralisation of the Divisional Officers to Northallerton, the fire prevention offices once again came under the auspices of Northallerton with the officers seconded to the department.

1994 – 1997	DO	K Isaacs
1997 – 2000	ADO	S Cluderay
2000 – 2002	ADO	K Dobson

The 2002 restructuring of the Service saw the end of any one individual being responsible for the fire safety department.

APPENDIX 6

SCARBOROUGH ENGINEER / MECHANICS

Originally the Superintendent of the fire brigade, who once the police took over the role of firefighting, would delegate the job to lower ranks, carried out the maintenance of the old hand pumps. The 1880's saw Fireman Ed Reed appointed to maintain the pumps.

Once it was decided to introduce a steam pump it was realised that an engineer with experience in maintenance of the mechanical side of the equipment was required. W Birkbeck was brought in from Manchester Fire Brigade where he had obtained this knowledge.

With the introduction of a motorised fire engine, in 1913, it again became obvious that an experienced mechanic was required to maintain the standards of the pumps.

ENGINEER / MECHANICS
W Birkbeck   1901 – 1920
A Clake   1920 – 1934

With the introduction of a fleet of police cars, vans, motorbikes, ambulance etc. it was decided to employ a mechanic purely for their maintenance.

MECHANICS
A Robinson   1934 – 1936
L Nightingale   1936 – 1942
G Alonze   1939 – 1942*

* With the advent of war an additional fireman / mechanic was employed

When the NFS was formed in 1942 Ezards Garage – Falsgrave Road (now Red Dragon restaurant) was made into workshops for fire service vehicles. Various firemen with mechanical backgrounds were used under the supervision of Section Officer E Hunt.

On the formation of the North Riding Fire Brigade maintenance was again moved back to Scarborough fire station and maintenance again fell to a dedicated mechanic.

NRFB MECHANICS

W Taylor	1948 – 1956
W Wright	1956 – 1969
J Howson	1969 – 1974

NYFB MECHANICS

J Howson	1974 – 1989
O Burrell	1974 – 1977
R Metcalf	1977 – 1989
M Miller	1989 –

Mick Miller

APPENDIX 7

SCARBOROUGH POLICE CHIEFS

CHIEFS OF SCARBOROUGH POLICE FORCE

1836 police run from Town Hall
St Nicholas Street

William Robinson	1836
John Ramsden	1836 – 1839
Richard Roberts	1840 – 1865

1861 uniforms introduced

William Pattison	1865 – 1898

1868 police station moves to Castle Rd

Henry Riches	1898 – 1902
William Basham	1902 – 1913
Henry Windsor	1913 – 1929
Walter Abbott	1929 – 1941
GF Goodman	1941 – 1943
John ES Browne	1943 – 1947

The following is a list of police chiefs who never took on the responsibility of Scarborough fire station.

NORTH RIDING POLICE

Pre-merger

Captain Thomas Hill	1856 – 1898
Major Sir Robert L Bower	1898 – 1929
Lieutenant Colonel John Clervaux Chayton	1929 – 1958

Post-merger

Lieutenant Colonel John Clervaux Chayton	1947 – 1958
James Robert Archer-Burton	1958 – 1965

1965 police station moves to
Northway

Harold Hubert Salisbury	1965 – 1968

YORK & NORTH EAST POLICE

Harold Hubert Salisbury	1968 – 1972
Robert Paul Boyes	1972 – 1974

NORTH YORKSHIRE POLICE

Robert Paul Boyes	1974 – 1977
John Woodcock	1977 – 1980
Kenneth Henshaw	1980 – 1985
Peter Noble	1985 – 1989
David Burke	1989 – 1997
David Kenworthy	1998 – 2002

2002 major alterations carried out on Northway Station

Della Cannings	2002 –

Mr Basham's Funeral

APPENDIX 8

SCARBOROUGH AMBULANCE CHIEFS

OFFICERS IN CHARGE OF THE AMBULANCE SECTION

William Pattison	(1865)	1880 – 1898
Henry Riches		1898 – 1902
William Basham		1902 – 1913
Henry Windsor (Order of St John)		1913 – 1929
(Motorised Ambulance Introduced)	*1916*	
Walter Abbott (Order of St John)		1929 – 1941
(Ambulance Station Built)	*1930*	
G F Goodman		1941 – 1943
John ES Browne		1943 – 1948

With the formation of the National Health System in 1947 the ambulance service was adopted by them. The Scarborough police however carried on running the ambulance service as a caretaker for some time after the takeover until the new service was sorted out.

CHIEFS OF NORTH RIDING AMBULANCE SERVICE
Ambulance Depot – Dean Road opened 1947

C F Hole	1948 – 1951
J Bedford	1951 – 1957
M R Smith	1957 – 1961
Edward J Draper	1961 – 1974

CHIEFS OF NORTH YORKSHIRE AMBULANCE SERVICE

Joe Field	1974 – 1979

Ambulance Station – Seamer Road opened 1974

Chris Abbott	1979 – 1984
Brian Dukes	1984 – 1989
Trevor Smith	1989 – 1994

CHIEF EXECUTIVES OF NORTH YORKSHIRE AMBULANCE TRUST

Mike King   1994 – 1997

Ambulance Station – Queen Margaret's Industrial Estate opened 1997

Ian Coulton   1997 – 1999

DIRECTORS OF TEES NORTH AND EAST YORKSHIRE AMBULANCE SERVICE

David Craig   1999 – 2001
Trevor Moulton   2001 – 2003 *
Jayne Barnes   2003 –

* Post temporarily filled by Director of West Yorkshire Metropolitan Ambulance Service

First Ambulance

APPENDIX 9

SCARBOROUGH WATER SUPPLIES

Pre 1300s	Public and private wells.
1319	Stone conduit run from Springhill.
1339	Private conduit run from Springhill to Friarage.
1485/1623	Stone conduits replaced by lead.
1808	Pot pipes run from Stoney Haggs spring.
1820's	Waterhouse Lane reservoir built.
1845	Scarborough Water Co. given Royal Assent.
1845	Cayton Bay works built,
	Steam pump fitted,
	Seacliff reservoir built.
1853	Larger steam pump fitted.
1855	Osgodby Top reservoir built,
	Seacliff reservoir abandoned.
1872	Osgodby Lane pumping station built.
1877	Referendum on water works.
1878	Referendum result in favour of Corporation.
1878	Scarborough Water Undertakings formed.
1884	Irton water works opened,
	Two steam pumps fitted,
	Two reservoirs built on Olivers Mount,
	Supply to town conduits discontinued,
	Waterhouse Lane reservoir discontinued.
1892	Olivers Mount top reservoir covered over.
1912	Gas power installed at Cayton Bay pumping station.
1928	Irton, second bore sunk,
	Irton, electric pumps installed,
	Olivers Mount, electric booster pump fitted,
	Springhill reservoir built,
	Osgodby reservoir covered over.
1939	Osgodby Lane, electricity installed.
1945	Water Act, Scarborough Co. includes Whitby.
1965	Irton, 4 electric pumps installed.
1971	Cayton Carrs, bore hole sunk.
1974	Regionalised -Yorkshire Water Authority.
	Privatised – Yorkshire Water.
2001	Olivers Mount 3rd reservoir built.

REFERENCES

In order not to distract from the flow of reading continual reference points have note been included in the text of the book, however the following is a list of references used in each chapter:

CHAPTER 1 – Early Scarborough

Baker J B   History of Scarbrough   Longmens, Green & Co.
    London   1882
Binns J   Did Scarborough Burn?   Scarborough
        – Transactions   Archaeological Society
    Scarborough   1999
Binns J   The History of Scarborough   Blackthorn Press
        – North Yorkshire
    Pickering   2001
Blackstone G V A History of the   Routledge & Kegan Paul
        British Fire Service
    London   1957
Crouch D &   Medieval Scarborough –   Yorkshire Archaeological
Pearson T   Occasional Paper 1   Society
    Leeds   2001
Debenham L S Scarborough's Water   Scarborough
        Supply   Archaeological Society
    Scarborough   1972
Edwards M   Scarborough 966 – 1966   Scarborough
        Archaeological Society
    Scarborough   1966
Farmer P G   Scarborough Harbour   Scarborough
        & Borough   Archaeological Society
    Scarborough   1976
Gamble S G   Outbreaks of Fire   C Griffin & Co. Ltd.
    London   1925
Hinderwell T   History of Scarborough   W Blanchar
    Scarborough   1798
Kirk J L   A History of Fire   Castle Museum
        Fighting
    York   1960
Knight A W   The Yorkshire Story   York Reference Library
    (Unpublished)   1974
Meadley C   Memorials of Scarborough   ETW Dennis
    Scarborough   1890
North Riding   The First Hundred Years   North Riding Police
Police
    Northallerton   1956
Rowntree A   History of Scarborough   J M Dent & Sons
    London   1931

Sun Fire Office <u>Policy Records</u>   Guildhall Library
        London   1710 -1860
Wright B   <u>A History of British</u>   Woodhead & Faulkner
                <u>Firemarks</u>
        London   1982

CHAPTER 2 – Improvement Commissioners
Minutes of the Scarborough Improvement Commissioners
Minutes of the Scarborough Council
        County Records Office Northallerton 1847 –1861
Scarborough Evening News
Scarborough Mercury
Scarborough Gazette
        Located at Scarborough Reference Library & the Scarborough &
District News Offices
North Riding Police   op cit
Blackstone   op cit

CHAPTER 3 – Sewer Committee
Minutes of Scarborough Street, Sewer Building and Fire Committee
Minutes of Scarborough Council
Minutes of Scarborough Watch Committee
        County Record Office, Northallerton 1861 – 1896
Scarborough Evening News
Scarborough Mercury
Scarborough Gazette
        Located at Scarborough Reference Library & the Scarborough &
District News Offices
Blakey J W   <u>Some Scarborough Faces</u>   Scarborough Gazette
        Scarborough   1901
North Riding   op cit
Police
Whittaker M   <u>The Book of Scarborough</u>   Barracuda Books
                <u>Spaw</u>
        Buckingham   1984
Debenham   op cit
Wright B   <u>Firmens Uniform</u>   Shire Album
        Aylesbury   1991
Wright B   <u>Fire Fighting Equipment</u>   Shire Album
        Aylesbury   1989
Roetter C   <u>Fire is their Enemy</u>   Angus & Robertson
        London   1962
Blackstone   op cit

CHAPTER 4 – The Fire King
Minutes of Scarborough Street, Sewer Building and Fire Committee
Minutes of Scarborough Council
    County Record Office, Northallerton 1896 – 1900
Scarborough Evening News
Scarborough Mercury
Scarborough Gazette
    Located at Scarborough Reference Library & the Scarborough &
District News Offices
Home Office   <u>Manual of Firemanship</u>   HMSO
              <u>Part One</u>
    London   1942
North Riding   op cit
Police
Burgess-Wise D <u>Fire Engines and Fire Fighting</u> Octopus Books
    London   1977

CHAPTER 5 – Central Fire Station
Minutes of Scarborough Street, Sewer Building and Fire Committee
Minutes of Scarborough Council
    County Record Office, Northallerton 1900 – 1903
Scarborough Evening News
Scarborough Mercury
    Located at Scarborough Reference Library & the Scarborough &
District News Offices
Oral Research with Miss Bertha Birkbeck (resident on Scarborough fire
Station from birth 1902 – 1920)

CHAPTER 6 – The Watch Committee
Minutes of Scarborough Council
Minutes of Scarborough Watch Committee
    County Record Office, Northallerton 1903 – 1920
Scarborough Evening News
Scarborough Mercury
Scarborough Pictorial Souvenir Edition
    Located at Scarborough Reference Library & the Scarborough &
District News Offices
Gamble   op cit
Boyes   <u>Boyes Stores The Story of</u>   Pindar Print
         <u>a Family</u>
    Scarborough   1981

CHAPTER 7 – Mr Clarke

Minutes of Scarborough Council
Minutes of Scarborough Watch Committee
    County Record Office, Northallerton 1919 – 1939
Scarborough Evening News
Scarborough Mercury
    Located at Scarborough Reference Library & the Scarborough &
District News Offices

CHAPTER 8 – AFS

Minutes of Scarborough Council
Minutes of Scarborough Watch Committee
    County Record Office, Northallerton 1939 – 1942
Scarborough Evening News
Scarborough Mercury
    Located at Scarborough Reference Library & the Scarborough &
District News Offices
Oral Research with
   1 Mr E Goodwin   (ex AFS, NFS, North Riding retained fireman)
   2 Mrs Greetham   (ex NFS)
   3 Mr T Hunt   (ex AFS, NFS, North Riding sub officer)
   4 Mr L Sowry   (ex AFS, NFS)
   5 Mr F Stevenson (ex AFS, NFS, North Riding chief fire officer)
   6 Mr F Swiers   (ex AFS,NFS)
   7 Mr N Ward   (ex AFS, NFS)
Blackstone   op cit
North Riding Fire Brigade
              Nor-rider   NYCC
   Northallerton   1950 – 1960

CHAPTER 9 – NFS

Minutes of Scarborough Council
Minutes of Scarborough Watch Committee
    County Record Office, Northallerton 1941 – 1948
Scarborough Evening News
Scarborough Mercury
    Located at Scarborough Reference Library & the Scarborough &
District News Offices
Oral Research   op cit 1 – 7
   8 Mr W Ramm   (ex NFS, NRFB, NYFB)
   9 Mrs B Cobb   (ex NFS)
   10 Mrs J Wallington {ex NFS)
Blackstone   op cit
Plaxtons

CHAPTER 10 – NRFB

Minutes of Scarborough Council
Minutes of Scarborough Watch Committee
    County Record Office, Northallerton 1947 – 1974
Scarborough Evening News
Scarborough Mercury
    Located at Scarborough Reference Library & the Scarborough &
District News Offices

Chief Fire Officer	Annual Reports	NYCC
Northallerton	1948 – 1974	
NRFB	Routine Orders	
Northallerton	1948 – 1974	
NYFB	Flashpoint Magazine	
Liverpool	Issues 1 – 18	
Atkinson G	The Birth of a	Flashpoint Magazine
	Fire Brigade	
Liverpool	Volume 2 – Issue 3	
Oral Research	op cit 1,4,7,8	
	11 Mr A Lee	(ex post war AFS)
Transport Information	Mr T Whelan	(fire brigade enthusiast)
North Riding Police	op cit	

CHAPTER 11 – NYFB

Scarborough Evening News
Scarborough Mercury
    Located at Scarborough Reference Library & the Scarborough &
District News Offices

NYFB	Routine Orders	
Northallerton	1977 – 1994	
Whelan T	op cit	
West S	Letter	1st Regiment Royal Horse
		Artillery
1993		
Barty-King H	Light Up the World	Quiller Press
	– Dales Story	
London	1985	

CHAPTER 12 – NYF&RS

Scarborough Evening News
    Located at Scarborough Reference Library & the Scarborough &
District News Offices

NYF&RS	Routine Orders	
	Northallerton	1994 – 2003

CHAPTER 13 – Other fire brigades
Scarborough Evening News
Scarborough Mercury
    Located at Scarborough Reference Library & the Scarborough &
District News Offices
Oral Research   Mr I Galbraith
                       Mr L Wellock
                       Mr A Brown

BIBLIOGRAPHY
Belfitt M   Many articles in various newspapers
Barty-King H   Light Up the World –   1985
                       Dales Electric Group Story
Binns J   The History of Scarborough –   2001
                       North Yorkshire
Blackstone G V A   History of the British Fire Service   1957
Boyes   Boyes Stores – The story of a family   1981
Debenham L S   Scarborough Water Supplies
                     Scarborough & District Archaeological   1972
                       Society
Gamble S G   A Practical Treatise on the Outbreaks   1926
                       of fire
Haydon A L   The Book of the Fire Brigade   1912
Home Office   Manual of Firemanship
                       parts 1 – 7 – HMSO
                         1943 reprinted and revised 1947, 1955, 1976, 1980
Home Office   Drill Book – HMSO
                       1942 reprinted and revised
Kirk Dr   History of Firefighting – Castle Museum York   1960
Knight A W   The Yorkshire Story – York Reference Library
                                                     unpublished
Meadley C   Memorials of Scarborough
NRFB   Nor-Rider fire brigade journal   1950 – 1960
NYFB   Flashpoint fire brigade journal – issues 1 – 18
Roetter C   Fire is their Enemy   1962
Rowntree   History of Scarborough
Scarborough & District Archaeological Society
                     Scarborough 966 – 1966   1966
Scarborough Mercury
Scarborough Council Meetings   – County Archives
Scarborough Evening News
Scarborough Gazette